FRONT COVER: "Icy Bay and Mount St. Elias."
(Vancouver's Voyages.)

FRONT ENDPAPERS: "Carte des Possessions Russes,
dressée par Pierron, d'après la Carte de
Mr. Brué," 1825, shows extent of Russia's
possessions in North America, according to
1825 treaty between Russia and Great Britain.

TITLE PAGE: "A view of New Arkhangel harbor from
the eastern redoubt," showing fort and settlement. Note fortified wall and five-cannon shore
battery at left. I.G. Voznesenskii drawing,
1843-1844.

COLONIAL RUSSIAN AMERICA

KYRILL T. KHLEBNIKOV'S REPORTS, 1817-1832

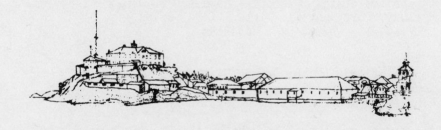

TRANSLATED WITH INTRODUCTION AND NOTES

BY BASIL DMYTRYSHYN
AND E. A. P. CROWNHART-VAUGHAN

OREGON HISTORICAL SOCIETY
PORTLAND, 1976

Published by the Oregon Historical Society
with the aid of the S.S. Johnson Foundation.

The Library of Congress Cataloged the First Printing
of the Title as Follows:

Khlebnikov, Kirill Timofeevish, 1776-1838.
  Colonial Russian America: Kyrill T. Khlebnikov's
reports, 1817-1832 / translated, with an introduction
and notes by Basil Dmytryshyn and E.A.P. Crownhart-Vaughan.
--Portland, Oregon Historical Society, 1976.
(North Pacific Studies Series, No. 2)
  Translation of that part of the author's manuscript
published in 1861 as a supplement to the periodical Morskoi
sbornik under title: "Materialy dha istorii russkikh
zaelenii po beregam vostochnago okeana."

Bibliography; p. [146]-152.
includes index.
ISBN 0-87595-053-9

  1. Rossiisko-amerkianskaia kompaniia--History--Sources.
2. Fort Ross, Calif.--History--Sources. 3. Russians in
the United States--History--Sources. I. Oregon Historical
Society, Portland. II. Title. III. Series.
F907.K47213   979.8'02   76-43154
                      MARC

Printed in the United States of America

CONTENTS

Appendixes

ILLUSTRATIONS

Aleksandr A. Baranov   facing p. 1

                                                  following p. 8
Ivan Kyrilov map of Russia, 1734
Plan of Pavlovsk Harbor, Kodiak Island, 1798
View of Pavlovsk Harbor, 1842-1843
View of Pavlovsk Settlement
An Aleut Woman
Aleut Hunter and Equipment
Aleut Sea Otter Hunting Equipment
Aleut Sea Otter Hunting Party
Aleuts Hunting Beluga
Diagram of Kodiak Baidarka

                                                  following p. 74
Bastion of New Arkhangel Fort
Drawing of New Arkhangel, circa 1830
Siberian Ostrog
Sitka Island, 1843-1844
Kolosh Dwellings Near New Arkhangel, 1843-1844
Sitka: Little and Big Iablochnye Islands
Funeral of a Kolosh Toion, 1844
Fur Warehouse at New Arkhangel, drawing, circa 1830's
Fur Warehouse at New Arkhangel, 1887 photo
New Arkhangel: The Cathedral, circa 1880
Inhabitants of Norton Bay, 1843
Redoubt of St. Michael, 1843
Main Street of New Arkhangel

                                                  following p. 106
Map of Northern California, 1848
Ross Settlement, circa 1840
Fort Ross
The Chernykh Ranch in Northern California, circa 1840
Honolulu, late 1830's
Map of Sitka Bay, 1850
Map of Northwest Coast of America, North and South of
   the Columbia River, with Chart of the Mouth, 1848
Map of Bodega, San Francisco and Monterey Bays, 1848

Source materials on the exploration of America and early contacts between native Americans and European voyagers are as rich and diverse as the explorers, traders and settlers themselves. Many accounts, especially those by the Spanish, French, English and Portuguese have been available in published editions either in the original or in translation almost from their inception. Unfortunately this has not been the case with accounts by Chinese, Japanese and Russian travelers along the Pacific coast of America.

In 1972 the Oregon Historical Society inaugurated a publishing venture entitled North Pacific Studies. Its purpose is to make available in English little known or hitherto unpublished works on the early history of the North Pacific Ocean and littorals. The first volume in the series, Explorations of Kamchatka, 1735-1741, is an account by a young Russian explorer-scientist, Stepan P. Krasheninnikov (1711-1755) during the famous Bering Expedition to Kamchatka and to the shores of Northwest America. The present volume, second in the series, is by Kirill Timofeevich Khlebnikov, also a Russian, who in his service as an official of the Russian American Company has left a rich account of the North Pacific.

Khlebnikov's notes were intended as an official investigatory report to the Directors of the Russian American Company. This manuscript eventually came into the possession of one of the directors, Ivan V. Prokofiev, and was apparently filed away with his personal papers. It was lost and forgotten for years, a classic misadventure. By a most fortuitous coincidence the naval historian A. P. Sokolov discovered the manuscript years later,"in a second-hand bookstore," bundled among papers belonging to Prokofiev's heirs. Sokolov immediately recognized the importance of his find, and part of the work was published in St. Petersburg in 1861, twenty-three years after Khlebnikov's death. It appeared as a supplement to the periodical Morskoi Sbornik [Naval Anthology], and was entitled "Materialy dlia istorii russkikh zaselenii po beregam vostochnago okeana: Zapiski K. Khlebnikova, o Amerike" ["Materials for a history of the Russian settlements along the shores of the Eastern (Pacific) Ocean: K. Khlebnikov's notes on America."]

This translation, with the exception of the eight appendixes here included which are taken from unpublished Khlebnikov material preserved in archives in the USSR, we have made from the 1861 publication. The second volume, now in preparation, will present the never published balance of Khlebnikov's manuscript on Russia's American colonies. We are pleased that this work, published in English for the first time, could appear on the 200th anniversary of Khlebnikov's birth and of the American year of colonial independence.

We have used the Library of Congress system of transliteration, but have omitted ligatures and apostrophes. For clarity we have used contemporary spellings for many place names: Sitka, Kodiak and Alaska, rather than Sitkha, Kadiak and Aliaska. Where a Russian name has been used, contemporary nomenclature follows in brackets: Kenai Bay [Cook Inlet]. Russian designations such as creole and Kolosh are explained in the glossary, which also includes notes on Russian weights, measures and dates. Plurals of untranslatable Russian words have been anglicized: promyshlenniks, prikashchiks. All footnotes are Khlebnikov's unless designated "-- Ed."

The translator-editors wish to express their deep gratitude to the many persons
and institutions in this country and in the USSR who have made this inter-
national publication project possible: The Academy of Sciences of the USSR,
Geographic Society of the USSR, Saltykov-Shchedrin State Public Library in
Leningrad, Museum of Anthropology and Ethnography (American Sector) in
Leningrad, Miklukho-Maklay Institute of Ethnography in Moscow, Lenin Library in
Moscow, Zhdanov State University Library in Irkutsk; James R. Gibson of York
University, Toronto; Roza G. Liapunova, Erna V. Siebert and Mikhail I. Belov of
Leningrad; Leonid A. Shur of Moscow; His Grace, The Right Reverend Grigorii,
Bishop of Sitka and Alaska; Thomas Vaughan, Director of the Oregon Historical
Society and General Editor of North Pacific Studies; Priscilla Knuth, Editor;
Mrs. Richard L. Godfrey, Nancy A. Hacker, Maurice Hodge and Connie H. Attebery;
and John Youell, Portland, chairman of the North Pacific (Irkutsk Archival)
Research Group of the Oregon Historical Society, under whose aegis and
sponsorship, together with the Louis and Maud Hill Family (Northwest Area)
Foundation, these materials were acquired and made available.

Our further thanks to Mr. and Mrs. Samuel S. Johnson, long time members of the
North Pacific (Irkutsk Archival) Research Group who generously offered the
major contribution toward the production of this volume.

INTRODUCTION

Kirill Timofeevich Khlebnikov (1776-1838), the author of this imposing account of
Russian colonial and imperial venture into North America, was born in 1776 in
Kungur, Perm gubernia, in the Ural region. In 1800 at the age of 24 he entered
the service of the recently chartered Russian American Company as prikashchik, or
agent, first in Irkutsk in eastern Siberia, and later (1801-1812) in Kamchatka.
He encountered many historically important travelers who put in at the magnificent
Kamchatka port of Petropavlovsk in Avacha Bay: Captain Ivan F. Krusenstern, the
circumnavigator; Georg Heinrich von Langsdorff, scientist with the Imperial
Russian Academy of Sciences; the courtier diplomat Nikolai P. Rezanov; the
Russian naval officers Nikolai A. Khvostov and Gavriil I. Davydov; and the
American shipmaster and world traveler, John d'Wolf.

After 13 years of grueling service and hardship, Khlebnikov in 1813 was transferred
back to the Company's Siberian administrative headquarters in Irkutsk, then later
to St. Petersburg. In the brilliant capital, exhilarated by the victories over
Napoleon, he accepted a new promotion as Administrator of the Company's head
office in America, recently transferred from Kodiak to New Arkhangel (now Sitka).
He departed for America in September 1816 aboard the ship Kutuzov, named in honor
of the Russian conqueror of Napoleon, under Captain Leontii Hagemeister. Upon
reaching New Arkhangel on November 20, 1817, Hagemeister was appointed Chief
Manager of all Russia's American colonies to replace the aging and ailing
Aleksandr A. Baranov. Khlebnikov was thus second in command over all of Russian
America under the new manager, and assisted in the difficult transition involved
in the transfer of power from the long established and legendary Baranov to the
new Chief Manager. The strongest indication of Khlebnikov's executive skill is
revealed by the fact that he subsequently assisted Hagemeister's successors:
Semen Ianovskii, Matvei Muraviev, P.E. Chistiakov and Ferdinand von Wrangell.

During the long voyage from the Gulf of Finland en route to his post in the
Russian colonies in America he stopped in Chile, Peru and Mexico. Later he
traveled on business to the Company's posts in Alaska, the Aleutian, Fox,
Pribylov and Komandorskie Islands and California, where he journeyed several
times during the 1820's as commercial agent. He stopped at Fort Ross, as well
as at the Spanish colonial villages of San Francisco, Santa Cruz, Monterey and
Santa Barbara, and became acquainted with influential Spanish officials.
Included in his accounts are important references to Governor Pablo V. de Solá,
Luis Argüello and José María Echeandia. He also worked with the Russian
administrators of Fort Ross: Ivan A. Kuskov, Carl J. Schmidt, P. I. Shelekhov
and Petr S. Kostromitinov. In the course of his travels and business contacts
he learned to read and speak both Spanish and English, and certainly he was one
of the best informed persons on the Pacific coast of America. And practically
speaking, in his official capacity Khlebnikov dealt with all of the Russian
employes as well as with the natives, both hostile and friendly, whom he
understood with unusual perception and endeavored to treat fairly.

Khlebnikov's broad experiences, unusual powers of observation, capacity for hard
and sustained work, and curiosity about all aspects of the world around him are

reflected in his numerous works, the most important of which are his reports
and travel diaries on Russian America. He wrote revealingly not only of
intricate business affairs, but of history, ethnology, geography, mythology,
natural science, navigation and the whole spectrum of economic activity. He
sent many important artifacts to the Museum of Curiosities, the first museum
founded by Peter the Great, now the Museum of Anthropology and Ethnography, and
to the Academy of Sciences in St. Petersburg.

Khlebnikov's seventeen-year sojourn in America ended in 1832 when he departed
for St. Petersburg. He reached the capital and the main headquarters of the
Russian American Company in September 1833. Because of his knowledge, price-
less experience and loyal service, he was made Chief Administrator of all the
Company's affairs. Khlebnikov's virtues were again recognized when he was
elected to the Governing Board of the Company. In recognition of his singular
contributions to knowledge, his associates in St. Petersburg made him a corresponding member of the already illustrious Academy of Sciences. Subsequently,
he was decorated with the coveted Order of St. Anne, third class.

During the last five years of his life Khlebnikov wrote prolifically, perhaps
stimulated by the literary outpouring of Russian authors during this special
era. In addition to the present work, Khlebnikov's published writings include:
"Zapiski o Kalifornii" ["Notes on California"] in Syn Otechestva, Nos. 124-125,
1829; "Pervonachalnoe poselenie russkikh v Amerike" ["The first settlement of
Russians in America"] in Raduga, books II, III and V, Reval, 1833; Zhizneopisanie
Aleksandra Andreevicha Baranova [Biography of Aleksandr Andreevich Baranov], St.
Petersburg, 1835; "Vzgliad na polveka moei zhizni" ["A glance at a half century
of my life"] in Syn Otechestva, 1838; "Otryvki iz zapisok russkago puteshestvennika
v Brazill" ["Excerpts from the notes of a Russian traveler in Brazil"] in
Severnaia Pchela, 1838; and several entries in the Entsiklopedicheskii Leksikon
on subjects familiar to him such as the Bering Sea, Bering Straits, and Alaskan
landmarks. But even today the greater part of his writing continues unnoticed,
and unpublished, in remote archives.

Khlebnikov's notes on America, here translated into English for the first time,
were published in 1861 in Russia. The published version includes two of six
parts which exist in manuscript form: New Arkhangel and Fort Ross, here presented
as the first of two volumes. The second volume, which we are now completing,
will include the four unpublished parts: Kodiak; Unalaska, the Alaskan peninsula
and the Fox Islands; Atka, the Andreanov, Komandorskie and Near Islands; and the
Pribylov Islands, St. Matthew Island and part of North America.

The history of Russia's American colonies is receiving vigorous new attention in
the Soviet Union, Canada and the United States. Ambitious publication programs
are now underway and in some instances a substantial exchange of materials and
scholars has been achieved, notably at the Oregon Historical Society. It is
encouraging to learn that recently discovered journals by Kirill Khlebnikov
relating to his California travels are being edited for publication in the USSR
by ethnographers, who have uncovered important unpublished Khlebnikov material
in archives in Leningrad, Moscow, Perm, Tartu and Kungur. It would be of
unusual, in fact extraordinary assistance to the scholars, analysts and readers
in this field to have all Khlebnikov's work, scattered and sometimes inaccessible,
brought together in a contemporary and comprehensive publication. To further

reveal the plight he suffers in his temporary anonymity, this recondite chronicler is not as yet mentioned in the comprehensive Bolshaia Sovetskaia Entsiklopediia. So great a servant of Russian interests and North American history is deserving of this final recognition--and an order from Clio, first class.

Basil Dmytryshyn
E.A.P. Crownhart-Vaughan
Portland, Oregon

GLOSSARY

Albion, **New Albion**. Term used by Russians to refer to northern California.

Americans. When used by Russians, refers to American natives.

Arroba. Spanish measure, equivalent to 1/4 **quintal**, 25.3 pounds.

Artel. Russian. A party of men organized under a leader on cooperative lines for work, hunting, harvesting, fishing, etc.

Arshin. Russian linear measure, 28 inches.

Baidara. Open boat made of hide (**lavtak**) stretched over a light wooden framework. Holds up to 25 persons.

Baidarka. A kayak. Smaller than a baidara, enclosed, with open hatches for one, two or three persons. The Russian American Company generally used the two-hatch baidarka for hunting, and the three-hatch for transport and exploration. Both are very light and maneuverable craft, easily righted if overturned, propelled with paddles.

Baidarshchik. Has various meanings: baidara construction supervisors, baidara crew overseer, baidara crew, steersman or owner.

Charka. Glassful, cupful. 10 charkas = 2.16 pints.

Chernozem. Black soil.

Chervonets. Russian currency; a 10-ruble banknote or gold piece.

Chetvert. Russian measure for dry goods; one chetvert of wheat = 49 pounds.

Chief Manager. In Russian, **glavnyi pravitel**.

Condorina. Spanish; small gold coin.

Creole. Term used by Russians to refer to a person of mixed Russian and native blood. They were often educated, trained and employed by the Russian American Company in various capacities.

Desiatina. Russian land measure; 2.7 acres.

Fanega. Spanish grain measure, 1.5 bushels.

Funt. Russian measure; 0.9 pound; .41 kilogram.

Governing Board. In Russian, **glavnoe pravlenie**.

Iukola. Siberian term for dried fish, generally salmon, used as a staple in the diet.

Kaiur. A native worker hired or drafted for service by the Russians.

Kalga. Kolosh [Tlingit] term for slave.

Kamlei. A circular waterproof garment made of cured sea mammal gut. Worn in cold or rainy weather, and when hunting at sea. Worn alone or over other garments.

Kazhim. Communal living quarters; men's barracks for Aleuts, Eskimos or Indians.

Kekur. Siberian term for a cliff or headland jutting out into the sea; in Alaska, a perpendicular cliff just off shore.

Kolosh. Russian term for Tlingit Indians.

Kopeck. 1/100 ruble; about 1/2 cent U.S. in 19 century.

Lavtak. Cured and processed seal or walrus hide, used to make baidaras and baidarkas.

Marki. Russian colonial currency, scrip.

Mednovtsi. Russian term for Copper River Indians.

Office Administrator. In Russian, pravitel kontory.

Phratry. Clan divisions, also the animal or other sign under which such a clan is recognized, such as wolf phratry, raven phratry, etc. Here applied to Kolosh.

Prikashchik. In medieval Russia, Muscovy and later in Siberia, an official of the prikaz, i.e. administrative department. In Alaska, a special agent employed by the Russian American Company, or the supercargo on a ship.

Promyshlennik. Russian term for fur trapper and trader, especially in Siberia and subsequently in Russia's American colonies.

Pud. Russian measure of weight; 36.11 pounds; 16.38 kilograms.

Quintal. Spanish measure; four arrobas, 101.2 pounds.

R.A.K. Rossiisko-Amerikanskaia Kompaniia.

Real. Spanish coin, silver.

Réaumur thermometer. A thermometer used in the 18 century; 0° indicates the freezing point of water and 80° the boiling point.

Rovduga. Siberian term for a reindeer hide used for barter. See zamshcha.

Ruble. Russian coin or banknote. In the early 19 century, one ruble = U.S. $.50.

Santim. Centime.

Sarana. The Kamchatka lily bulb, used for food.

Sazhen. Russian linear measure; 7 feet; 2.13 meters.

Shtoff. Russian liquid measure; 1.2 litres.

Sitka. In the context of this book, refers to the island then known as Sitka, presently named Baranov Island.

Toion. A Yakut word meaning "leader." The Russians applied the term to Siberian tribal elders of large Koriak, Chukchee and Kamchadal tribes, and similarly to Aleuts and American Indians. The word is not native to any of these peoples.

Tolkushka. Food prepared by natives of Siberia and Alaska consisting of dried meat or fish, fat and dried berries or roots; pemmican.

Uezd. Russian administrative unit; roughly corresponds to a county.

Vara. Spanish measure; 33 inches.

Vedro. Russian liquid or grain measure. (Literally, "pailful"). 2.70 gallons. 12 vedros = 1 barrel approximately.

Vershok. Russian, 1.75 inches.

Zamshcha. A cured reindeer hide used for barter among the Kolosh.

A note on dates: all dates are given according to the Julian calendar in official use in Russia from 1700 to January 26, 1918. In the 18 century that calendar was 11, and in the 19 century, 12 days behind the Gregorian calendar used in the West.

COLONIAL RUSSIAN AMERICA:
KHLEBNIKOV'S REPORTS

Александръ Андрѣевичь

БАРАНОВЪ,

Little known preliminary sketch for a portrait of Aleksandr A. Baranov,
first Chief Manager of Russia's American colonies; his face reveals much
more than the more finished portraits familiar to us. Baranov's labors
have been rewarded with the Order of Saint Anne, second class. The
artist is Mikhail Tikhonov, 1789-1862, who sailed to the west coast of
America aboard the naval corvette Kamchatka under command of Capt.
Vasilii M. Golovnin, 1817-1819. (Archive MAE AN SSSR. published in
Leonid A. Shur, "El Pintor Viajero Mijail Tijanov," America Latina, No.
1, 1975.)

1. NEW ARKHANGEL ON BARANOV ISLAND. SITKA.
REASONS FOR ITS ESTABLISHMENT.

It is a known fact that the number of sea otters gradually decreased within a few years after [Grigorii Ivanovich] Shelekhov's company occupied Kodiak Island in 1783, and in the years just after that when the Lebedev-Lastochin Company artels occupied Kenai [Cook Inlet] and Chugach [Prince William Sound] Bays and nearby areas. The primary reason for establishing these settlements was to hunt sea otters. It was for this reason that the Chief Manager of the colony, [Aleksandr Andreevich] Baranov, suggested sending parties of Aleuts in baidarkas farther southeast along the coast of America. The first of these hunting parties, under the leadership of [Egor] Purtov, reached Yakutat Bay (Bering Bay) in 1794 and took some 2,000 pelts.*

In 1795 a vessel was sent to take persons to settle Yakutat, but the leader exercised poor judgment and the group had to return to Kodiak, for lack of [fresh] water.

In the following year, 1796, in accordance with an Imperial order, a fort was built, with an adjacent settlement. This was done in order to develop agriculture and raise livestock. The Governor General of Siberia, [Ivan Alferevich] Pil, in an instruction dated May 11, 1794 addressed to Shelekhov** states, "According to Imperial decree, you are to build shipyards at Cape St. Elias, and send twenty families of settlers and ten families of agricultural workers there, or to some appropriate location on the mainland of the American continent. These persons have been assigned 36 rubles per annum, which is to be paid to them at the earliest opportunity." Yakutat Bay, which had been surveyed by Purtov and later by Baranov himself, was preferable to Cape Elias because of the advantage of having a good harbor and a forest around the harbor, and because contact had been established with the savages known as Koluzh or Kolosh [Tlingit].

There are both deciduous and coniferous trees in the forest around Yakutat Bay. The terrain is primarily hilly, but there are also meadows where tall grasses grow. The fact that grain will not ripen is apparently due to the ocean air; however there have been several attempts to grow it. The bay lies in 59-1/2° north latitude, and off to the WNW, at a distance of some 60 miles, one can see Mount St. Elias, the highest peak in North America+, in all its magnificence.

---

*There were some 500 baidarkas on that expedition. Generally from 100 to 200 baidarkas were sent to other parts of the coast of Kodiak Island and along the shore of Alaska. They could bring together as many as 700 baidarkas on Kodiak; these came from the Kenais and Chugach. Occasionally even more could be assembled.

**In the first winter after the fort was built, there was a shortage of food; seven settlers and 13 promyshlenniks died from scurvy in Yakutat, and this number does not include their wives and children. The two prikashchiks assigned to the region were very hostile toward one another and quarreled constantly.

+Khlebnikov obviously never saw Mount McKinley, 20,320 feet -- Ed.

According to the observations of [Jean Francois de Galaup de] LaPerouse, this peak lies in 60°23" [north] latitude and 140°45" longitude west of Greenwich. By his calculations the mountain is 12,672 English feet high. The Spanish navigator [Alejandro] Malaspina set the height at 2,793 tuazas, or 18,829 feet [actual height: 18,008 feet]. If these measurements are correct, then the mountain is as high as those in South America, and higher than Mauna Kea in the Sandwich Islands. I mention this in such detail only because this is contrary to the view of naturalists who maintain that mountains tend to be lower toward the poles than in equatorial regions.

From 1796 on, groups of Aleuts were constantly sent out from Kodiak, far from the settlement used as a supply depot for hunting. They left with their baidarkas and were subsequently carried on board sailing ships. In 1798 they reached Khuntsovsk [Kootznahoo] Inlet, and in 1799 they discovered sea otter breeding grounds in various smaller bays. The catch sometimes numbered from 3,000 to 5,000 pelts. A party of Aleuts generally consisted of 250 to 300 baidarkas under the leadership of two or three deputized Russian prikashchiks [agents]. The settlement at Yakutat served as a resting place, but because of its distance from the hunting party, it was necessary to have a place to store the pelts collected on the hunt.

Parties were nearly always sent out without the support of sailing vessels. They went such great distances that they would be gone until late fall, when they were endangered by storms. The coast from Snow Sound to Yakutat and all the way to Chugach Bay is either rocky or full of shoals. There are very few places where even baidarkas can land. Thus if the baidarka parties had such good hunting that they went even further, or if they were delayed on their return voyage home, they were in certain danger of being wrecked during the autumn storms, or they might have to stay out all winter and face a shortage of supplies and the enmity of the Kolosh [Tlingits].

Baranov also had political motives for spreading out Russia's possessions: to prevent other nations from laying claim to the coast. The government approved this reasoning. In a letter to [Stefan Grigorevich] Larionov dated June 24, 1800, Baranov referred to the Sitka settlement as follows: "We are in these places now not only because of trade advantages, but also: 1) because of what we know of local conditions; 2) in order to prevent the English and Americans from trading with the savages, to whom they supply firearms; and to prevent them from settling places which have been discovered by Russian seafarers."

In July of 1799 Baranov came to Sitka [Island] aboard the galley Olga which he personally commanded; a group of persons was to meet him there, but did not wait for him and left for Kodiak with a catch of 1,500 sea otter.* Medvednikov, who had been appointed supervisor of the settlement, arrived there with his people aboard the Orel.

---

*The following day, after the party left Sitka, the Aleuts ate some black mussels as usual. They immediately suffered cramps and nausea, and within two hours more than 100 died. In order to stop the vomiting, the leaders dosed the victims with tobacco mixed with gunpowder, and this stopped the epidemic, but not before an additional 15 men had died. Because of this disaster the bay was named Perish Bay, and it is so called to the present time.

Baranov chose an advantageous location, gave the natives presents and offered them protection and defense against their neighbors. They left 50 Aleuts there to help with the work, and the crew of the ship Ekaterina, which had gone to look over Bucareli Bay, also assisted. Baranov wrote, "We first built a large balagan where we cached the supplies of food which we had unloaded from the ship; next, a small black [windowless] bath house, which I moved into in October. Before that I had lived in a little shack in rainy weather, and I suffered there the entire winter because of smoke, and because of a leaking roof I was rained on until the end of February. Next we built a two-story warehouse with two watch towers which were eight sazhens [56 feet] long and four [28 feet] wide. After that we built barracks for the Aleuts." The fort was named for the Archangel Michael.

During the winter the Aleuts and the Russians caught 40 sea lions and 150 seals for food. In spring they caught halibut, and in March great schools of herring came. During the winter the Aleuts caught some 300 sea otter near the settlement. During Baranov's sojourn, five foreign ships put in there and he became acquainted with the persons on board. He familiarized himself with their transactions and became keenly aware of the profits lost to us by their trade.

The Kolosh initially treated us with indifference, but when they realized that we were building a substantial permanent settlement, which they had not expected, they armed themselves with spears and tried several times to seize it from us. They were unsuccessful, however, due to Baranov's vigilance and caution. On April 20, 1800, Baranov left to sail to Kodiak on a galley, and put Medvednikov in charge as administrator, with 20 Russians. The garrison was careless, and the Kolosh attacked and destroyed the settlement in 1802.

With the aid of the ship Neva which had arrived from Russia, Baranov seized the Kolosh strongholds on October 8, 1804. He built a fort nearby which he named New Arkhangel. Thanks to God's help the fort is still standing at the present time.

2. PROFITS FORMERLY RECEIVED, AND RESULTS FOLLOWING BARANOV'S ADMINISTRATION

Baranov decided to establish the main office here. Even earlier he had brought to the attention of the Governing Board of the Company the fact that the advantages of this location would bring much profit to the Empire. Consider the fact that English and American vessels had been putting in here for ten years, six to ten times per year, to trade for 2,000 to 3,000 pelts in various places. An average for the six vessels might be considered to be 2,000 pelts. One must thus conclude that some 12,000 pelts were being taken out each year. Even if that figure were reduced to 10,000, it is apparent that over a period of ten years some 100,000 pelts were exported. These sold for 30 piastres or 45 rubles apiece in Kamchatka; thus the revenue was 4,500,000 rubles. If the cost of procuring the pelts was 1,500,000 rubles, then the net profit over the ten-year period would be 3,000,000 rubles. Baranov went on to declare, "These same circumstances which profit our country are the very incentives which led me to establish the settlement on Sitka. In spite of our inadequate number of personnel, and the circumstances of the Company, it is our decision to establish the first settlement, familiarize ourselves with existing conditions, and in time expect important results."

This opinion was important also in that we thus concealed our weakness and prevented the likelihood of attack. Once we had established our presence here, Aleuts could be put to work and thus obviate the necessity for sending new persons out from Kodiak each year. The deep water and abundant forests made it possible to build a shipyard. And finally, there were obvious advantages in establishing relations with the Americans who after trading along the northwest coast on their homeward voyages, would dispose of their [surplus] goods at moderate prices. This cannot be considered a very great advantage, however, for if the Americans knew that the Company would buy their goods, they would willingly come to Kodiak and even more remote places.

Our first commercial encounter with them took place on Kodiak, where there was a serious shortage of supplies (due to the disaster [shipwreck] suffered by the ship Phoenix). In May, 1801, we bought 12,000 rubles worth of goods from them, which we paid for in fox pelts. In 1802 the Englishman, [Henry] Barber, and the American, [John] Ebbets, ransomed several prisoners from the Kolosh and brought them to Kodiak. We bought goods from them [Barber and Ebbets] worth more than 70,000 rubles. In 1803 the American, [Joseph] O'Cain, sold goods to us, and we concluded an agreement regarding the sea otter hunt in California.

During the 14-year period between the time Sitka was settled and the time Baranov was replaced, it is apparent, on the basis of what developed, that he changed his mind a good deal as a result of various circumstances. Fur trade took a different direction, and shipbuilding was not always successful, but trade with the Americans increased significantly. Through them we acquired a new route for trade with Canton. Let us examine these remarkable developments in detail.

The Sea Otter Hunt In The Vicinity Of Sitka

A year after Sitka was settled, in June 1805, a party of Aleuts in 300 baidarkas was sent out into the sound to hunt sea otters under the leadership of Bykadorov. Two sailing vessels, Ermak and Rostislav, accompanied them for protection. They hunted in Chatham Strait and Frederick Sound until the 21st of August, but took only 1,645 pelts because of constant harrassment on the part of the Kolosh. When the party returned to Sitka, 200 of the baidarkas were sent to Kodiak under the leadership of Demianenkov. En route this group learned from some Kolosh who had been sold to us that the Kolosh had destroyed the Yakutat settlement. Accordingly, the leader of the hunting party acted with extreme caution. They reached the settlement at night and witnessed the disaster. They had been traveling by baidarka for several days and were very tired, but there was no safe place to rest. It was impossible to go along the shore safely, so the leader and many of the Aleuts in the group set out for Nuchek. Those who were too exhausted to go on, some 31 baidarkas, put themselves into God's hands and approached the coast. Soon a violent storm blew in from the southwest, and all who had put out to sea were drowned. Those who had gone ashore were fortunately not apprehended by the Kolosh. They continued on their way and found the baidarkas and the bodies of their ill-fated companions which had washed ashore.

This disaster halted the successful hunts. In 1806 no hunting parties put out
from Sitka. In 1807 a group of 75 baidarkas led by Eremin went around the Cape of
Oman to Chatham Strait, intending to go to Kaigan Strait; however they met with
fierce Kolosh opposition and returned with little profit. [Ivan Aleksandrovich]
Kuskov, who had remained on Sitka, redirected them to the Bay of Islands, where
they took about 300 pelts and returned on September 10.

In March 1808 a hunting party of 100 baidarkas was sent to the Bay of Islands, and
returned on April 22 with 130 pelts. 95 more baidarkas joined them, and they
went around the Cape of Oman to Kenai Bay [Cook Inlet] under the protection of the
ship Nikolai, commanded by [C. M.] Benzeman.* The ship Kodiak was sent there to
trade with the Kolosh. The hunting party took some 1,700 pelts, but they did not
trade with the Kolosh, who were unwilling to barter their sea otter pelts. When
the party returned on July 21, all 110 baidarkas were sent out again, to Cape
Echka. They returned August 30 with 170 pelts.

On June 16, 1809, a hunting group went to the Sound with Kuglinov in charge, and
the schooner Chirikov accompanied them for protection. The men returned in
September. The Kolosh had everywhere opposed them in their hunt for sea otters.

On March 10, 1810, Shvetsov took a hunting party to the Bay of Islands. They
spent ten days there and took about 150 pelts. According to Shvetsov's report,
the Aleuts became ill with diarrhea from contaminated water; as a result of this,
52 of the baidarkas from Kodiak and the Fox Islands could not take part in the
hunt. Only two persons died, however.

In May of that same year a hunting party was sent to the Sound. Both for protection and to trade with the Kolosh, two large sailing vessels accompanied the
party, the Juno under Benzeman, and the Americanets Winship. Kuskov commanded the
expedition. The party reached Dundas Island, near the Queen Charlotte Islands,
and began their hunt, but they were constantly harrassed by the Kolosh. There
were American ships trading there at the time, and a certain [Samuel] Hill openly
expressed his dissatisfaction and threatened Kuskov that he would unite with the
Kolosh and use every possible means to prevent us from hunting. At one time
several ships with armed men surrounded our two vessels, and Hill, on board his
ship, stood off at a distance ready to support them. In order to avoid conflict
Kuskov decided to turn back, for eight of his Aleuts had already been killed in
various encounters. On his return voyage he put into land at every opportunity,
but he everywhere encountered well armed Kolosh ready to attack on the slightest
provocation. Kuskov returned on August 2 with both of his ships and 1,400 pelts.
After his voyage, no further hunting parties were sent to the Sound. But in the
meantime a new opportunity for hunting sea otter along the California coast
opened up.

In 1815 the ship Otkrytie, under command of [Iakov Ankievich] Podushkin, was sent
along the Sound to trade. The prikashchik Toropogritskii traded with the Kolosh

---

*Christopher M. Benjamin of Danzig had served the Russian American Company since
1807. He married a native woman in Alaska, and in 1823 petitioned to be made a
Russian subject, at which time his name was changed to Khristofor Benzeman. -- Ed.

for 340 large sea otters, 107 medium and 39 small. The voyage lasted 46 days. Hunting parties near Sitka took 276 prime* sea otters and 73 yearlings.

In 1816 hunting parties took 63 sea otters. Between 1815 and 1818 they traded with the Kolosh on Sitka for 108 prime sea otters, 37 yearlings and 18 cubs.

Hunting Sea Otters Along The California Coast
Together With Foreigners

When the American O'Cain arrived in Kodiak in 1803 on Eclipse, he sold part of his goods to Baranov, and informed him that he had discovered a new island off the coast of California which abounded in sea otters. He was the first to suggest that Baranov supply him with baidarkas to use for hunting sea otter, and that they then divide the catch. Baranov was immediately favorable to this idea, and they reached an agreement. As security, O'Cain gave Baranov goods worth 12,000 rubles. Shvetsov and [Timofei] Tarakanov were appointed to this expedition and were assigned 20 baidarkas. They left Kodiak October 26, 1803 and put in at the port of San Diego. They then went to San Quentin, where they took 1,100 pelts. O'Cain bought about 700 sea otter pelts from missionaries and Spanish officials in various places, and paid no more than three piastres apiece for them. Shvetsov learned from one of the sailors that his captain had not actually discovered the island, but he had been there in 1801 and had seen great numbers of sea otters; and since he had no way to take them, he decided to involve Baranov. O'Cain returned safely to Kodiak in June 1804, and because of the success of this first venture, Baranov turned his attention to the California coast.

In 1804 and 1805 the occupation of Sitka and [Nikolai Petrovich] Rezanov's visit served to strengthen these ties. In May 1806 an agreement was concluded with [Jonathan] Winship which would give him 70 baidarkas under the leadership of [Sysoi] Slobodchikov.** He would go to the mouth of the Columbia River to begin hunting, and continue all the way to Cape Barro de Arena.+ While in California Winship quarreled with Slobodchikov; the latter, while on the island of Seros, bought the schooner Nikolai in exchange for 100 large sea otter pelts and 50 medium, and persuaded an American to sail it to the Sandwich Islands and then to Sitka, where he arrived August 22, 1807. Winship and his party returned September 8. The entire catch consisted of 3,006 prime sea otters, 1,264 yearlings and 594 cubs. These were divided up in Sitka. After Winship left, Baranov went to Kodiak, where he met an American named Campbell. On October 25,

---

*Prime sea otter pelts run up to six feet. -- Ed.

**Slobodchikov is thought to have drawn a map of the mouth of the Columbia River. See Svetlana G. Fedorova, THE RUSSIAN POPULATION IN ALASKA AND CALIFORNIA, p. 349. -- Ed.

+The hunt was to last from 10 to 14 months, with the catch to be divided equally. The leader of the hunting party had the rank of captain. The Company provided food for the Aleuts. The captain was to pay the Aleuts 2-1/2 piastres for each prime sea otter, 1-1/2 for a yearling, and 1 for a cub. If an Aleut were to be taken prisoner by the Spaniards, or killed by savages, the captain was to pay his family a sum of 250 talers.

1806, they made an agreement that 12 baidarkas under Tarakanov's supervision would go along the California coast and begin hunting from the Bay of Trinidad, but that they would not approach any Spanish settlements. Campbell was successful, and returned to New Arkhangel on August 3. The catch consisted of 753 prime sea otters, 222 yearlings and 250 cubs.

[George W.] Ayers, master of Mercury, agreed in May 1818 to take 25 baidarkas under Shvetsov's supervision.

They left Kodiak on June 26, went to the Queen Charlotte Islands and to the Columbia River to trade, then began hunting at Trinidad. They were also in Bodega and San Francisco bays. When Ayers returned to Sitka he gave the Company its share which consisted of 844 prime sea otters, 128 yearlings and 68 cubs. Shvetsov had also purchased 37 pelts of various sea animals, and 190 river beaver pelts.

Other hunting contracts were successfully concluded: in December 1809 with Jonathan Winship, master of O'Cain; in October 1810 with Nathan Winship, master of Albatross; in November, 1811, with Thomas Meek and William Blanchard of Amethyst and Katherine; with William Davis, of Isabella; and in 1813 with [Isaac] Whittemore, master of the Charon. All of them took baidarkas along and all successfully fulfilled their purpose. The table below indicates the large profits which were made through cooperation with the Americans.

THE COMPANY'S SHARE [of pelts]

	Prime	Yearling	Cub	Total
Jonathan Winship	2,251	267	208	2,726
Nathan Winship, Albatross	389	70	101	560
William Davis, Isabella	989	216	283	1,488
Thomas Meek, Amethyst	655	49	17	721
William Blanchard, Katherine	626	93	39	758
[Isaac] Whittemore, Charon	798	68	30	896
	5,708	763	678	7,149

Acquisition Of Sea Otters In California
By The Company's Own Hunting Parties

Since Baranov had no information about California, he learned about the climate and natural resources of the land through persons he had sent out with the hunting parties; and he waited for an opportune time to attempt to use only his own men to hunt sea otters along that coast. When he returned from Kodiak in August, 1808, Baranov sent the schooner Nikolai, under command of [Nikolai Isaakovich] Bulagin, to trade and hunt for sea otters, this latter assignment under the direction of the prikashchik [Timofei] Tarakanov. They were ordered to go to the Columbia River, then from there to proceed to Gray's Harbor to rendezvous with the ship Kodiak. The shipwreck of the Nikolai and the subsequent capture of the crew have been described by Tarakanov and published in the HISTORY OF SHIPWRECKS. On October 20 Kodiak was sent out under command of navigator Petrov, and Kuskov, Baranov's energetic associate, accompanied him. They were

instructed to familiarize themselves with places hitherto unknown. Strong
headwinds prevented them from approaching Gray's Harbor, but they put in at
Trinidad and from there went on to Bodega on December 15. They began hunting in
this latter place, and took 1,453 large sea otters, 406 medium, and 491 small.
They left Bodega on August 18, but because of headwinds it took them 49 days to
reach Sitka. While Kodiak was at Bodega, five of her crew, both Russian and
American, deserted ship. On January 22, 1811, Kuskov again sailed for
California aboard the schooner Chirikov, under command of Benjamin. They
reached Bodega on February 21, but hunting was not good there so they sent 22
baidarkas to San Francisco Bay where they found Tarakanov with a hunting party
of 48 baidarkas which had been left there by Davis on Isabella, and another
group of 60 baidarkas sent by Winship. During a three-month hunt, Kuskov's
party took 1,160 prime pelts and 78 yearlings. At first the Spaniards did not
raise any objection, but later they decided to prevent them from taking on fresh
water. They posted guards at all fresh water sources, with instructions to
capture any Aleuts. Consequently, the hunting party was forced to withdraw.
The brig put out from Bodega on June 20 and stopped at the Farallon Islands to
take seals. They reached Sitka on July 28.

In November of that same year Baranov again sent Kuskov out aboard the schooner
Chirikov. He took Aleut hunters and 40 baidarkas and carried instructions to
establish a settlement along the coast of Albion, in some region that had an
abundance of sea otters and was suitable for the development of agriculture.
With the assistance of the crew from Chirikov, this group built Ross settlement
in June, 1812. During this same period, hunting parties were sent out whenever
conditions permitted. Between March 1812 and 1815 they took 714 prime and 143
yearling sea otters. In 1815 they took 114 prime and 39 yearling, in 1816, 84
prime and 13 yearling; and in 1817, 44 prime and 11 yearling. It is apparent
from these figures that the size of the catch diminished. The reason is not so
much any hindrance on the part of the Spaniards, who did not permit hunting near
their possessions, as the fact that the Aleuts caused the dispersal of the sea
otters.

In 1815 Baranov sent out the brig Ilmen with a party of Aleuts under Tarakanov,
and trading goods with the prikashchik Nikiforov. The captain of the ship was
an American named Vosdwit [Wosdwith (Bancroft) or Wadsworth (Okun)]. The chief
commissioner was also an American, Dr. [John] Eliot. The party obtained and
sent to Sitka 322 prime sea otters, 50 yearling and 20 cubs. Eliot cleared
10,000 piastres in cash. He continued to smuggle along the coast and was eventually apprehended by the Spaniards, who also took a number of Russians and many
Aleuts. Because of strong tides Ilmen could not go directly to Sitka, and so
returned to the Sandwich Islands, reaching there May 2, 1816; there the ship was
under the jurisdiction of Dr. [Georg Anton; in Russian, Egor Antonovich]
Scheffer, whom Baranov had appointed to the post of administrator of the Islands.

Importation Of Wheat From California

After an attempt to establish trade in California undertaken by order of
Chancellor N. P. Rezanov in 1806, there was no further opportunity to pursue
this aim; however, through Americans who went with hunting groups, they sometimes received local produce such as wheat, barley, beans, lard, salt and salted
beef. Kuskov established himself on the shores of Albion and became acquainted

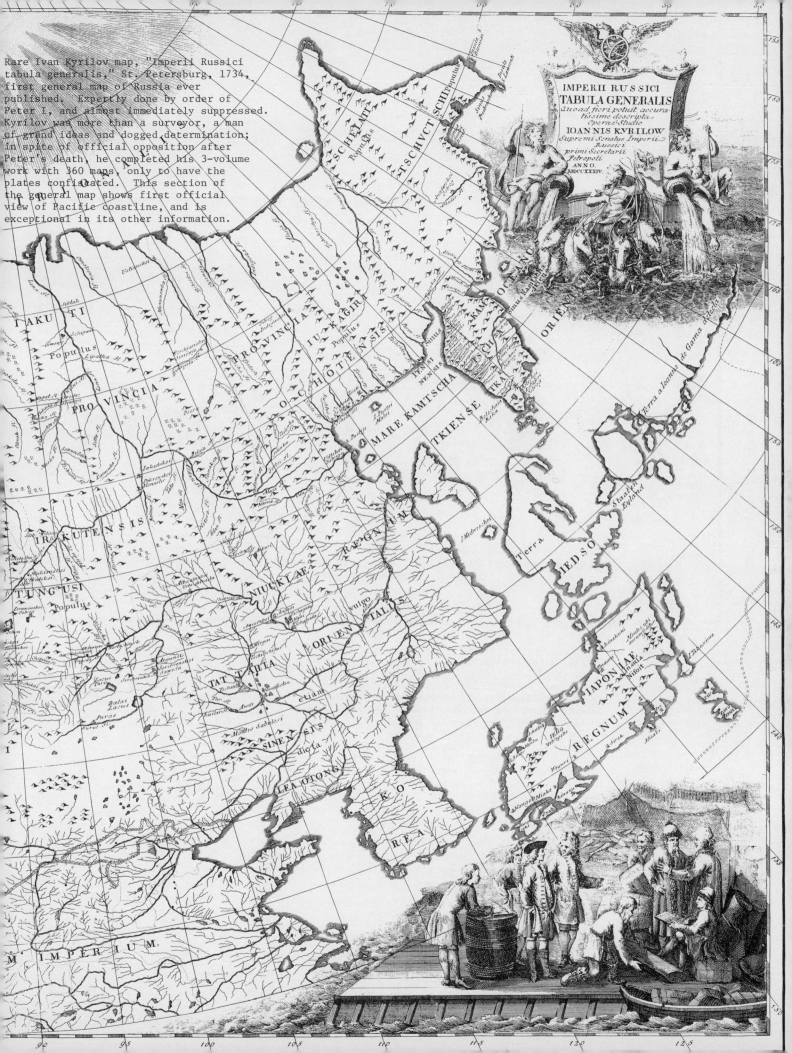

Rare Ivan Kyrilov map, "Imperii Russici tabula generalis," St. Petersburg, 1734, first general map of Russia ever published. Expertly done by order of Peter I, and almost immediately suppressed. Kyrilov was more than a surveyor, a man of grand ideas and dogged determination; In spite of official opposition after Peter's death, he completed his 3-volume work with 360 maps, only to have the plates confiscated. This section of the general map shows first official view of Pacific coastline, and is exceptional in its other information.

IMPERII RUSSICI
TABULA GENERALIS
Quo ad fieri potuit accura-
tissime descripta
Operae et Studio
IOANNIS KYRILOW
Supremi Senatus Imperii
Russici
primi Secretarii
Petropoli
ANNO
MDCCXXXIV.

Plan of Pavlovsk Harbor on Kodiak Island, an exceptional compacted view
from the steep slope above the harbor, dated 1798 but unsigned. This
rare early view clearly reveals several important structures in the then
Company headquarters, which had just previously been moved from Three
Saints Harbor on the same island, and would soon move again to New
Arkhangel on Sitka Island. The Administrator's building with the flag
atop is in the foreground, and behind it one can see the Church of the
Resurrection, functioning today at approximately the same site. The
unknown artist thoughtfully included a languishing vegetable garden and
the "treeless island" which made a protected anchorage for ships and
traders. (From A.V. Efimov, Atlas Geograficheskikh Otkrytii v Sibiri
i v Severo-Zapadnoi Amerike [Atlas of Geographical Discoveries in
Siberia and Northwest America], Moscow, 1964.)

"A view of Pavlovsk Harbor on Kodiak Island," by I.G. Voznesenskii,
1842 or 1843. For 20 years Kodiak was the administrative center of the
Russian American Company, first at Three Saints Harbor, then at
Pavlovsk, the present townsite of Kodiak. Here one sees the narrow
channel and protected harbor. Two Aleuts paddle a three-hatch
baidarka, transporting a Russian priest. In the distance two smaller
baidarkas are busy near the two-masted sailing vessel. Above the
administrative office waves the red-white-and-green tricolor of the
Company, emblazoned with the Imperial double-headed eagle. (Archive of
the Museum of Anthropology and Ethnography of the Academy of Sciences
of the USSR [hereafter MAE AN SSSR], Leningrad.)

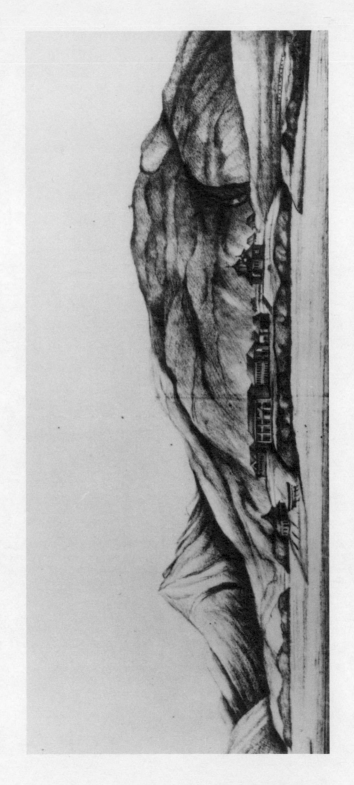

"A view of Pavlovsk Settlement on Kodiak Island," by I.G. Voznesenskii, 1842 or 1843. The center part of the Russian American Company settlement is shown in this view. Atop the low rise stands the little Church of the Resurrection; there is at present a lovely small Russian Orthodox church in the same location. Downhill and slightly to the left, to the rear of the two-story warehouse and barracks, stands the factor's warehouse, built in 1792. It has been preserved to the present day and is listed in the National Register of Historic Places as the Erskine House, maintained by the Kodiak Historical Society. (Archive MAE AN SSSR.)

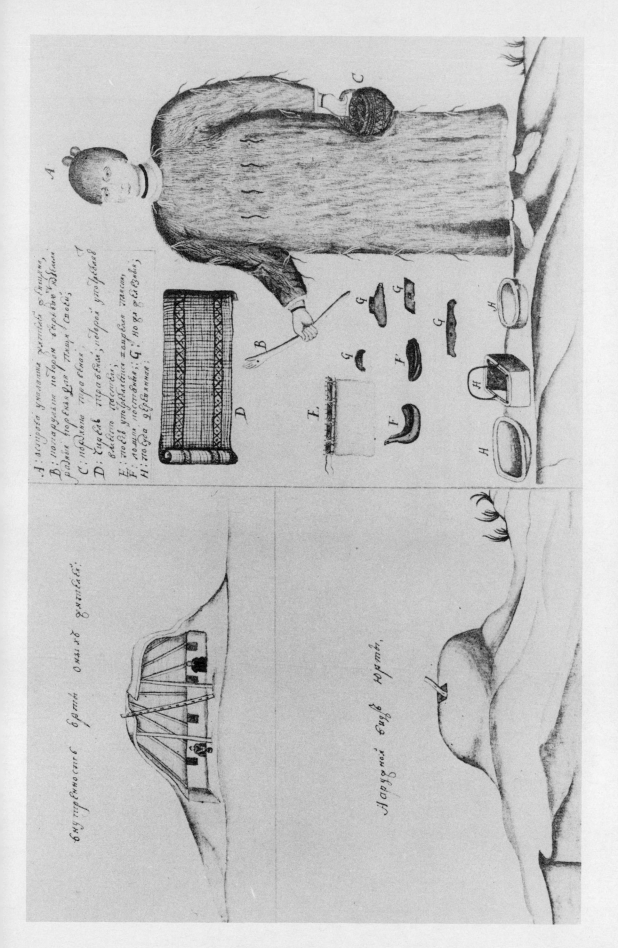

Drawing by M.D. Levashov (1760's) shows Aleut woman of Unalaska and simple implements of her daily life before native traditions were modified by foreign influences. She wears full-length cloak of bird skins and holds wooden digging stick, B. Her other belongings are C, finely woven grass basket for which Aleuts are famous; D, grass mat for sitting or sleeping; E, belt worn during dancing; F, bone spoon; G, iron knife blade; H, wooden table implements. Large earthen iurt on left was a practical solution to problem of shelter on treeless islands. (Roza G. Liapunova, "Etnograpficheskoe znachenie ekspeditsii kapitanov P.K. Krenitsyna i M.D. Levashova na Aleutskie Ostrova, 1764-1769 gg" [Ethnographic Significance of the Expedition of Captains P.K. Krenitsyn and M.D. Levashov to the Aleutian Islands, 1764-1769], Sovetskaia Etnografiia, 1971, no. 6.)

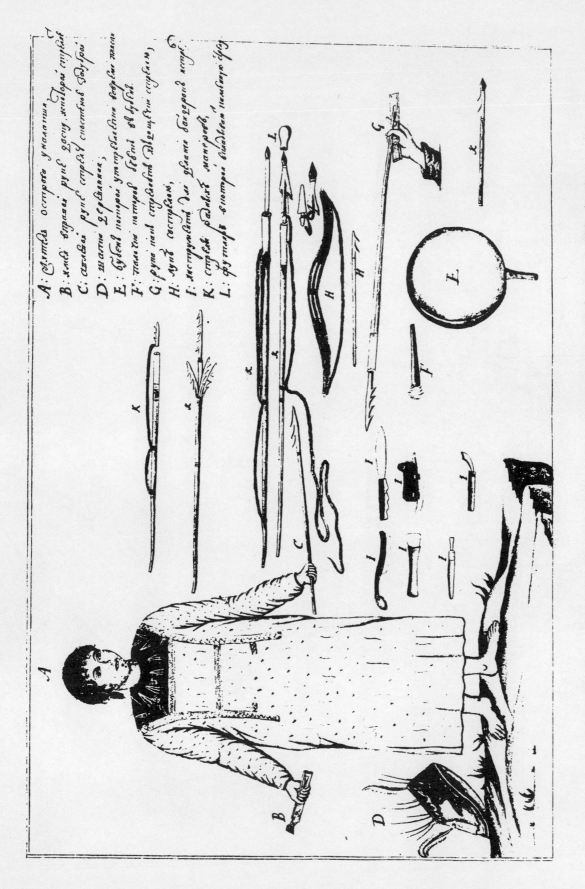

Aleut hunter of 1760's wore waterproof kamlei made of gut trimmed with feathers. This drawing by Levashov shows him holding throwing board, B used to hurl spear, C, which has notched bone head. Other items are D, wooden hunting hat; E, tambourine used during dances; F, drumstick used to beat tambourine; G, closeup view of hand in position with throwing board ready to hurl spear; H, bow and arrow; I, instrument used to make baidarkas and arrows; K, various kinds of arrows; L, case for stone arrowhead. (Liapunova, "Etnograficheskoe znachenie...")

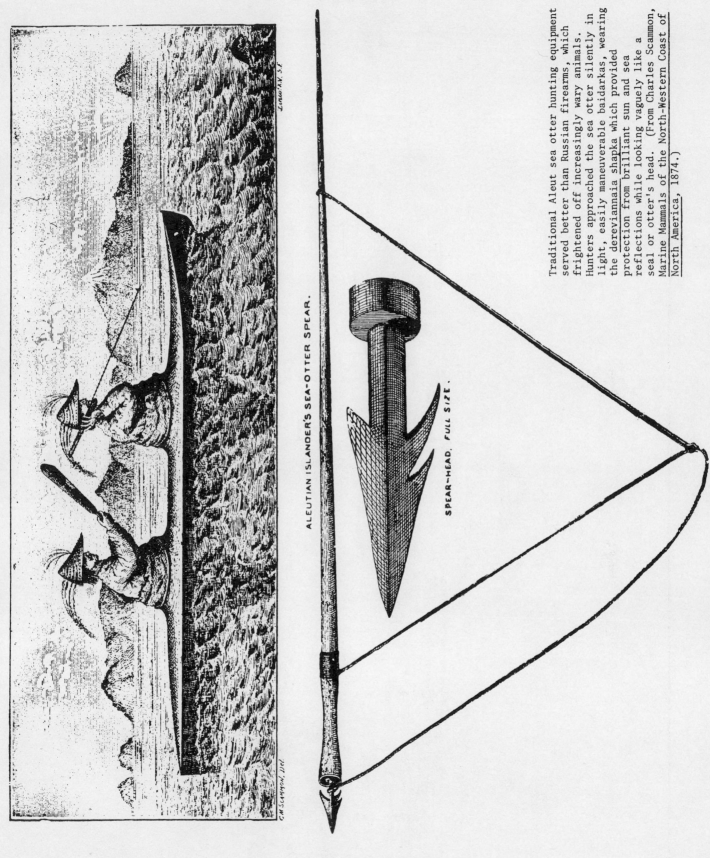

ALEUTIAN ISLANDERS' SEA OTTER CANOE, OR BAIDARKA, WITH HUNTERS ENGAGED IN THE CHASE.

ALEUTIAN ISLANDER'S SEA-OTTER SPEAR.

SPEAR-HEAD. FULL SIZE.

Traditional Aleut sea otter hunting equipment served better than Russian firearms, which frightened off increasingly wary animals. Hunters approached the sea otter silently in light, easily maneuverable baidarkas, wearing the dereviannaia shapka which provided protection from brilliant sun and sea reflections while looking vaguely like a seal or otter's head. (From Charles Scammon, Marine Mammals of the North-Western Coast of North America, 1874.)

Aleutes Sea Otter Hunting; south of Saanak Island.
The Aleutes Waiting for the otter to rise again.

Drawing by Henry Wood Elliott (1870's) shows technique of sea otter hunting party of Aleuts in
two and three-man baidarkas. An otter has dived, but his sounding has been marked, and
experienced hunters know he must soon surface, probably within their ring. Each hunter has
incised his harpoon heads and lances with his own identifying mark for practical convenience.
(OHS photo collections. Original now in National Museum.)

Natives hunting the White Whale (Beluga) Cooks Inlet, Alaska.
Iliama or Illiamna volcano

Aleut hunters harpoon a "white whale" (beluga) in Cook Inlet, using
detachable points and bladder floats to tire the great mammal while
marking its location. Still active Iliamna volcano in distance.

Drawing by Henry Wood Elliott (1870s). (OHS photo collections.
Original now in National Museum.)

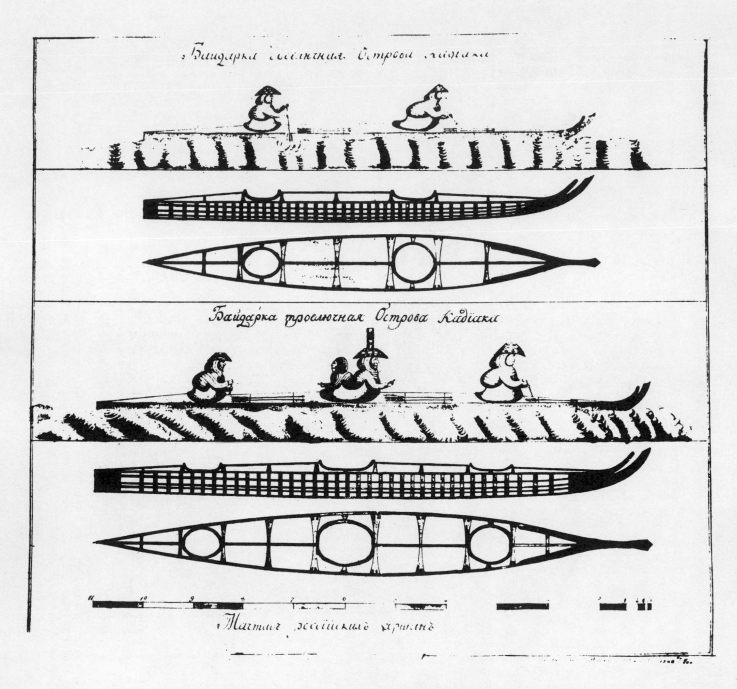

Diagrams of standard Kodiak Island two and three-person (and a babe in this case) baidarkas. The light and beautifully constructed three-seat vessel is 11 arshins in length, or about 25 2/3rds feet. Drawings by a missionary, May 4, 1793. (Holy Synod Archives, copy in University of Washington Library.)

with missionaries and with several officials. He visited the port of San Francisco and traded for 2,886 puds [36 pound unit] of wheat in 1813 and for 1,695 puds in 1815. Commissioner Eliot supplied Fort Ross with 4,838 puds, and Kuskov sent 8,022-1/2 puds to Sitka. Governor de Solá, who came to California in 1816, had a different attitude from the previous administration. Indignant over the fact that a settlement had been established, he terminated relations and trade. He also gave the order that the Russians should be watched carefully wherever they hunted.

Shipbuilding In Sitka

Rezanov came to Sitka in 1805. Noting the shortage of sailing vessels, which were necessary for a projected expedition to Japan, he ordered a tender to be built. Two shipwrights began building it in September, and it was launched the following June and named Avos. [Gavriil I.] Davydov commanded this tender, which was sent on an expedition to Japan, wintered in Kamchatka, and was later ship-wrecked near Cross Sound by Karpinskii.

Baranov could not manage the shipwrights and had to send them both back to Russia. Meanwhile, since he did not have enough ships, he bought some from the Americans, but considered that it would be more to his advantage to undertake the building of some. With that in mind, in 1806 he concluded an agreement with an American named Lincoln, who in the following year built the brig Sitka, for which he received 2,000 rubles. An older ship, the Aleksandr, was retimbered. In June, 1807, the keel was laid for Otkrytie, which was launched July 16, 1808. Lincoln received 2,500 rubles for its construction. The same year repairs were made on Juno, and the keel was laid for Chirikov, at the same price. After Lincoln left in September, 1809, no more new ships were built. A promyshlennik named Mukin undertook the repair of old ships with some success. The ships built by Lincoln deserve mention. Sitka, a beautiful boat, was shipwrecked along the coast of Kamchatka. Chirikov was in use until 1825. Otkrytie, after 1820, was in use for five years more as a storehouse for wheat.

Meanwhile in the Ross settlement a promyshlennik named Grudinin, who had been Lincoln's assistant, volunteered to build a ship. He chose a variety of oak he was unfamiliar with, and in 1816 the keel was laid for Rumiantsev.

Trade With Foreigners On Sitka

Mention was made earlier of commercial transactions between American and English crews on Kodiak. After the occupation of Sitka, from May 1805 on, foreign ships began to put in there regularly. Because of a shortage of goods and provisions, Rezanov bought the ship Juno from [John d'] Wolf, with its entire cargo.*

Trade with Americans on Sitka reached a sum of 1,170,000 rubles, which included the purchase of five ships: Juno, Myrtle (renamed Kodiak), Lydia (renamed Ilmen),

---

   *See Crownhart-Vaughan and Vaughan, "Dnevnik amerikanskogo puteshestvennika nachala XIX v. Dzhona deVulfa kak istoricheskii istochnik." ["The diary of the American traveler of the early 19 century John d'Wolf as historical source material."] -- Ed.

Atahualpa (renamed Bering) and Amethyst. Payment was made to the Americans in sea otter pelts, 4,884 of all sizes, 3,845 sea otter tails, 9,694 river beavers, 362,730 fur seals, 864 river otters, and 235 foxes; and 94,587.50 piastres were transferred to the administrative account. Baranov computed the piastre exchange rate at two rubles, but when it was devalued in Russia, the Company lost heavily on the exchange.

The table below indicates that in trading, prime sea otter pelts brought from 40 to 50 piastres: that is, 80 to 100 rubles; medium, 20 to 25 piastres or 40 to 50 rubles; fur seals, a principal item of trade, 3/4 to 1-1/2 piastres, or 1.50 rubles to 3 rubles.

TABLE SHOWING WHEN AND AT WHAT PRICE BASIC COMMODITIES WERE PURCHASED FROM FOREIGNERS

Item	1803 from Trescott & d'Wolf	1806 from Winship	1808 from Ayers	1810 from Davis	1811 from Ebbets & Whittemore
Buckwheat flour, small barrel	piastres 10			16	
Salt beef, small barrel	25		13	10	
Rum & brandy, gallon	3.50	4	3-3.50	3-4	1.50
Treacle, gallon	1.50	1.75	1.25	1	1
Virginia tobacco, 100	25	25	50	15	9
Resin, small barrel	10				
Soap, 100	25	25		20	
Rifles with bayonets	6				
Frieze, yard. From 1.50 to 2.14			4	2	2
Plates, dozen		3			
Coffee, pound		.75			
White wine, gallon		3		2	
Vinegar, gallon		.75	1		.30
Resin and pitch, small barrel		11.25			9
Millet, cwt.			7.50	7	2 pud
Blue Chinese cotton, bolt			1.50		
Large blankets, each			3.50		2
Salt, cwt.				4	
Rock sugar				16.80 for 5 puds	
English flour, cwt.				8.72	
Granulated sugar, cwt.					15

Trade In Canton Through The Americans

Captain O'Cain of Eclipse, who had made a commercial transaction with Baranov on Kodiak in 1803 and was the first to suggest the possibility of sea otter hunting along the California coast, came to New Arkhangel in August 1806 with a proposal to explore trade possibilities in Nagasaki, Canton or ports in eastern India. Baranov sent a considerable number of pelts with him and assigned Bykadorov and Toropogritskii as his deputies to go with him. O'Cain exchanged the pelts in Canton at almost no profit. On his return voyage he put in at Kamchatka where he gave the local commissioner, Miasnikov, 200,000 rubles worth of Chinese cotton and other goods. He proceeded toward Kodiak with the rest, but his ship was wrecked on Sanak Island, and almost the entire cargo was lost.

When Baranov received word of this situation, he felt that it was impossible for his deputies to retrieve anything from the loss, and felt strongly that O'Cain had duped him. However, since O'Cain had been killed in the shipwreck on the island, the matter was concluded.

Ebbets was employed by the wealthy and powerful merchant [John Jacob] Astor, and was a man Baranov had known for some time and trusted in trade. He came to Sitka in July 1810 and negotiated an agreement to take Company furs to exchange in Canton. Ebbets was to receive five percent of the transaction as his share. Baranov agreed to pay 18,000 piastres as freight on his goods to Canton and on Chinese goods from Canton. Ebbets was responsible for all expenses in Canton. In the following table are listed the goods Baranov sent, and what they were sold for in Canton.

Sent from the colonies		[piastres]
2,391 sea otters, pelts, prime	@ 50	119,550
112 yearlings	20	2,240
165 cubs	6	495
356 cubs	3	1,068
67 cubs	1	67
3,055 prime sea otter tails	3	9,165
13 yearling tails	1	13
326 prime river otters	8	2,608
285 yearling river otters	8	1,710
183 cub river otters	3	549
21 little river otters	1.50	31.50
31 river beaver, various sizes		167
30 white polar fox		30
122 sables		89.60
61 mink		30.50
100 Kodiak fox		200
30 cross fox		150
10 black-brown fox	15	150
6,220 fur seals		6,220

Exchanged in Canton		[piastres]
2,503 prime and yearling sea otters	@ 21.50	53,814.50
518 cub sea otters	4	2,072
3,555 tails	2.15	7,643.25
822 river otters	4	3,288
28 river beavers	6.50	182
3 small river beavers	2	6
Fox:	1.50	255
30 white fox		
30 cross fox		
10 black-brown fox		
100 red fox		
6,405 fur seals	1	6,405
200 defective fur seals		100
11 sable tippets		132
75 mink	25	18.75
101 puds 36 pounds whale bone		63
17 puds 33 pounds teeth*		42
Piastres		74,021.50

or 148,043 rubles

| 17 puds 33 pounds teeth | 10 | 178.25 |
| 101 puds 36 pounds whale bone | 5 | 509.50 |

Rubles: 145,611 rubles 35 kopecks

	Tel	Mes**
123 pikols 55 katti rock sugar	10	7
24 pikols 65 katti rock sugar	11	7
273 pikols 95 katti rock sugar	7	9
1,000 pikols wheat	3	4
	8,637	7

Figuring 1 piastre = 82 kondorinas: 11,996.80 piastres

---

*The Russian American Company exported walrus teeth to Turkey and Persia. Okun, p. 56. -- Ed.

**1 tel = 10 mes; 1 mes = 10 kondorils; 1 kondoril = 10 kem. 100 katti = 1 pikol = 133 English pounds = ¹48 Russian pounds.

4,000 pieces of nankeen @ 90 santim

[piastres]

2,000 blue Chinese cotton	1.20
800 unbleached Chinese cotton	.90
300 black Chinese cotton	2.75
200 bombazine	2
600 cotton	from 3.50 - 6.50
10 velvet	28
250 demicotton	1.50
10 pikols thread	100

6,250 English pounds 48 pikols 90 katti	Hysson tea	45
13,515 English pounds 101 pikols 36 katti	Pekoe tea	54.50
13,400 English pounds 100 pikols 50 katti	Sushop tea	35
5,085 English pounds 38 pikols 14 katti	Gunpowder tea	62

Tels	13,606.08
at 72 kondorils	18,896.33

[piastres]

10 cases tea services	2.40
22 cases table china	23
2 cases plates	50
55 bolts seersucker	4
595 silk gilets	840
500 bolts silk	9.20
500 bolts silk	6.85
200 bolts silk	5
147 bolts atlas satin	20.25
50 cases kerchiefs	9.75
170 bolts satin	18 - 19.75
50 bolts satin	16.50
30 bolts taffeta	12.75
28 katti silk	6.50
5 bolts raw wool camelot	26

Total for all goods	64,388.34

Baranov received all of these goods, along with accurate accounts and documents which Ebbets gave him, and was fully satisfied with the exchange. As noted previously, throughout Baranov's administration he figured one piastre as equal to two rubles. On that basis he placed a 60 percent markup on purchased goods, and imposed a tax on their sale in the colonies.

	Length in arshins	Width in vershoks	Price on Sitka	Price in various departments
Rock sugar			16	18 & 20
Millet, pud			5.50	6
Unbleached Chinese cotton, bolt	8-14/16	9	3	3.50
Unglazed red Chinese cotton	14	7-1/2	4	4.20
Black Chinese cotton	13-15/16	12-1/2	8.80	9
Demicotton	14-1/4	8	5	5.50
White bombazine	14-1/4	8-1/2	6.50	7
First quality Bengal	47	10	21	25
Third quality Bengal	47	10	18	22
Fourth quality Bengal	48-1/2	8-1/2	14	18
Velvet			89.60	
Thread, pound			3	4.20
Seersucker			7	9
Table service			80	100
Very precious tea (gunpowder)			2.25	2.50
Green tea (Assam)			1.70	2
Black tea (pekoe)			2	2.50
Dried tea			1.30	1.60
Taffeta	22-1/2		29	35
Fine Chinese silk	20-1/2	11-1/4	22	28
Atlas satin	16-3/4		17	20
Flowered satin	23-6/16		65	70
Black satin	23	16	62	68
Blue satin	16		65	70
Fabric for an ensemble	37	1	60	65
Chinese kancha silk	23-1/2	1	42	50
Serge suit			1.75	2
Silk	1-58/96 Russian measure		16	18

3. THE REPLACEMENT OF BARANOV AND THE CONDITION OF THE COMPANY AT THAT TIME

1817. In the month of November the ship Kutuzov docked at Sitka under the command of Captain-Lieutenant L. A. [Leontii Andreianovich] Hagemeister. The cargo which the ship carried was to have been placed at Baranov's disposal, but the advanced age of this esteemed individual had weakened his health and impaired his mental faculties. There was no competent person to assist him, and therefore Hagemeister was forced to replace him in order to obviate further mismanagement. He gave instructions to this effect:

"The Council created by Imperial will on behalf of the Governing Board of the Russian American Company, which is under the protection of His Imperial Majesty, send this directive to the New Arkhangel Office.

"The advanced years of the Chief Manager of the American territories, the Collegiate Councillor and Cavalier Baranov, as well as his ill health, his 25-year stay there, constant work and worry, have given him the right to request to be released from these obligations. Twice a man has been sent to replace him: [Ivan Gavrilovich] Koch and [Tertii Stepanovich] Bornovolokov. However both men died before reaching this region. Since then, the administration has been unable to find a third qualified person. Now a qualified person has been found, Navy Captain-Lieutenant and Cavalier Leontii Andreianovich Hagemeister, commander of the ships Kutuzov and Suvorov. Consequently, the Council of the Russian American Company has decided on this course of action, and Hagemeister has sent a notice in writing to Baranov requesting that he formally relinquish his authority, operating capital and business affairs. The New Arkhangel Office, naval officers, and all officials and employes of the Company must be advised of this change, and each in his own capacity must obey the newly appointed chief, Hagemeister. Should any person fail to obey this order, he will be subject to severe punishment according to law.

"Given in St. Petersburg, August 25, 1816.

Signed: Gavriil Sarychev
Ivan Veidemeier
Iakov Druzhinin
Mikhailo Buldakov
Venedik Kramer
Andrei Severin
Legal Councillor Ivan Zelenskii"

Makeup Of The Population, Particularly On Sitka, And The Status Of The Russian Employes, Creoles And Aleuts

On January 11, 1818, Hagemeister summoned Z. I. [Zakhar Ivanovich] Ponafidin, captain of the Suvorov, then went to Baranov and announced the instructions of the directive of the Council. While in no way denigrating the important services Baranov rendered to the country and to the Company, the fact should not be concealed that during the latter years of his administration he paid only superficial attention to business; and because he had no competent persons to assist him, he at last realized that business was unprofitable.* He had tried to gloss over these misfortunes in his old age, in order not to show the obvious dereliction of duty in which he was actually deeply entrenched. Hagemeister was forced to make the replacement; he announced this to Baranov, and immediately appointed a commissioner of his ship as the administrator of the Office, forwarded the directive of the Council to the Office, and issued a formal statement concerning the replacement of Baranov to all officials and functionaries. The next day they began to take inventory of capital here, and in bringing together information on business matters, they collected data on the makeup of the population. According to census lists drawn up in various places in 1815 and in 1817, the population

---

*Baranov himself acknowledged this fact several times. He wrote to certain persons, referring to the unfortunate outcome of O'Cain's expedition to Canton, and to D. [Doctor] Scheffer's in the Sandwich Islands.

consisted of the following:

	Male	Female
Kodiak Islanders	1,483	1,769
In New Arkhangel: Kodiaks	142	35
Fox Islanders	42	26
Along [the] Alaska [Peninsula]	402	467
Kenai Bay [Cook Inlet]	723	747
Chugach Bay [Prince William Sound]	172	188
In various places of the Kodiak Department	345	425
Unalaska and other Fox Islands	463	559
Department of the Northern Islands	188	191
	3,960	4,407

(Total for both sexes: 8,367)

In New Arkhangel there were:

Russians, males with children	190	
Creoles, males with children	72	
Aleuts, males with children	173	435
Women, married to Russians and Creoles, with children	110	
Women, married to Aleuts	75	185
Total:		620

In addition to the above, there were some persons from this Department who had been left on the Sandwich Islands from Dr. Scheffer's expedition: 24 Russians and Creoles, 37 Aleut males and three Aleut females; in all, 64 persons.

About one-half of the 190 service people were engaged in hunting, but not the Chief Manager. One hundred and one were on salary. The Chief Manager set the pay rate for the Aleuts for the sea otter hunt; this was set at about one-tenth of the catch, after taxes; sometimes it was more. They were given lavtaks* for their baidarkas and kamleis** from the hunt account.

At the last division this amounted to between 1,000 and 1,200 over the four-year

———

*Lavtak: a cured hide, seal or walrus, used to make a baidarka.

**Kamlei: a waterproof garment made of marine animal gut.

period. Average annual expenditures were as follows:

Chief Manager, 13 shares @ 600*		7,800 [rubles]
Three prikashchiks, half-shares, donative	6 shares	
Promyshlenniks and other participants	183	
Creoles	3	
Aleuts	1	
	193 @ 300	57,900

In addition to half-shares, three persons
  received salaries   1,500

Creoles and Aleuts	45 persons at 60 rubles	2,700 rubles
	19 80	1,500
	5 100	500
	9 120	1,080 [sic]
	8 150	1,200
		7,000

Creole apprentices	1 180	180
	2 400	800
	1 450	450
		1,450

Burtsov	1,000
Navigator Benzeman	2,000
Navigators Jones and Young @ 1,500	3,000
Navigator Domashnev	2,450
	8,450

Lieutenant [Iakov Anikievich] Podushkin, salary	5,000
Lodging 600 piastres	3,000
	8,000

Prikashchik Nosov	3,000
Two Sukhanovs	4,000
Office employe	600
Priest	600
	8,200

Special bonuses, distributed annually	6,850
	Rubles 120,000

---

*According to the agreement, Baranov received ten donative shares, plus three as his due as the administrator in Sitka, one and one-half of which were paid to his assistant, Kuskov, who according to the contract received five donative shares.

In addition to the above listed laborers, they used up to 20 Aleuts for work; they were called kaiurs,* and were sent into the forest and assigned to other jobs. Such persons did not receive salaries, but did receive clothing and foot-wear appropriate for the season of the year from the Company.

Capital Goods In New Arkhangel. Ships.
Basic Commodities And Their Prices

The capital goods received from Baranov during the year 1818 consisted of the following:

Russian and foreign goods, materials, and supplies in warehouses, the store and in other shops	1,066,904r	43k**
Pelts of sea animals and land animals	202,750	70
Economic goods, such as lavtaks, kishka (intestines) and kamlei	21,784	62
Debts of officials, promyshlenniks and Aleuts	338,903	96
Debts of Aleuts for 2,534 sea otter pelts	21,698	96
Sailing and rowing vessels	125,363	12
Total:	1,777,404	61

Buildings were at first entered without a value, but subsequently, so that accounts might be put in order, they were appraised. However, at the time Baranov was replaced, only one large warehouse, out of the entire complex of buildings, was of any value. In general, the rest of the buildings were worth-less. The barracks had no heat, were empty, and on the verge of collapse; thus there were no living quarters for personnel. A few of the promyshlenniks had built five small dwellings behind the fortress.

The sailing and rowing vessels were appraised as follows:

Otkrytie	45,550 rubles
Ilmen	35,440
Chirikov	28,030
Konstantin	6,400
Zlatoust	4,300
Platov	2,000
Amethyst, used as a storehouse,	3,000
and two rowing vessels	650
	125,370 rubles

---

*Kaiur was originally a Kamchatkan word for a hired worker. In Alaska, the term came to be used to refer to a native, generally Aleut, pressed into Company service. -- Ed.

**Included in these goods were also supplies that were delivered from St. Petersburg aboard Suvorov and Kutuzov.

At that time the brig Finlandia was here, but it is not included under capital because it belonged to the Atkhinsk Department; however it was in use here for almost two years because of the shortage of ships.

The principal goods from foreign exchanges were received in the following amounts:

1,550 Bolts blue Chinese cotton
48 Bolts black Chinese cotton
165 Bolts cotton
360 Black serge kerchiefs
1,664 Bengal cotton kerchiefs
1,180 Second quality Bengal kerchiefs
1,467 Arshins frieze
712 Arshins low quality cloth, @ 8 rubles
822 Arshins frieze
556 Arshins flannel
1,596 Arshins bombazine
400 Frieze blankets
45 Bolts Canton silk
187 Puds granulated sugar
323 Puds rock sugar
6,060 Pounds Canton tea, various kinds
920 Puds lead grapeshot
220 Puds powder
115 English leather soles
19 Cases gin
540 Vedros rum
40 Puds Virginia tobacco
220 Barrels tar and pitch
2,500 Puds salt from Sandwich Islands and California
568 Puds treacle
654 Puds millet
9 Puds Boston crackers
2,717 Puds Boston flour
596 Puds California wheat
596 Puds barley
43 Puds coffee
290 Bolts Bengal and Canton calico

The new Chief Manager noted that since the piastre had been devalued, the sale price of foreign goods should be set without taking its value into consideration; he therefore ordered the office to arrive at the actual cost as closely as possible, using the present value of the piastre, and not figuring expenditures, nor including the usual commercial interest. This was done so as not to arouse dissatisfaction among the service personnel, since the exchange was uncertain. The tax he suggested was approved and publicly posted in the store.

However the previously set sale prices were not constant. They fluctuated according to the prices that goods were purchased for. Also, one must note the unfair distribution of prices: for example, sugar candy cost 16 rubles in New Arkhangel, while at other offices it cost 18 or 20 rubles per pud, even though its purchase price was taken into account. In general a 10% to 25% markup was imposed on goods for sale, even though all service personnel, in each and every place, had the same rights.

On the basis of the new regulations, it was impossible to lower the exchange rate of piastres, and as a result there was an increase in the price of commodities, especially for new goods and provisions. For example, 100 English pounds of millet sold for 8 piastres; with the exchange rate of one piastre equal to 5 rubles, this amounted to 40 rubles, or roughly 14 rubles per pud. Taking into consideration unavoidable loss from rat damage, it could not be sold for less than 16 rubles per pud. But supposing the exchange rate rose to 6 rubles, the price would treble. In a gradual transition, this equalization was not so obvious.

Subsequently the Governing Board stipulated in directive No. 523, Paragraph 11: "Common cloth, heavy workcloth, ticking and molasses should be sold at the lowest possible prices. Add a 30% markup to goods purchased in St. Petersburg for expenses, and add a 10% to 15% markup to those purchased elsewhere, to cover transportation, not to show a profit. In general it is suggested that the Company take a profit only from various imported goods, furs, and from trade with foreigners. (Paragraph 10). Married men with families should receive bread according to the size of the family, at cost, so that the Company will not take a profit from this."

Goods were given out to workers from the store, upon authorization of the Chief Manager, and were put on their accounts; this took place once a month or sometimes every three months. At such times they received several pounds of flour and other provisions. However this transaction was very complicated, both for the workers and for the authorities. The former were not always able to receive supplies at will, and the latter accumulated such a great number of petty bills that they could not always prepare a satisfactory account. It was true, that business affairs were impossible to understand, not only during the time they stayed there, but also when a change took place in the stores.

4. REORGANIZATION OF THE COLONIES BY HAGEMEISTER

Hagemeister introduced a number of directives from the Governing Board which had hitherto not applied to all areas. He sent out to all the offices regulations about the duties of the Chief Manager and of the offices, according to the directive of May 1811. These articles referred to relationships with the islanders, which he explained to the offices. He put into effect almost all the instructions of the Governing Board, sent out in the name of the New Arkhangel Office June 23, 1817, in directive No. 523, as can be seen in the following review.

An Agreement With Workers For Pay Instead Of Shares

On February 20 he ordered the office to make known to the promyshlenniks the intent of the Governing Board contained in paragraph 14 of the above mentioned directive, that instead of shares they would receive 300 rubles in pay and one pud of flour per month. The office published this proposal, and all promyshlenniks on Sitka at that time submitted the following response:

"In verification of Your Excellency's proposal dated February 20 and sent to this office, which details the intent of the Board of Directors and which has been explained to us, requesting the consent of each person to substitute a payment in money for payment in a share of the furs; with the Company to supply food and possibly flour, should the supply from California come on a regular basis; so that we would receive 300 rubles per year, and one pud of flour free per month; we accept this proposal on the following conditions:

"1) We propose that the substitution of payment in money, 300 rubles apiece, be retroactive to the last pay period, May, 1815. Since the Governing Board proposes to give each man one pud of flour per month, we hope that they will be humane in considering our needs; we owe the Company some amounts of money; the Governing Board should deduct such sums from our earnings, but based on the average prices current on the day such debts were incurred.
"2) Should it happen that there is no regular shipment of food supplies and the proposed amount of grain is not distributed, then we propose that we should receive pay instead.
"3) From henceforth for the duration of our service with the Company, we humbly ask that prices not be increased on necessary and indispensable goods such as footwear and clothing, or on provisions, above the set tax which is presently imposed and in effect at the store.
"4) Those of us who distinguish themselves in service to the benefit of the Company expect a bonus over and above the proposed 300 rubles per year, at the discretion of Your Excellency, at the expense of the Company.
"5) Should sickness, accident or disability befall us in the course of our service, there should be no deduction taken from our pay.
"6) We humbly ask that our needs be taken into consideration in making decrees and setting prices on goods that are necessary to our livelihood, and that a stable annual tax be approved. We know that the Company will not suffer any loss from this."

After this agreement had been concluded, Hagemeister ordered that promyshlenniks be issued one pud of flour per month, pending the approval of the administration.

The proposal to pay men in money rather than shares was outlined by the late Rezanov. In a memorandum to Baranov dated September 9, 1805, this is well expressed in paragraph IV, on hunting: "...hunting is performed by American natives; [other] persons who enter the Company's service are used for construction, security, seafaring and defense. The entire force in America numbers less than 400 men on shares. These men keep the natives in submission, help in construction, and although they comprise a very small force, nevertheless they protect the whole coast of America insofar as possible. In return for their work they receive half shares or a fraction of a share of the animals taken. Masters sometimes receive full shares. The number of persons, considering the widespread extent of the settlements, is insufficient and hinders success; but to increase their number, on the present terms, would be a great burden on both Company and on them, for this would diminish the profit from the hunt and both parties would suffer. In addition, promyshlenniks suffer from the uncertainty of their status for the duration of the four-year period after which the distribution of bonuses takes place. Instead of the bonus they expect, they could easily lose the entire fruit of their work. Rather than expand its activity, the Company should look for profit in trade in which only the Company and not the promyshlenniks would participate. Promyshlenniks cannot continue to operate for long on the present terms. I believe that gradually the number of half-share participants will decrease and that eventually the Company will receive all the profit and that all its employes will be paid on a cash basis."

This reorganization went into effect almost without opposition. Naturally the old promyshlenniks who had had the opportunity prior to 1803 to receive skins made a real profit. But in the subsequent three periods, when animals were taxed, on the basis of a half-share they could not make more than 1,531 rubles in four years. It is true that the number of furs secured by the promyshlenniks was sometimes very large, and in fact, larger than before; but at the same time the number of personnel increased, and some officials received a large salary in cash from the general sum, which as a result decreased. And furthermore, promyshlenniks, and even many other persons, lived in the hopes of the unknown future, rather than being content with the definite and constant situation. With the introduction of salaries, everyone knew at all times what his pay was.

No one can deny that promyshlenniks could make a living by working on terms with previous companies where they received only shares, that is, animal pelts, which they then sold at the going price and made a profit. But when the prices changed by agreement, this profit was totally erased. Those who had good sense noted later that the new arrangement was both more optimistic and profitable than the earlier one.

Instructions For Aleuts For Hunting Sea Otters
And Other Animals

In order to carry out the instructions of the Governing Board, in paragraphs 7 and 8 of the above mentioned directive No. 533, Hagemeister instructed the Office to issue [to the Aleuts] at Company expense, lavtaks for baidarkas, a whalegut kamlei and a birdskin parka to each man. In exchange for the pelts taken in the hunt, they were to be paid in goods which were to be taxed at 20% of the set price, as stipulated in the contract for all promyshlenniks. The kaiurs were to be paid enough to cover the cost of clothing and footwear.

Various Useful Changes Introduced By Hagemeister
And His Successor

1) Because of inadequate pay to the Creoles, Hagemeister instructed the office to issue them, in addition to their pay, the kind of clothing worn by sailors, two pairs of boots, and one kamlei, at a cost of about 35 rubles.

2) From this time on scrip entered into general circulation, and notes were no longer issued when goods were purchased. Each employe received scrip every month and used it to purchase goods he needed. In directive No. 177 Hagemeister ordered that one-third of the pay be withheld from the salary of all persons who owed money to the Company, and that they be given two-thirds for their living expenses.

3) Responsible promyshlenniks previously on the share system were now used as prikashchiks, but this did not give them enough to live on, and so it was

directed that they be given 25 rubles per month during the time they were at sea.

4) In order to eliminate illegal trapping and to clearly establish trapping under the jurisdiction of the Office, it was decreed that each pelt be stamped with the symbol R.A.K. [Rossiisko-Amerikanskaia Kompaniia], which was to signify good quality.

5) From the beginning of Hagemeister's administration, business affairs in the offices were put into order. Prikashchiks who were in charge of stores and warehouses presented accounts three times a year. Commissioners and prikashchiks on ships who were sent out on various assignments presented accounts to the office immediately upon their return. The office administrator who was in charge of cash presented monthly accounts, and the office prepared an accounting every third month and submitted it to the Chief Manager.

6) Hagemeister appointed Lieutenant Ianovskii as his successor on October 23, 1818, and sailed to Russia aboard the ship Kutuzov. His successor introduced two useful procedures: he instructed the ships' commanders who did not receive scrip in accordance with the agreement to issue foodstuffs to the sailors each month for the duration of the voyage:

To the Commander		To the Crew	
Flour	1 pud	Biscuits, per day	1 pound
Salt pork	30 pounds	Meat--sea lion or beef	1/2 pound
Butter	10 pounds	Groats, per month	6-64/96 pounds
Tea	1 pounds	Peas	8 pounds
Granulated sugar	12 pounds	Lard	8 pounds
Peas	10 pounds	Rum	5 cups
Rum	1-1/2 tankards		

At current prices these came to 36 rubles 45 kopecks per month.

5. THE LOCATION OF NEW ARKHANGEL

In mentioning Sitka, I have said nothing regarding the climate and resources of the region, which either were or still are the occasion for settlement; thus it is necessary to examine them in detail.

All hills are covered with a heavy growth of coniferous forest, but only at the higher elevations is there permanent snow. Sitka is an island separated from the mainland by Chatham Strait, and is separated by smaller straits from the northern parts. The entire extent of the island is almost two degrees, extending from Cape Oman to Icy Strait. There is probably no flat area one square mile in extent. There are mountain ridges everywhere; these consist for the most part of granite of various sorts, of gneiss and mica shale. Small plains and meadows and even mountain slopes are covered with wet tundra overlain with moss. Old stands of trees have been felled by wind and undercut by the flow of snow water; they are piled in great heaps and are covered over with moss; they rot, and create

completely impassable barriers. This wild condition gives rise to fog and
fierce winds. On the basis of a good many observations it is possible to say
truly that in a good year there is bad weather for 2/3 of the time, and only
1/3 of the days are clear or moderate; but there are times when only one-fifth
of a year is clear. Constant gloom, drizzle and biting air are usual atmospheric
conditions. But, here as everywhere, there are no rules without exceptions, and
good weather does occur. The winter is usually mild, occasionally snow falls and
melts as it turns into rain; infrequently there is a real winter. Occasionally
the temperature reaches 10 or even 14 degrees (1820) on the Reámur thermometer.
Spring sometimes comes early, with raspberries blooming in February (1825) and
berries ripening in May. It is beautiful then to see these shrubs, still
leafless, but with lovely blossoms. But again, sometimes there may be eight
degrees of frost in the morning in March, and four degrees in April. And by May
there may be barely a trace of green showing (1826). Sometimes there is snow
from November until February (1824), but the usual weather condition is to have
clouds and rain, so that it is like autumn the year around. Winds on land are
usually gusty, and sometimes so fierce that trees are uprooted.

If the weather is clear on the third day after a new moon, then one may expect
it to continue for the entire lunar month. There is frequently entirely different weather at sea from that along the coast. Sometimes one can put out from
shore, creeping through gradually diminishing fog, and then find oneself under
a clear sky. From there one can see the black clouds which encircle the snow
covered mountain peaks. At sea the winds are variable, but generally east and
south in spring and summer, and southwest and northwest in fall. There are
sometimes northeast and northwest winds in spring and summer, and sometimes they
continue on into the fall and winter months; but sometimes exactly the opposite
happens.

6. THE INDIGENOUS POPULATION OF SITKA AND OF THE ENTIRE NORTHWEST COAST OF AMERICA

The Koliush or Kolosh, with various of their tribes, inhabit the northwest
coast from the 40th to the 60th degrees of latitude. If the natives of Trinidad
Bay are different from those of the Columbia River, then the degree of difference is the same as between the latter and those of the Straits of Juan de Fuca,
and so on. According to the accounts of Russians and Aleuts who have visited
those areas, the inhabitants of Trinidad Bay more closely resemble the Kolosh
than they do the Indians who live south of Cape Mendocino. For this reason I
would probably number them among the Kolosh (this similarity is most remarkable
in their ceremonies and their way of life.)

Indians of New Albion do not understand one another if they come from areas ten
miles apart. Consequently it is entirely possible that peoples spread out over
20 degrees will quite naturally, by virtue of intermixing with inhabitants of
the interior of America, have an even greater diversity in their way of life
and their language, than do the Kolosh of Bering and Trinidad bays.

In order to understand a people such as the Kolosh, one must study them thoroughly and in detail. It is possible that one tribe may be more intelligent than another, and consequently may have better understanding and more knowledge. It is very likely that over a distance of 20 degrees, climate and other factors will have an influence on customs.

We have been familiar with the Kolosh since 1783, but the first travellers without interpreters did not have an opportunity to gather information about their ideas. Following the occupation of Yakutat in 1794 and Sitka in 1799 Baranov of course gathered necessary data, but these are presently not known. Data which I have collected consist of the following:

The Kolosh do not comprehend the existence of a higher being, a Creator of the World; but their understanding has led them to wonder about the beginning of all things in their environs. They view all living creatures as actual beings; man is considered a half-god, and crows are viewed as life-givers in the mythology of the Sitka Kolosh.

"Kitkh-ugin-si, the first living being in the land, had a sister; he killed her children when they were born, in order that the size of the tribe be not increased. In addition to him there were other beings in the land over whom he wielded power, and for their sins he punished them with a flood, but he could not destroy all of them, for some people saved themselves on top of rafts and boats and on the peaks of high mountains which the flood did not reach. They tied up their boats to the rocks with rope, and thus saved themselves. Rafts and ropes are still preserved atop the mountains to the very present day.

"The sister of Kitkh-ugin-si, weary of suffering abuse from her brother, decided to flee. She went far off to the seashore, and built herself a hut there from the bark of a tree. One clear day she went down to the shore and saw whales playing in the sea. Not knowing who such creatures might be, she began to shout to them, inviting them to come visit her and bring her food, for she was suffering from hunger. The whales made no answer, and hid. In the evening of that same day a fine looking man came to her hut and asked her why she was alone there, suffering from hunger. She told him how her brother had not allowed her to bring up her children, about how she was sorrowful over their fate and had to run away and suffered from hunger. The man who had come sent one of his people (a slave) to the shore and ordered him to bring a small round pebble which he placed on the fire and then gave her something to eat. When she had finished he told her that afterward she would give birth to a son, whom no one would be able to kill, and then he vanished.

"Soon thereafter she realized that she was with child, and gave birth to a son, Elkh. While she was bringing him up, she bathed him in sea water each morning; and when he began to grow up, she made him an arrow and showed him how to use it, how to kill birds with it. Hiking through the forest he killed many humming birds, and his mother made a cloak for herself from the birdskins. Once when he was in the forest he saw something large in the top of a tree. He shot and killed a large bird. He skinned it, and donned the skin, and examining the wings, realized that the bird used them to fly in the air. When he understood this he said, 'How happy I should be if I could fly like a bird.' With these words, he leaped into the air, but as he did not know how to use his wings, he hid behind a cloud and feeling downcast said sorrowfully, 'It would have been better if I had stayed with mother!' And after these words, he suddenly appeared beside her in the hut.

"After they had lived together for some time, his mother told him about the sins of Kitkh-ugin-si, and how he had killed her children, and why they were now in this place. The young man, feeling his strength, begged his mother to let him take revenge on his uncle. But his mother would not permit this, for fear that he would not return to her alive. But at last, after his ceaseless pleas, she consented, and he left. When he came to his uncle's dwelling, he discovered he was not at home. Persons (slaves) told him that his uncle was out. The uncle was very jealous, so that when he went away he locked his wife in a large box and hoisted it into the middle of his hut. The young guest asked what it contained, and they told him it was his uncle's wife. So he disregarded their protests, broke open the lid of the box, and let her free. Several days later they noticed that Kitkh-ugin-si's boat was approaching from the sea, so they hurriedly put his wife back in the box and hoisted it up again.

"When Kitkh-ugin-si came up to the shore, he noticed that there was a change in his dwelling; and when he left the boat, he asked who had broken the box. In great trepidation his people replied that it was his nephew, whom they were not strong enough to restrain. When the old man came home, he gathered all living persons in his dwelling, and ordered the water to rise and drown all those who were not present with him. His nephew was sitting on top of the hut, and was wearing the birdskin; he was not frightened by his uncle's threats, but ordered the waters to recede immediately. After that, he came down, locked up the cottage tightly, so they could not get out, and ordered the waters to rise, while he used his bird wings to fly up to heaven. He flew for a long time, but finally became weak and fell to ground and bruised himself badly on a rock. It was for this reason that people after that began to experience painful accidents. He lay without moving for a long time in that place, but one morning, after he had fallen soundly asleep, he heard a voice saying, 'Go! They are calling you!'

"He awoke, but he saw no one and thought that this was just a dream and fell asleep again. But the voice repeated the words for a second time. He woke again, but still saw no one; he gathered his strength and went down to the shore. He saw otters swimming out at sea and thought, could it be that these sea creatures were calling me? A swimming otter answered, 'Sit down on my back. I will carry you where you are being called!' 'Will you drown me?' asked Elkh. 'Close your eyes, and sit down. Do not fear anything,' replied the otter. Obeying the voice, he sat on the otter's back, and they swam for rather a long time. Then the otter told him, 'Open your eyes and look!' Looking up, he saw the shore and a multitude of people there. The otter told him, 'Go, you will find your mother and your uncle there.'

"When he came ashore he saw his mother and his uncle; they were very happy and wished to entertain him; but he could not eat anything. His uncle summoned to his side all the people who were there; there was one guest who had two stomachs and ate a great deal. Elkh asked how this had come about. At first the two-stomach man did not wish to say anything, but finally at Elkh's request he confided that he once had seen a sick raven who had asked him to scrape the skin off one of the raven's feet, beneath his body, and he did so until water came from it. Subsequently the raven was able to eat any living creature. He ordered the two-stomach man to eat the skin that had been scratched from his foot, and from that time on the man became gluttonous.

"In this way Elkh became acquainted with the raven, and received the right from him to be the founder of the Kolosh."

But how this tribe appeared, and what the power of the raven is, they did not know. They maintain that this is how it should be. However, even through the haze of this fable, the story of a worldwide deluge emerges. The rest is obviously subsequent invention.

The Kolosh believe in evil spirits, and think that they bring illness to people, that they inhabit water, and that therefore illnesses come from eating fish and shellfish which are sent by evil spirits. They are appeased by shamans in order to avoid illness, but no honor is given them. They believe that herring asked the evil spirits to give Kabachakov to them, because he did not give them any peace. The spirits told this to the shamans.

After a person dies, the Kolosh burn the body, and wealthy persons erect monuments on the spot. They believe that the spirit does not die, but that it does not receive anything in another world in the way of rewards for good deeds or punishment for bad deeds. Spirits exist in the same condition in the other world as in this world, especially leaders and subordinates. If a dead toion's [leader's] slaves are sacrificed alongside his body, then those spirits remain eternal servants of the spirit of the leader.

When a boy is born, his mother stays in bed in the hut for a month. After this period of time she bathes herself, bathes the infant, washes all of her clothes, and dresses in fresh clothing. Then the relatives are called in to celebrate, at which time the mother gives the newborn son his name, which she takes from one of her dead relatives. With this, the ceremony ends. Women give birth to as many as six to eight children, but seldom to as many as ten.

The mother nurses the infant until such time as he begins to walk; she places half-chewed morsels of dried salmon into its mouth until the child's teeth come through and he can feed himself. They make clothing from animal pelts for little boys. And when the child starts to talk, his relatives, uncles and others, must bathe him every morning either in river water or sea water, regardless of the frost, until the young boy becomes accustomed to the cold. Fathers and mothers stay completely away from this whole custom, because the tears and weeping of the children would cause them grief. It is customary however for the uncles to beat children with sticks if they are insubordinate or shriek. In all stages of their growth children are obedient to their parents, and even more remarkable, the aged and the infirm are attended with great care.*

----

 *Orphans and children without relatives, who are unable to take care of themselves because of illness, are cared for by those who have means and who will be responsible for bringing them up.

In general, children belong to the maternal side of the family, and the right of succession is considered to follow along the maternal line. The Kolosh have strong bodies, are of medium height, and have regular facial features; their hair is coarse and black and they do not wear a beard, for although they do grow a thin beard, they pluck it out with clamshells. Women pierce the lower lip and insert a wooden labret, which usually gives the face a repulsive appearance. This practice is now becoming rare.

A man who enters into marriage must be strong enough to undertake any kind of work, and be able to use weapons. He asks and receives permission of the parents [of the intended bride] to go to their settlement where he wishes to marry; he sends a man with his proposal to the woman he plans to marry. If the bride and her father agree, he then brings gifts to the parents of the bride, and to her close relatives, and is given his bride. Later he and his wife go to her parents and receive gifts from them, which must be more valuable than the initial gifts from the groom. These gifts consist of animal pelts, items from Europe, weapons, and frequently slaves. There have been cases where the bride would not consent to certain terms, and the marriage was dissolved. For example, one bride demanded that if a certain toion [leader] wished to marry her, he must send his first wife off to her relatives. But the toion liked that wife and so did not agree, and the marriage was not consummated. They never use shamans for marriage ceremonies, nor do they offer any sacrifices.

Wealthy and influential Kolosh may have as many as five wives, and sometimes more. They try to receive large dowries through these ties, and to acquire a large number of relatives in order to strengthen their position thereby. In some tribes it is the custom to marry before puberty. There are cases of jealousy among wives which often lead to a quarrel and sometimes to fights with knives and cudgels. If a wife is unfaithful, and is caught, then the husband kills her and her lover, with no vengeance on the part of the relatives, to whom he may pay something in the line of clothing or other items of value. This punishment applies to a man who has no blood ties with the husband. Should he be related, then the insulted husband forces him to take his wife and keep her as a concubine. Hot-tempered and passionate persons do not always observe this moderation, with the result that relatives often become victims of the anger of the insulted husband. There are some indulgent husbands who will allow an elder wife to have a young male assistant who lives with them in the hut and takes care of all the work, and in the absence of the husband takes his place in bed.

There have been no instances of anyone marrying his mother, daughter, or even a relative. A wife is always selected from another tribe. However, one must note that after the death of an uncle, the nephew is supposed to take his wife regardless of the age difference. It is possible that two sisters may become wives of the same man.

Women are usually busy with their work such as preparing fish that have been caught, sewing, weaving baskets, making blankets from animal wool, etc. They are also responsible for such domestic duties as preparing wood, bark, etc. In time of war or negotiations with neighboring tribes, women are not accepted into the councils; rather, the men keep their plans a secret from them. But in matters of trade, holiday celebrations and various business decisions they participate directly, and often the husbands merely carry out their orders.

When a man dies, before a grave is dug, they gather friends and relatives, carry the body to a selected place and burn it there, at which time the relatives vent their grief with shrieks and cries. At an earlier time, before they came to know Europeans, when a prominent toion died they would kill his slaves, as mentioned previously. The relatives of the deceased cut off their hair, and to express their grief, paint their faces black; they may mourn for an entire year.

The Kolosh of Sitka begin preparing food in February when the herring come in. They do not preserve this fish because it molds and spoils easily; but they do preserve the roe. The Kolosh know when the herring spawn, and prepare a wicker container, tie it, and submerge it with stones in the water near the shore. The released roe settle on the wicker, which is then taken from the water and dried in sun or just in the air. When the roe is dry, they remove it from the wicker and keep it to use. After the herring, there is constant preparing of food, which begins with the arrival of sea fish of all kinds into the rivers; this generally continues until July. Salmon is preserved by removing the meat from the bones, drying it in the air, or smoking it. They try to prepare enough of this to last a whole year, and usually it lasts until new fish come. Halibut can be caught at any time of year, and thus can be used in place of dried food. In addition to fish, raspberries are preserved and eaten with herring roe, thus making a tolkushka. In spring sap is taken from trees, is dried and preserved. Edible roots of all kinds are also preserved. Seal, dolphin, sea lions and whale foetuses which have washed up on shore are also consumed as food; the fat of these creatures is considered a delicacy, and during festivities it is used to drink. Of the quadrupeds in this area, reindeer and mountain ram are used for food, but bear is not eaten. All kinds of birds are eaten except for the crow, which is sacred.

The Kolosh never eat human flesh under any circumstances. But they say that there are people who live in the mountains to the north who are called Konians, who do eat humans if there is a famine. These people sometimes come to Chilkat to trade. They are different from the Kolosh in their way of life as well as in their language. In earlier times they had bows and stone-headed arrows for weapons, but now they receive firearms from the Chilkat Kolosh in exchange for fox and sable pelts and native copper. The toion Saigakakh assured us that these people have dealings with the Mednovsk and Chugats people across the mountains, and that the Chilkat Kolosh spend time with them there.

The Kolosh, as earlier mentioned, are robust, and no one has noted that they are subject to indigenous illness. Generally any ill health they experience stems from their way of life and affects the eyes, head and stomach. The smoke in their huts and other factors cause eye and head aches. Stomach disorders are frequently caused by food, but not all are fatal. Sometimes they come down with a fever which is fatal because they do not know how to treat it. According to Saigakakh there was an epidemic of small pox there some 50 years ago, that is, about 1770. He was a small child and barely remembers it, but he knows for a fact that there were only one or two persons left in each family. According to him it spread from Stakhin (Stikine) to Sitka, but did not go further north. The Kolosh supposed that this illness was visited on them by the crow as a punishment for the endless wars they waged among themselves. Treating sickness is the responsibility of an old woman who uses all kinds of herbs and roots, but the Kolosh do not have faith in the old woman's knowledge. Shamans do not take part in curing sickness; they only are asked whether the sick person is going to

recover from the illness or is going to die. For a good answer they receive
various presents. There are, however, shamans who do engage in curing persons,
and they deserve mention because they are so rare.

The people lead a sybaritic existence in their huts. If food has been
prepared, an affluent Kolosh will lie between his wives all day long. If he
becomes bored he puts on his cloak, goes down to the beach and sits on the rocks
or lies in the sand. They eat two or three times a day.* They often bathe in
water but seldom warm themselves around a fire. Many of them are very fond of
playing stick games; they may lose everything - clothes, sea otters, weapons,
slaves - and there have even been cases when they lost their wives. When they
are short of food, the Kolosh go to sea and catch halibut. Wood and water are
carried by the women. They prepare all the food and care for all domestic
needs. The Kolosh have a basic conception about matters which fall within the
realm of their comprehension. They are eager for trade and exchange; with a
childlike eagerness they always grab for trivial things and pay extraordinary
prices for them; then when they tire of the item, they dispose of it without
compensation. They have European clothing, some have a good deal of it, but
they rarely wear it. Once in a while you will see a person change his clothes
three or four times in a day. Others wear shirts. But the usual and principal
item of clothing is a cloak or mantle made out of a flannel blanket or a length
of frieze about three arshins [seven feet] long; for winter time it is made of
sable, fox, black bear, mink, marmot or other fur.

The wars of the Kolosh are always internecine, but must be differentiated into
intertribal and intratribal. The former occurs when a disagreement develops
between two clans in one settlement, such as between the Wolf and the Crow, and
one person dies as a result of the dispute. The relatives of the dead person
demand payment for him, and in case the opposing side refuses, open fighting
breaks out. In such a case neither side uses firearms, but rather fight with
daggers and try only to wound, not to kill. If they should demonstrate their
superiority, then they force payment for the dead person and negotiations
commence. If the attacking tribe retreats, then a temporary truce is agreed
upon, and they await the opportunity of avenging the death by killing any one
of their adversaries. This blood feud continues for several years, among
people who are living, so to speak, under one roof.

Women always appear to be the cause of disputes and quarrels. The intratribal
battles, though quite often stemming from the same cause, often involve honor.
If it comes to the strong versus the weak, the pride of the savages is not
bridled by temperance or moderation, but is prompted by greed and vengeance.
If it happens that for some reason a man is killed who belongs to another
settlement or region, then vengeance fills the minds of the relatives of the
dead man. They try not to betray their plans until they are ready to take the
offensive. For this reason all councils of warriors are kept secret from the
women who, being tied by blood with other settlements, would not miss the
opportunity of warning their tribes about the danger. Thus prepared, the men
depart aboard war canoes and seek to approach the enemy settlement at daybreak.
Prior to the attack they put on armor made of wood intertwined with strands of

---

*When the Kolosh arise early in the morning they do not wash but immediately
begin to eat; likewise at noon and in the evening. This is not invariable, but
usually, when a person thinks about eating, he eats.

whale sinew, which encloses their chests and backs. On their heads they wear wooden masks that have carved images of wild animals or other creatures, with terrifying visages. Over the masks they wear heavy wooden hats with similar expressions; these paraphernelia they fasten with ties, leaving only slits for eyes and ears. When they launch a surprise attack they do not spare any man, but kill all; but they generally spare the women and take them into slavery (kuukh).

The defeated subsequently seek an opportunity to avenge the dead, and if they do not attain the goal during their lifetime, then the vendetta remains the inheritance of the tribe. There are cases where the quarrel is resolved through negotiation, and the defeated receive payment for the dead; at such a time peace hostages are exchanged. A strange ceremony is performed during this exchange. Both sides gather together on level ground, carrying daggers, both men and women. First the men try to seize a hostage (the top man of the adversaries, one most respected by virtue of family ties as well as age); they look as if they were attacking and lash out with lances and daggers; they yell and penetrate into the midst of the enemy and seize the selected hostage who hides in the midst of his party. Then with shouts which express joy and the fulfilling of their desires, and the end of war, they lift him on their hands and carry him to their side. Another similar exchange having also taken place, each side keeps its hostage in good condition, providing him all possible service; they do not permit him to walk, but always carry him on their hands, etc. The peace ceremony is concluded with dancing from morning to night and with feasting. Savages almost everywhere consider three things the most satisfying in their lives: a surfeit of food, especially fat and oily foods, lovemaking and dancing. In these are centered the complete essence of freedom and independence.

At last the hostages are taken to the settlement of their new friends, where they live for a year or more, and then are returned and with new dances they affirm the permanence of the alliance.

Recollections about deceased friends and relatives, about amusing happenings, new unions, new acquaintances, military clashes, new plans and other satisfying aspects of life are celebrated with dances accompanied by feasting. There are two kinds of dances: one seems to be a dance for families and close neighbors; these are annual occurrences. The other kind is a public dance, with friends and acquaintances being invited from distant areas on the basis of renown, wealth and position.

The former are held in the fall when there is a good supply of fish, fat, berries and edible roots. At such a time the leader of any tribe will invite neighbors and entertain them for several days. They dance without interruption, taking turns; then the guests are presented with animal pelts, blankets, clothing, etc. The head of the first house goes to the next house and so on, whoever is ready. They are careful to see that gifts are never presented irrevocably.

Public dances are not given by one family but by entire tribes. Invitations to persons in far off places will be given more than a month in advance. In the settlement where the entertainment is planned, each iurt has a carved totem pole depicting some animal or bird or a similar distinctive phratry recognizable to all. During the time the celebration goes on, a iurt is no longer referred to by the name of the owner, but rather according to the image above it. When they have danced in one iurt, they agree to move on to the phratry of the eagle, the crow, sun, moon, bear, etc. These totems are prepared by special artists who carve them skillfully and are paid by receiving a reindeer pelt, or elk, or sometimes a slave for each one he makes.

Arriving guests are presented with gifts according to status, and in expectation of receiving no less valuable gifts in the future. Dancing goes on from morning to night, and consists of gyrating while standing and dancing in one place. To prepare themselves for the dance, the Kolosh paint various figures on their faces, and put eagle feathers in their hair; they toss feathers on persons around them. They carry various rattles in their hands, and some persons beat on a drum.

The shamans acquire their position by their own efforts. When they wish to take on this vocation from a relative who was a shaman and who died, young persons are designated to this; they prepare themselves by fasting and by training for several years; when they feel they are ready, they are accepted for this sorcery. Their chief responsibility is to foretell the future; sometimes they cure sicknesses caused by evil spirits. If someone falls desperately ill or dies suddenly, such a case is usually attributed to spoiled food, and people run to the shaman who calls out the names of persons he thinks might be responsible for poisoning or injuring. The unfortunate suspect is then either beaten severely or killed.

Slaves

It was noted earlier that slaves or kalgas were taken during wartime. At present in the vicinity of Sitka there are seldom intertribal wars and therefore slaves are rare. But they are purchased from Kolosh who live along the shore and near the Queen Charlotte Islands. They have complete authority over the life of a slave. Even today they are sometimes killed during a gift ceremony or during dances or when an important leader dies. Poor and sick and weak slaves who cannot be sold or given away are killed. During such rituals they sometimes free the slaves, who may then live wherever they wish.

It is interesting that the Kolosh never practice suicide and even the lowest and most oppressed slaves never resort to this violent means of terminating their lives.

Toions

The toions or leaders in each tribe are acknowledged as elders, but they have no authority over anyone. They cannot assign anyone to a particular job or service. A toion will be assisted in general work only as a gesture of good will. The status of toions is hereditary.

Wealth And The Value Of Things

The status of a Kolosh is established according to the number of relatives; but his wealth consists of slaves, of whom they have 20, 30 or 40, of both sexes.

Instead of money the Kolosh have in circulation reindeer hides, zamshchas, which in Siberia are called rovdugas. These are not used for clothing, but are carefully prepared to be used as exchange in transactions. They pay 15 or 20 for a slave, five or six for a sea otter, and 10 or 15 for a good boat. In general, every new item is evaluated according to a number of rovdugas.

How The Kolosh Regard Other Peoples

The first foreigners to appear along these shores were the Spanish, English, French and Russians. They stopped at various places and were looked on as gods. The Kolosh say that when they approached a ship they did not have the courage to stop; but after they were enticed with various signs, they decided to send an old man. When he returned alive, and with gifts, they were emboldened to become acquainted and they began to trade.

Handcrafts

The major art of the Kolosh is building boats and canoes which are very light to navigate and which will accommodate from two to six persons in the smaller ones, and from 40 to 60 men in the larger ones; usually they hold from 10 to 20 persons. They are propelled by short paddles on both sides; no rowed boat can compare with them for speed.

Men carve war masks with faces of men and women resembling natural features; these are made of wood or slate. They carve pipes from copper or bone. They make arm bracelets; spoons from wild ram horns; and wooden dishes which look like pottery bowls, and are decorated with bones and shells. At present some of them also make weapons. I saw a Kolosh-made dagger which resembled an English dirk and in beauty of craftsmanship was in no way inferior to the original. They make the common two-edged daggers from iron and decorate them with colorful shells.

Women make beautiful blankets from soft goat hair. They weave baskets out of grass roots, and use them to carry and store water. Small baskets with pockets are woven from colored roots and are used by the women to store their sewing supplies.

At present they make European-style hats from these roots; they are very light, useful, and quite beautiful.

Waters

There are no large rivers on Sitka island, but there are small ones which flow over a rocky course. These waters are pure, and in summer they have many fish. All of these rise in the mountains. Two rather large rivers have waterfalls. One is near the fortress, about three hours away, in Silver Bay; the fall is more than 100 feet high, and after the water falls it divides into two streams. The river has its source in a lake; it takes about an hour to walk along the winding river course from the source to the falls. The lake is surrounded by high cliffs. The other important waterfall empties into a deep lake near the lake redoubt. There are also many small falls which cascade noisily all around, especially in the spring when the snow melts.

There are many lakes on the island; the largest is near the lake redoubt and is about 10 miles long; in some places they have measured a depth of 190 sazhens, and in other places they have not been able to reach bottom. It lies between mountains and by virtue of its location, it is apparent that it was created by an earthquake, because massive cliffs that stand in one place show that they have

been created by some powerful force. The unusual depth serves as an additional
indication. It is located slightly above sea level; its water and that in
other lakes is fresh, but there are no fish.

The lake near the New Arkhangel fortress has a muddy marshy bottom; there are
leeches, but not the kind used for bleeding.

There are mineral springs in various places along the shore. Near the lake
redoubt there are sulphurous hot springs. These have been known to the Kolosh,
who used them to treat various illnesses. Today many persons use them as a cure.
They heal wounds quickly and cure arthritis and scurvy. As the water flows from
the source to the mouth it leaves a sulphurous deposit on the rocks. At the
source the water is very hot, but it can be drunk. At first the taste is
unpleasant, but once one becomes accustomed to it, the smell is not repulsive
when it is hot. No one can bathe in it for more than 15 minutes; after that
length of time one experiences a great lassitude and the head begins to spin.

On various small islands there are cold waters that have a sour taste, whose
salubrious qualities the Aleuts have learned through experience.

Sea Otters And The Hunt

The most valuable product of these seas has been and still is sea beavers,
which the English refer to as sea otters, and the Spanish call nutria. The
Russians were the first to appreciate their pelts; soon after the Bering
Expedition of 1741 brought back some 900 pelts, the Russians set out from
Kamchatka to hunt these animals. The Spaniards knew about them earlier, that
is, from the time they occupied California; but they were interested in minerals
and did not care to become involved in a hunt which required both work and time.
After [James] Cook discovered the port at Nootka, he noted both there and along
the entire coast a good many sea otters, and he took back several hundred pelts
on his ship, [Resolution] which introduced the English to this new trade item in
1784 and 1786. The first ships to be sent to the northwest shores put out from
Macao and the East Indies; the next year they returned to Canton where they
commenced trading. In 1787 LaPerouse took aboard his ships 600 pelts which had
been collected along the shore; and from that time on, there were uninterrupted
yearly shipments.

We earlier noted Baranov's calculation in the year 1800 that during the previous
10 years a minimum of 100,000 pelts has been taken out. It is important to
state that this view is not exaggerated. Shemelin, while in Canton, picked up
the information that the Americans had brought 8,200 pelts there in 1804, and
14,000 in 1805, and that 4,628 had been brought aboard Russian American Company
ships. It is apparent that the number of sea otters gradually began to decrease,
not only because so many were killed, but because they were frightened off by
the shots and by being so frequently dispersed; they have moved off to areas
where they have not yet been rediscovered. One notable observer, carried away
by fervor for his mother country, remarked once that the sea otters will be
exterminated only when all the cod have been fished out of the sea at Arkhangel.
It is presently the case that there are only two areas along the whole span of
coast from Cape Oman to Cook Inlet where the hunt can be carried on, namely
Lituya Bay and Yakutat [Bay]; but even here they are no longer native to the

area, but are coming to hide from areas further along the coast to the southeast, where they have been increasingly threatened. They have almost completely disappeared from around Sitka, and there are ever fewer and fewer in the countless bays to the 46th parallel. The Kolosh have profited greatly from the hunt; they plunge in wholeheartedly and do not pass over a single place where sea otters might be hiding. An esteemed visitor to the colonies, commenting on the above mentioned suggestion about an abundance of sea otters, accurately observed that "cod spawn roe, but sea otters give birth to only one or two young; and thus, due to this inequality, they can be completely exterminated."

Sea otters of the northwest coast, according to present knowledge, can be placed in three [sic] classes, according to quality: 1) those from the Kurile and Kamchatka regions; 2) those taken from the Andreanovskii and Fox Islands; 3) those from the northwest coast; and 4) from Albion and California. Those in the first three groups grow to a large size, and their fur is longer and denser. In the best pelts the fur is quite black, with a fine gloss which is considered very desirable in Russia. In Canton the sides of a pelt are examined first, and then it is graded according to quality. Pelts from regions more to the south are generally smaller. The winter catch is black, but the fur is short and has no gloss [sic]. The advantage of the winter catch is that the fur is glossier and there are fewer immature animals, because the young by then have grown to adult size.

The Aleuts are the only persons who have an innate passion for hunting sea otter. They set out in hunting parties of five to ten baidarkas. When they spot a sea otter, they surround it, and the person who first sighted it emerging from the water harpoons it and claims the catch. The sea otter can stay under water for up to a quarter of an hour; the more severely wounded he is, the more frequently he has to surface. It is impossible for him to escape the keen hand of the harpooner.

The Kolosh formerly killed sea otters with bow and arrow, but at present they have guns and kill them with muskets. The sound of the shots frightens the sea otters so that they leave their native places. We know that in areas where once there were many, such as Cook Inlet, Prince William Sound and around Sitka, they are now quite rare. Where they have already been hunted out, they may reappear after hunting has been stopped, such as along the shores of the Andreanovskii and Fox Islands, and in the bays of Yakutat and Lituya.

Whales, Sea Lions And Seals

Whales appear along these shores from time to time, but neither the Kolosh nor the Aleuts hunt for them. It occasionally occurs that they are washed ashore near the fortress, and if the Aleuts find them, they immediately send baidarkas to strip off the blubber and bring it back to the fort. Several times whales have been found nearby and towed to the settlement to be cut up there. Generally they are small, not more than six sazhens long.

The sea lions bask on the rocks near Cape Eskom [Edgecumbe?] and at the southern tip of the island. On the nearby islands there are few of them, and because it is very difficult, persons are rarely sent out to hunt for them on distant islands. The best catch is between December and March, but seldom are ten skins

obtained in a year. Seals have also been totally killed off, and it is a rare
occurrence to have one appear anywhere. It was earlier mentioned that in 1800,
during Baranov's first winter here, the Aleuts killed 40 sea lions and 150
seals. After that, as a result of settlement and hunting expeditions, these
creatures could no longer exist here; they were either killed or moved off.
Some evidence has been discovered that sea lions have been killed here with
Albion [California] Indian arrowheads in their bodies. This is an indication
that they migrate from north to south and back.

Fish And Shellfish

Fish which are here all year around include halibut, cod, eel-pout and sea
perch; the first two can be taken in large numbers and are always abundant;
sometimes there are more halibut, and sometimes more cod. Generally, halibut
is the basic food for the native population. The flavor is good from fall to
spring. Fish which appear periodically are the following: herring come in large
schools in February or March and stay along the shores until May. Sometimes
they appear in fall or even during winter, but one cannot count on this, and at
that time they are of inferior quality. From May on, fish come in which
resemble the same kind of salmon as one finds in Kamchatka. They are called
by the same names here as there. In May, June, July and August, the chinook
and humpback come; in August the silver salmon appear and stay until the end of
October. In addition to these there are various small fish such as flounder;
the sculpin is always to be found here and white-fish and loach come every
spring.*

Among shellfish, there are large crabs here, shrimp, and various sorts of
mollusks used for food. The best of these is the mamai in a round white
striped shell which makes a delicious broth and is very good cooked like a
cutlet. Shellfish known as "baidarkas" have to be pickled in vinegar. The
cuttlefish is known as "button-shell" here. Sea crabs are the most abundant
of all shell fish. All of these types of shellfish are used as food by the
Kolosh as well as by the Aleuts and the Russians, and many can be used in the
preparation of fine dishes. Sometimes, however, they all taste the same. In
summer the flavor is very strong and not good. It is better from September on,
and continues good until May. Sometimes they are quite poisonous. There have
been cases when people died after eating shellfish. The famous Doctor B.
[Eduard Blaschke] stated, in regard to this latter, that is, sea urchin, that
it is a fact that this crustacean is a link between all three kingdoms of
nature: mineral, vegetable and animal. The shell is formed from a familiar
matter that belongs to the first; the spines on the surface of the shell are

————

*It is not unusual that after a long storm the shores may be filled with
every kind of fish. Crabs crawl out of the sea and assemble in great schools,
and die while they are out of the water. The sea all around the shore looks
red. This was noted on Sitka in 1816 and on Kodiak in October, 1825. At that
time they could not fish for anything at all until spring.

vegetable and smell like vegetables;* and then inside is the living creature. This man believes that nature in this fashion endows poor lands to equalize them with others. He finds the demand for sea urchin great, for in addition to a delicious flavor, it has healing properties. It can cure stones, also tuberculosis in its early stages. In fact, it is a universal medicine for all illnesses. Without rejecting the views of scholars, one can suppose that nature has not created anything without a purpose: some things can be used as food, some as delicacies; but not everything.

Land Animals, Amphibians And Others

Sitka is an island, and therefore there are obviously many kinds of animals. The most important are: the bear which has a beautiful black fur, foxes of various kinds and the mountain ram which provides the only meat for human consumption. There are many small animals: the marmot, which belongs to the ant-bear family, the mink, many rats which were brought here aboard various ships from Okhotsk and Kamchatka, the Sandwich Islands and Canton, and small mice. Of the amphibians there are river beavers and otters, but not in any large quantity.

On the mainland, which is separated from the island by a strait, there are these same animals, plus large numbers of elk, reindeer, wolverine, sable, wolf, and one kind of mountain ram whose hair provides a fine yarn from which the Kolosh weave blankets and the Russians knit stockings and hats.

Birds

Birds which are native to the cliffs and forests of northwest America are not small and delicate. If we exclude the birds who come up from the south to spend the summer, which beautify the forests, the water and the air, then the following forest birds can be considered native to this region: a medium sized white eagle which nests in high inaccessible places in mountain ravines, the crow and the small eagle-owl. The crow is found everywhere, and one can always hear its wild cawing. A few birds of the sparrow family and a few swallows appear in the spring. Black geese and ptarmigan are to be found in forests far from the sea. In very cold winters the black geese cannot find anything to eat on the snow-covered cliffs and comes in close to shore, at which time they can be killed in great numbers.

Migratory birds appear in spring, sometimes in March but more often about the middle of April. These include geese, ducks, cranes, herons and swans. They spread out through the mainland of North America and the islands to bring up their young. They start to fly back about the middle of August. Occasionally some will spend the winter here.

---

*The odor comes from a tiny opening on the point of the spine, but the spines themselves are made of a material rather like limestone. The spines of large sea urchin can be used like an engraving instrument to write on slate.

In spring, in the month of May, hummingbirds appear; they are three and a half inches long, including a long thin bill and tail; but counting only the body and head, they measure one and six-tenths of an inch, and without the head, one inch. The flame color on the throat of this bird looks like a red-hot coal. Sometimes there will be whole flocks of them during a warm period, which may remain two or occasionally three months, and then will disappear. Hummingbirds are also found in California; they are about one inch in length. The throats of those birds are emblazoned with a raspberry color, but not as beautiful. By virtue of this difference they appear to be a different species; obviously those that are found along these shores are native and not migratory, and like some insects, they hibernate for the winter and are revived by the life-giving rays of the spring sun.

Marine birds native to this climate include ducks of all kinds, which have a poor taste because their diet consists of fish. There are puffin, cormorant, divers and seagulls. The first three nest in rocks; the latter appears mainly when schools of herring come in to the shore. Grey albatross may be found along the sea close to shore. Pratincoles of various kinds are found here in spring and summer.

Bats and flying mice appear in summer and fly away in the fall.

Vegetation

The massive mountain cliffs, deep ravines and wet tundra are all covered with a primeval forest. Eroded granite on cliffs that support scarcely any soil is covered with dense moss, and has a lush growth of conifers. Old trees that have been blown down by strong winds and have rotted give rise to new growth; all together this comprises a dense impenetrable cover for wild animals. The principal forest tree of the conifers is the fir, then the larch, then a variety of cypress with a pungent odor. Small pines grow sparsely here and there. In the deciduous forests one finds alder, willow and the so-called apple tree. Low growing brushy vegetation with berries include the raspberry, which has a very watery taste, the mountain ash, currant, blackberry, which also has an inferior flavor, elderberry and some others. One plant [devil's club] belongs to the thorn family and is covered with countless sharp thorns. It grows between forested areas along the shore and adds to the impenetrability. Along the shore there is a shrub that produces good berries called "velvet berries." In the tundra grow cowberries, crowberries, cranberries and cloudberries. V[asilii] N. Berkh noted that persons in China prefer our native ginseng to that from Canada. But the root which he calls ginseng is actually maun, or valerian; and we now know that the Americans took it to Canton and that it was not called ginseng, and that it is no longer taken there. Medicinal herbs, in addition to that root, include milifolium, which is known and used by the natives. Wild grasses which are gathered in spring and used as food include young nettles, parsley, sorrel and chicory.*

---

*We do not know where this grows, but the Kolosh gather a fine moss which grows on rocks in the mountains. They use it to make a dye to color the wool of the mountain ram, from which they weave blankets which only toions or distinguished elders have the right to wear.

The following trees are used in ship building. Cypress, which is known here as the dushmiannoe tree is used for the frame and sides of sailing ships; it is somewhat yellowish, good to work with, and light. Fir is used for beams and deck, and for the mast they use a tree that grows near rocks. Vegetation that grows in the wet tundra has a soft growth and contains a great deal of moisture, and consequently will rot easily. Ash is used for planking and sometimes for the deck. It can be used straight or it can also be easily bent for rudders and pumps. Because of its strength, the apple tree is used as needed for blocks and pulleys. Fir is used to build homes, for it is a straight and even tree, and sometimes will have no knots for 14 or 15 sazhens. The bark is stripped off cypress trees in spring and used to cover dwellings. Usually trees are full of moisture and when they are cut in the fall, they are used in construction the following summer. They soon rot, because they do not dry out very well and are constantly exposed to moisture; in construction they do not last more than 20 years. It is important to note that this condition is an advantage for forests, for they are fire resistant. It is impossible to set a forest on fire in the dry summer season, when trees are full of pitch; for this reason buildings are not subject to fire.

There are several species of mushrooms and saffron milk cap on Sitka, but they do not occur in large quantities. There are many milk-agaric in Yakutat Bay.

Minerals

Mountains on the island of Sitka consist of granite and other composite rocks, including kinds of shieferion here and there. Gneiss, schist and granite are found in Lituya Bay and Yakutat. And in many places there is quartz, hornstone, hornblende, chlorite, serpentine and talc. Large garnets can be found in schist, some as large as one and two-tenths inch in diameter. They are seldom perfect, however; generally there are flaws. Because of the shortage of lead, the Kolosh use them instead of shot to kill sea animals. Small ones, similar to those just mentioned, are used to kill birds. Obviously, guns are damaged from their use. One can also find white and grey marble, limespar, sometimes cornelian and chalcedony, occurring in round chunks. The Kolosh make smoking pipes out of slate, and decorate them with carved representations of bird eyes and beaks. They used to make serpentine labrets which women wore inserted into their lips. One such labret, which had been used for a long time, was two and one-tenth inches long, two inches wide, and seven and one-half inches around. Near Mount Edgecumbe there is much pumice, and in various places around there one can find several kinds of volcanic rocks with bits of olivine, zeolite and volcanic blends.

The Colonial Status Of New Arkhangel

New Arkhangel became the chief port after Baranov left, and was also the place where the chief administrators lived. There were then and still are many points of view in regard to its advantages and disadvantages. The advantage of this port cannot be matched by any other places. The disadvantages lie in the great expense and the fact that it is impossible to pacify the natives. Both are important. Both will for some time to come be the subject of discussion and disagreement. We must examine all of these in regard to reality and detail.

Population Of The Fort

As of January 1, 1825, the population of the fort was as follows:

SERVICE PERSONNEL

Officials, churchmen, promyshlenniks and other Russians	309	
Creoles	58	
Kodiak Aleuts	17	
Fox Island Aleuts	13	
Indian Aleuts	3	
	Total	400

NON-SERVICE PERSONNEL

Kodiak creoles	8	
Kodiak Aleuts	129	
Fox Island Aleuts	8	
Indians	2	
	Total	147
Boys	66	
Women	133	
Girls	67	
	Total	200
	In all	813

The breakdown of the 400 service people noted above is as follows:

Chief Manager	1
His secretary	1
Office Manager and assistants	6
Naval officers	1
Navigators	8
Assistant navigators	6
Warehouse supervisors	3
Assistant supervisors	5
Priest, elder, cantor	3
Supervisor and assistants for the arsenal	3
Medical worker and infirmary assistants	5
Chief Manager's service personnel	6
Teacher and supervisor	2
Law enforcement personnel	4
Total	54

Crew of ships at sea

Brig Baikal	22	
Brig Buldakov	20	
Brig Volga	13	
Brig Riurik, government seamen	28	
Brig Okhotsk	10	
Schooner Fortuna	14	
Sloop Konstantin	16	
Cutter Baranov	8	
Total		131

In Okhotsk, discharged from the service	13	
Dispatched to various departments	11	

In the harbor

Orderly and supervisor of materials	2	
Boatwrights, joiners, turners	10	
Blacksmith and assistants	6	
Metal workers and apprentices	6	
Copper smiths and assistants	11	
Coopers	4	
Spinners	4	
Baidarshchiks [in charge of Aleut baidarka hunters]	2	
Stovemakers	2	
Tailors	2	
Roofer, glazier, painter	3	
Coal heaver	1	
Fisherman	1	
Shipwrights and carpenters	21	
Woodcutters	14	
Chalkers	2	
Total	[91]	93

Sentries	22	
Cooks	4	
Interpreters	2	
Bookkeepers	2	
In the lake redoubt	24	
Total		54

Remaining	43	
Total		400

It is evident that, not counting the 43 who had no official responsibilities and who were working as general laborers in procuring coal, and excluding those who were ill, one could not even make up a crew of 16 men for a longboat. During the time ships were sent to sea in 1825, the personnel in the harbor consisted of 180 males, including young apprentices who worked in various shops.

Having described all jobs in detail, it is obvious that there is no surplus of personnel anywhere. In fact, we cannot operate without at least 300 trained persons. If Sitka were not the main settled area, and if it existed because of some other circumstance, its garrison should consist of not less than 100 men able to use firearms. Today, taking into account all the work and shipbuilding, that number is just barely sufficient.

Relations Of Officials And Promyshlenniks To The Company

All officials, from the Chief Manager on down, are paid a salary, and in addition receive from the Company their living quarters, wood, candles and fish, as needed. All the rest of the necessities of life they buy from their wages, which are sufficient. They are given schoolage boys as servants. Goods and supplies are issued to them in exchange for money at the store; these supplies are kept in warehouses, and although they are sometimes available only in limited quantity, nonetheless there is always something available. Officials receive their salaries, in colonial money, every month from the cashier. The term of service lasts from three to five years. A year or more prior to the end of his term of service, an official must give notice as to whether he wishes to continue in service or to leave. The return voyage is of course guaranteed under the conditions of service. Allowances and salary during travel are determined according to rank as well as the length of time in service. Officials pledge not to purchase any furs at all.

In the past promyshlenniks were hired under an overall contract. On December 14, 1820, however, the Board of Directors issued a directive outlining the terms on which workers are to be accepted for hunting and other Company duties in the American colonies. The terms of this directive are as follows:

A) Upon entering the service, this statement is to be read to the employe, and by signing it, he obligates himself to fulfill it. The Company will secure for him a passport valid for seven years, and will give him the necessary money to cover the cost of his transportation. Prior to his departure, the Company will give him money for food in the amount of 70 kopecks per day. When the employes are en route around the world aboard ships, they are required to carry out sailors' duties and to help wherever possible. They must obey the captain, and if they disobey, they will be subject to punishment under naval regulations. In Kronstadt they are to be provided with prepared rations, and aboard ship they are to receive standard ship's rations. Those who are sent across Siberia are to receive a food allowance of one ruble per day, as far as the Lena River. While they are sailing on the Lena to Yakutsk, they will receive prepared rations. They must travel on foot from Yakutsk to Okhotsk, because of the shortage of horses. During that time they receive prepared rations from the Company.

B) When they reach Okhotsk they will be under the jurisdiction of the Company office there, and in accordance with the instructions of that office, they will board a ship which will take them to America. They are to pledge themselves to carry out all jobs. Both in Okhotsk and for the duration of the voyage at sea they are to be provided for at the Company's expense. When they leave Okhotsk, their accounts will be taken aboard ship with them.

C) When they arrive in the colonies, they are under the jurisdiction of the Chief Manager or the various office administrators, and they must carry out their professional duties or other work, according to their training; they pledge to obey the administration at all times.

D) A promyshlennik must promise not to engage in any trading with the savages or with foreigners, under threat of loss of his contract and of his profit.

E) Every new arrival must pledge to avoid the following vices: drunkenness, extravagance, quarreling and other offenses, and not to accumulate large unpaid debts.

F) The term of service is seven years; at the end of this period, if the employe has no debts and decides to return home, the Company shall not hinder this decision, and the employe shall be sent by the first available transport to Okhotsk, or around the world, at Company expense. At the time of his departure he shall receive an accurate accounting, and within a month after the journey via either Okhotsk or St. Petersburg, he is completely discharged from service. Those who have debts must pay them through service, and must neither ask nor petition to be released from their contracts.

G) Those who return from the colonies via Kronstadt or Okhotsk shall not leave service before the ship is unloaded.

For its part, the Company promises the following to those who enter its service:

1) To issue salaries, upon arrival in Okhotsk, of 350 rubles per year from the day of boarding ship to the return to their homeland.* Those who return around the world shall receive pay equal to that given to the ship's crew; those who go via Okhotsk shall receive 15 rubles per month for the duration of the voyage, including the unloading of the ship.

2) The Company pledges not to deduct debts from pay before reaching the colony. In the colonies, salaries will be paid monthly, with up to one-third being deducted for payment of debts.

3) During their stay in the colonies, the Company will issue a flour ration in addition to salary. Each employe will receive one pud per month of whatever flour the Chief Manager has available. Those who are there will receive this amount until the day of their departure for their homeland. At sea they will be

---

*According to the rules established by Chief Manager Matvei Ivanovich Muraviev, the salary was raised as follows: master craftsmen such as smiths and metal-workers, coppersmiths, carpenters, shipbuilders and others, from 400 to 450 rubles; boatswain first class, 450; boatswain second class, 400 rubles.

supplied with ship's rations. In case there is a shortage of flour, they will receive money, equivalent to five rubles per pud.

4) [The Company] will pay government taxes on behalf of the employe as follows: those who designate relatives as recipients will have deducted from their salaries, over and above the one-third amount, an annual sum which will not exceed 50 rubles.

5) In case of illness they will be cared for, and after the medical official has made his report, shall be provided with all necessities at the Company's expense. The Company shall not deduct any money from salaries for this.

6) The Company shall have in the colonies everything necessary to supply them with clothing and footwear; employes shall pay a price set by the Chief Manager depending on local conditions.

7) Colonial provisions should be dispersed by the Company without payment of money, in an amount to be determined by the Administration. Sea rations are also to be issued at Company expense.

8) If an employe distinguishes himself, the Company shall reward him, through the Chief Manager, in accordance with his authority.*

This regulation was made known to everyone entering the service as part of the mutual agreement. The Chief Manager Matvei Ivanovich Muraviev, agreed to sell from the store each month, over and above the portion of flour allotted:

1) To an unmarried promyshlennik, 15 pounds of flour,** six pounds of groats and six pounds of peas.

2) To a married promyshlennik without children, 30 pounds of flour, eight pounds of groats and 10 pounds of peas.

3) To a married promyshlennik with family, flour, groats and peas, the same as above; and for each child, four pounds of groats and six pounds of peas.

Depending on availability, each person receives a monthly allotment from other supplies as follows: from three-quarters to one pound of tea, two to three pounds of granulated sugar, one bottle of molasses and one pound of tobacco.

Any surplus goods are distributed freely.

---

*The Chief Manager has the right to give bonuses, beginning at five rubles per year, which are distributed annually to all promyshlenniks engaged in trade; those who perform work as sailors, or other work, receive from 25 to 100 rubles or more.

**When an adequate supply of flour came in from California, the Chief Manager in 1824 agreed to sell 20 pounds of flour to each unmarried man, and three pounds of groats and three pounds of peas.

On his birthday, each promyshlennik and creole receives a bottle of rum from the store; foremen receive two; and they pay for this. On major holidays each person may buy half a bottle or sometimes a cup per person. When there is a surplus of rum, sales may be made more frequently; when there is a shortage, less often.

In accordance with a directive of the Chief Manager, Hagemeister, a cup of rum is given out at the Company's expense eight times a year, on the following holidays: 1. Epiphany. 2. Easter. 3. Archangel Michael's day, November 8, which is a church feast day. 4. Christmas. 5, 6, 7 and 8. The birthday, saint's day, day of ascension to the throne, and day of coronation of the Sovereign Emperor.

Relationship Between The Creoles And The Company

The Board of Directors decreed the following, in a dispatch dated February 28, 1822, No. 157, sent out to the Chief Manager:

"The administration of the Company directs you to take note of the fact, at all times and in all places, that creoles born of legal marriages who are left without a father, as well as those born of a non-legalized union, are without exception to be educated at the Company's expense, wherever and however possible. Until they reach the age of 16, they should receive the same support as apprentices; from 16 to 20 they are to be assigned to various occupations according to their abilities; and depending on the work they do, they are to be provided with necessities appropriate to the position they occupy. Between the ages of 20 and 29 they are also to be employed on the basis of their training and ability, and they are to receive salaries on the basis of their productivity and dedication to service, of from 100 to 350 rubles, including clothing and food. Those who demonstrate character and distinguish themselves by exemplary behavior and zeal may advance to become prikashchiks or office managers; in special cases they should be singled out to be given privileges and appropriate titles."

Creoles who have received Imperial privileges through the Company form a separate class, and their rights are defined in paragraph 41. Chief Manager Matvei Ivanovich Muraviev, in distributing Imperial privileges, explained this matter of privileges in a directive, No. 336, which was issued from the New Arkhangel office in December 1822.

"Creoles who do not belong to their fathers' families, that is, those whose birth has not been legitimized and who are not registered anywhere in the latest census, are citizens of the colonies, that is, they are Russian subjects. They have all the rights of subjects and legal protection, and are at the same time obliged to obey the laws, and are accountable under them. The government frees them from all debts, and assigns them to the protection of the Chief Manager and his office, and he is obligated to look after their well-being and their property. That this goal may be attained, colonial authorities should observe their rights judiciously and not allow them to return to a savage condition. They must be concerned and use all the resources at their disposal to ensure that the creoles who have become familiar with a European way of life will not fall away from it. Those who have some ability and inclination to perform household work or agriculture or gardening should receive every assistance from the Company. Married persons with children should obviously be given preference. But colonial authorities should see to it that this assistance from the Company is not given in vain, but rather benefits those most capable.

"Other persons who are not qualified for such assistance - those who are single and have no children, who have been working as tradesmen or seamen for some time, may enter the service of the Company quite freely, but this freedom should be limited by the same conditions as those which apply to Russian promyshlenniks, namely, superior performance of duties and payment of debts owed to the Company. Creoles are by and large obligated to the Company for their initial upbringing, and those educated under these conditions, in accordance with the regulation of the Board of Directors, are obliged to serve the Company for as long as 29 years.

"Creoles who have not entered Company service may not under any circumstances be used for any Company work without pay or without their consent. They shall have complete freedom to hunt, on the basis of the rules outlined in paragraph No. 51, and everything they acquire shall be their inalienable property. It is understood that they may not and shall not acquire or aspire to privileges. In accordance with the Imperial charter of the Company, no one but the Company has the right to purchase furs; they may use the fruits of their labor for their personal needs. They have no right to ask salary, provisions or any other special treatment from the Company. In case of some mishap, the Company will not refuse to give them assistance, but this hope should not be allowed to cause laziness; a person unable to support himself because of laziness or vagrancy should be immediately taken into the service of the Company for one year, but given less pay. If he has a family they should be kept together; if his wife and children are employed in some capacity in Company service, they should receive equal pay so that there is no hardship.

"Before the Office Administrator decides on this course of action, he should assemble accurate data regarding the adverse behavior of the wayward person, and register it in the penalty book. If illness or some disaster causes an extreme case of suffering, then the Company official should immediately assist, to whatever extent his resources allow. In granting advantages and privileges to the creoles, the government delegated their supervision to the Chief Manager and to the offices, and for this reason, the following has been decreed:

1) The office shall prepare an accurate list of creoles, both male and female, indicating age and present status, and shall append a recommendation as to where each should be assigned. The Office Administrator shall attest to their capabilities and conduct, and sign this statement. No matter where creoles live, they should be registered in one of two offices, either Kodiak or Unalaska, because their mothers are from these two places, with a few exceptions, which should not change the rule. An Unalaska-born person may be registered as a resident of Kodiak and vice versa, because marriage or other family ties may put him in either place. Henceforth, a person wishing to change his place of residence must request this in writing at the office, indicating his reasons. When he receives permission to transfer, he is entered into the register of one office and removed from the register of the other. It is forbidden to transfer without this specific permission; such action is considered vagrancy.

2) All creoles shall be assembled in the office, and all the privileges and regulations granted by the Emperor shall be read to them, as well as this supplement to paragraph 41.

3) They should be asked who wishes to remain in the Company's service. Those who express this desire should be paid from 100 to 300 rubles, making certain that this payment will be adequate for his necessities, and will properly reward his service. It should be given according to his capabilities, and the benefit expected from his service. It should be explained to them that when they enter Company service they are subject to the same rules as Russian promyshlenniks in the colonies, except for the length of the term of service. I believe that the term of service for creoles should be three years. Each person who enters service signs an appropriate agreement. If there are some who do not wish to enter Company service, but have the right to do so; that is, who have no debts to the Company, and wish to live on their own (and such persons should be honest, industrious and intelligent), then the office should ask them how they expect to make a living and where they plan to settle. They should then be informed that they are under the jurisdiction of the nearest artel, and that in regard to any need or request they should consult the local administrator, whose permission is needed should they wish to change their place of residence. This person has jurisdiction over them; if they are dissatisfied, they should petition the Office Administrator or even the Chief Manager himself. The office billets each creole where he is registered. The office may give him his choice of place to live (providing this does not interfere with the rights of others), and will give him any necessary assistance to establish himself, being careful that such assistance is not insufficient. If a creole who lives on his own wants to go on a hunt with his relatives, he should not be denied this right, but should participate in that undertaking in accordance with the general rules."

When Chief Manager Matvei Ivanovich Muraviev took over on December 15, 1820, he issued the following directive regarding schools, in memorandum No. 105:

"In an effort to carry out the good intentions of the Russian American Company, I have resolved to organize a staff to care for and clothe the pupils in New Arkhangel. Although this staff is to be organized on an economical basis, nonetheless it will be adequately provided for. The office shall administer and carry out this matter. The office should note that the food supplies listed here may be in insufficient quantity. This has come about because of the extreme difficulty of securing these provisions, and because in addition to the things listed here, pupils should also be supplied with such edibles as garden produce, fresh fish, salted fish and whale and seal meat. Fats and oils, etc. should also be supplied as well as possible. In addition to a teacher and his assistant the school should have one person to supervise the young children, who will look after all of their food, linens and clothing. A woman of good standing, an Aleut, should be chosen to keep the pupils washed and clean; she should be paid 100 rubles per year. All of these expenses should be paid from the account designated for charitable institutions."

REQUIRED CLOTHING AND FOOD FOR 30 PUPILS

1 set of warm grey woolen clothing lined with crash	30 sets @	12.50 r.	375	r.
1 set summer clothing made of ticking	30	6.50	195	
3 fur hats apiece	90	.50	135 [sic]	
3 linen shirts apiece	90	2.50	202.50 [sic]	
1 cap apiece	30	.50	15	
3 arshins crash, for leggings	90	.30	27	

949.50 r.

Provisions

Monthly ration for each:

flour, 10 pounds; for all, 7 puds, 20 pounds
groats, 5 pounds   3 puds, 30 pounds
peas   5 pounds   3 puds, 30 pounds

Per year, 90 puds flour @ 5   r.   450 r.
          45 puds groats   4.80   240
          45 puds peas   4.80   240   930

Paper, ink, pencils, etc.   70.50
Salary for laundress   100

Total for year   2,050 r.

Nothing is mentioned in the regulation from the Board of Directors and the Chief
Manager about issuing rations to the creoles in case of shortages, but from this
time on they all were to receive one pud or half a pud of flour each month; and
those who had sea duty received regular sea rations.

A shortage of fish, which rarely occurs on Sitka, forced them to be permitted to
purchase the following supplies at the store, in addition to their rations:
married men -- six pounds of groats and six pounds of peas; and for each child,
four pounds of groats and four pounds of peas.

The wealth and strength of this area consists of the people. At this point it
should be explained what the advantages are which the late Active Chancellor
Rezanov foresaw when he visited the colonies. Directive No. 478, part 5,
states: "The true strength of these regions lies in increasing the number of
settlements and the population. The first objective of each administration
should be to increase the population. This will enable us to increase all
aspects of industry to satisfy private and public needs, such as agriculture,
construction, crafts and various other economic enterprises. This will also
provide indispensable resources for the protection and defense of these regions
by military forces. As native industry grows, these people will acquire more
means to take care of themselves as well as to increase their numbers to meet
the needs of defense."

Part 3 of that same directive states: "Persons of responsible families who have
been educated by the Company should have instilled in them from the time they
are young the desire to hunt and to work. Such persons should be appointed to
various positions according to their abilities." Part 6, referring to schools,
says, "By this means you will have military forces, agriculturalists, master
craftsmen, prikashchiks, accountants, and in time, administrators as well. By
increasing the number of schools, you will care for orphans and make a fine
contribution to humanity."

What, then, has education accomplished? In 1805 Rezanov believed that within
20 years this society would produce capable seamen, accountants, prikashchiks,
and a number of experienced artisans and fine master craftsmen. It is
unfortunate that because of inadequate basic education they do not have maturity

and strong character, and that although they understand Russian rules for good behaviour, they do not abide by them, but rather imitate the vices. They frequently use hard liquor which becomes a deadly habit for many.*

Let us hope that this generation will be successfully brought up, for the well-being and the advantage of the Company and the fatherland.

It was formerly considered helpful to send creoles to St. Petersburg to study navigation and seamanship. But experience has demonstrated that the necessary education is better learned on the job, without the great expense involved in instructing and maintaining them in the capitol. There have been cases of some who studied shipbuilding and returned quite unfamiliar with both theory and practice and as a result were of no use here. Some of the pupils learned navigation quite well, but at the same time they acquired a taste for luxuries and learned bad habits. Young people are always guided by example. In a small group dominated by one individual, who, with a paternal attitude supervises the conduct of each and every one, there cannot be so many open vices and evil tendencies as might occur in a large city. Here such sins as thievery and deceit cannot be hidden, and the guilty person is found out right away. The guilty one is punished immediately according to his offence. But it is not apparent to someone who goes into a worldly city how transgressions are found out and punished. As a result, such transgressions are rare here. There used to be some persons here who were steeped in vice; but we would not tolerate such sins, and so in time they completely abandoned their inclinations and became useful citizens.

Drinking is one of the problems of these natives. But this is understandable; where drinking is freely done, it is available at any time; and where can one not find people who would not avail themselves of this evil? Here, when they receive it rather rarely, some are satisfied with the fact that they have an opportunity for a merry time. Furthermore, there is not a steady supply in the colonies to nurture this vice.

On the basis of examples we see that creoles who were educated here perform their work quite well. There are a number of navigation students who are skippers of small sea vessels, and there are accountants and prikashchiks who know their jobs; there are masters of the art of bronzing and coppersmiths who are obviously not inferior to their teachers. It is now possible to look forward to having praiseworthy students of medicine, surgery and navigation.

It would be a good thing, and helpful toward increasing population, if a prohibition were instituted against Russians marrying creole women and taking them

---

*One must agree that in a wet and unsalubrious climate the moderate use of liquor is one of the best means of staying in good health. Experience has demonstrated that scurvy, which was once very widespread here, is today quite unknown. It is possible that rum, tea and potatoes are responsible for this. Every service person receives four or five cups of rum per month during the rainy season. They drink tea twice a day and always have potatoes. Sometimes these are distributed by the Company, and sometimes purchased from the artel.

to Russia, where they experience the change of climate and do not live long, or where they are abandoned by their husbands and are miserable. It would be very desirable to tie these people with bonds of marriage and homemaking; only in this way can stable citizens be created.

Relations Between The Aleuts And The Company

Among the privileges granted to the Company by the Emperor there are rules stating the relationship of the island natives to the Company, as per paragraphs 43 through 57. Chief Manager Muraviev, in carrying out these rules, elaborated on them in his directives to offices of the Company, numbers 337, 338 and 339, for the year 1822, and numbers 55, 59, 98 and 211, for the year 1823, which specify:

"Maintain the inhabitants of the islands in their present way of life, and keep account of the population, of both sexes, both births and deaths; keep track of those who have been or are about to be baptized, and differentiate between creoles and American natives; report who are present and who are absent; differentiate by sex and by age. Other offices should send such information to the New Arkhangel office, where there should be a special desk to keep that data.

"Islanders should be governed by their own native toions, under the supervision of elders. In order to accomplish this, two such persons should be appointed from among Russian service personnel, who shall be responsible, together with the toions, for taking care of and supervising the islanders who have been placed in their trust. They should settle personal quarrels and dissatisfactions, and help them as needed. However if a disagreement arises between these islanders and the toions, this should be resolved by the administrator of the office.

"The islanders, that is all males between the ages of 18 and 50, are obligated to assist the Company in catching sea animals. Half of these should be used for Company service, and the islanders should be informed of this in the month of January. For that purpose zakashchiks [Company officials] and toions should meet in the main settlement and receive instructions from the office admin- istrators. The office should see to it that those selected wherever possible be from a family with more than one male member, so that a wife and children will not be left without a provider.

"Colonial authorities should try to acquaint the islanders with the advantages of civilized life, and they should give them a sufficient plot of ground to introduce them to gardening, and assist them not only with advice, but also with agricultural equipment and with seeds. The administrator of the office may give this assistance at the Company's expense. In order to encourage gardening, the most successful persons should be singled out and presented to the Chief Manager each year, and should receive some individual reward.

"Islanders are subjects of Russia and are subject to the law; and thus their property and their persons are inviolable. The office is obliged to punish severely anyone who violates this. American natives who are not in the Company service, but who hunt with their own equipment and resources, with no assistance from the Company, have the full right to hunt land and sea animals in the vicinity of their dwellings, but they cannot go far off without permission from the authorities. Everything they catch is their own property; obviously, it is understood that if they wish to sell their catch, they may only sell to the Company. Persons who are organized into hunting parties and who receive assistance from the Company do not have the right to keep their catch for themselves, but must hand over the entire catch to the Company, which is obliged to pay the hunters as agreed. This is the only obligation of these natives to the Russian State and the Company takes every advantage of this circumstance since the Company makes a good deal of investment in organizing the [hunting] party.

"Islanders should be paid for their pelts not less than one-fifth of the amount earlier Russian promyshlenniks received, when they had a contract based on the gross catch."

This is the first definitive statement of the relationship between the island natives and the Company, and is still in force today.

It was earlier noted that in 1816 the Company decided to issue lavtaks [hides] for each baidarka and clothing for the Aleuts, as follows:

For each two-man baidarka

6 lavtaks from male walruses	3 r	18 r
2 whale gut kamlei	5 r	10 r
7 pounds whale whiskers for tying, and whale sinew for sewing		2 r
An issue of whale oil		—
Total		30 r

When an Aleut hunting party sets out, the Company supplies the baidarka crew with firearms and enough ammunition to kill seals for food. They are also issued fishhooks and line for fishing, and a pound or two of tobacco for each man. If necessary, the crew receives two or three cups of rum apiece. When they travel on sailing vessels, they are supplied with bread, and the hunting party also is issued some flour.

Whenever they are needed to work in the harbor or in the forest or in the Company gardens, the Company employs however many Aleuts are needed, and pays them at the rate of one ruble per day. When there is no work, they receive a cup of vodka. In summer the Aleut women clean fish for the Company at the lake redoubt and at the harbor, and are paid 50 kopecks [one-half ruble] per day.

If it is necessary to build or repair Company baidarkas, then the Company pays for each one separately. For a new three-man baidarka they pay 15 rubles; and for repairing one, depending on the work involved, from 5 to 10 rubles.

In general, neither Aleut men nor their women are put to work without pay. If a baidarka is sent to the lake redoubt or to the hot springs during winter or spring, without payment, then the men receive lavtaks from the Company to use in making their own baidarkas for fall and winter; they use these baidarkas for their own needs.

When Aleuts are sent out as a [hunting] party, they draw, on account, their necessary supplies which cost from 10 to 30 rubles per baidarka; and this amount is deducted from the profit of the hunt. But many try not to do this, so that if there is a successful hunt they will receive the full amount of profit from it. They receive money through various sources and are permitted to buy any commodities that may be for sale in the store. In cases of need, they may sometimes be given provisions of food. On the same basis as service personnel, the Aleuts receive an issue of rum during holidays, and they are permitted to buy a cup of rum for themselves whenever such a sale is arranged for all the employes.

Payment for sea otters has been set, on the basis of regulations from the Governing Board, at one-fifth of the official [sale] price, that is, 10 rubles for a large male or female pelt, four rubles for a medium, and 80 kopecks for a small. Taking into account the fact that prices on agricultural produce have risen considerably as well as those on Russian and foreign goods, and that sea otter pelts bring higher prices, the present Chief Manager, P. E. Chistiakov, has ordered that payment for pelts be increased by 50% over the stated prices, and he has requested approval for this from the Governing Board.

One article of the rules and privileges granted by the Emperor to the Company still remains unaltered to the present: paragraph 56, which permits the islanders to sell their catch to the Company at the official rate which the Company is to submit to the government for approval.*

In order to ascertain the advantages the Company receives, compared to those the islanders receive, it should be noted that they receive pay for their catch according to government regulations, but never more than the price set by the general contract. Obviously the value of furs has increased; but in order to purchase goods overseas, one has to have a ship for transport, and there is the expenditure of money to pay the crew. Even today where there is a 100% markup, we still operate at a loss. In such trade, in order to show a profit, there must be a 200% gain from the fur trade, or it will be impossible to stay in business. [Italics ours. -- Ed.]

If the Aleuts supply large quantities of pelts, they also profit, because the Company supplies their baidarkas. The Company should use traps to take land animals; the Aleuts are not familiar with these and cannot operate them because of a shortage of necessary supplies which the local authorities distribute at appropriate times.

There is no denying the fact that persons in the service of the Company who do not fill their quotas of pelts may have to pay twice as much as the Company does [for pelts to make up the quota], hoping somehow to be able to hide the fact they have not taken enough. But this cannot and should not be an example, since they are protected from abuse by law.

---

*This article, to the present time, has not been submitted to the government for approval.

It would be more nearly correct to say that the Company, in order to satisfy both the Russians and the island natives, brings goods around the world from St. Petersburg, and imposes a 30% markup on them, and a 10 to 15% markup on goods it purchases [in the islands]. Consequently, without gaining any profit, it merely distributes goods at cost. If a merchant has expenditures and does not receive interest on his capital, he loses all advantage. From the Company's point of view this implies the right to equal compliance by the islanders, for without this equalization, the Company would lose its balance on the one hand, and its profit on the other.

Means Of Provisioning The People

When the decision was made to put the promyshlenniks on salary, that is, at the time Baranov was replaced, the Company had to provide the people with flour, and for this purpose ships were sent every year to California where they traded for wheat, barley and other grains. It has been noted above which persons from the lower ranks might purchase flour, and in what amounts.

In New Arkhangel the flour ration during the winter reaches more than 300 puds, and in summer, 200; and in addition, up to 200 puds of flour, peas, groats and other grains are sold in the winter, and up to 100 puds in summer.

Ship biscuits are baked at the harbor; two bakeries have been especially built for this purpose. Two or three persons are employed there for the entire winter. Between 500 and 600 puds of these are prepared. One pud of flour makes 28 pounds of biscuits.*

Aside from bread, fish represents the chief food, and the Company prepares it in the following manner.

In February and March herring appear near the shore; they are taken in nets in various places near the fort. The promyshlenniks will not eat fresh herring, and therefore herring from the first catch are salted and given out in that condition. As long as they run, they are continuously salted, and they are stored in from six to eight tubs or in from 20 to 30 barrels. Blueback salmon are taken in traps set in the lake redoubt. At first there are only a few, but from the middle of June on, there are more and more. This is followed by the humpback salmon, dog salmon, and then the silver salmon. As long as the run of fish is small, they do not salt it, but send the fresh fish by baidarka to the port for consumption. Salting begins in June and continues until September. Between 120 and 180 barrels of fish of all kinds are salted in the redoubt. This requires five puds of salt per barrel. The amount of salted fish per barrel may be stated as follows: blueback,

-----

*It is important to note that: 1) millet has been used as an absolutely necessary provision for travel if there were no groats or peas in the warehouses. But it is now sold as a commodity for money. 2) The brig Kiakhta was sent to Kodiak with a full load of wheat, which should last for five or at least four years. 3) In addition to the above expenditures, the ship Elena at the time of its departure had 228 and 1/40 [puds] of flour, 201 puds and 16 pounds of ship biscuits and, 4) in all of these expenditure accounts, the loss in warehouses has not been entered; this amounts to about 100 puds.

200; dog salmon and silver salmon, 100; considering an average to be 150 per barrel, this means that some 20,000 fish are salted in the redoubt. In addition, the Aleuts dry about 10,000 fish for iukola,* which is done, however, only with great difficulty, because of the continuous dampness, and even dried fish molds and spoils, so that less than half is fit for consumption.

At the end of June and in July the humpback salmon comes in near the fort, then the dog salmon and silver salmon, which are taken with nets. For this purpose, they use a special boat with nine men. This catch supplies all three forts with fresh fish, and in addition provides from 20 to 30 barrels of salted fish.

It takes one and a half barrels a day in winter to provide food for the people. Of this amount, 35 fish are given to the artels in the barracks, and 25 go to a general kettle, from which all persons who live in their own dwellings receive a share. The most exceptional are issued special rations.

From November on the Aleuts go out in one or two rowing vessels to fish for halibut. They are hired for 10 rubles per month apiece, and there are eight rowers and two masters in each boat. They go to the hot springs, and from there into the bays in appropriate places, where they set up their fishing gear. The following chart will indicate the catch of that fish:

1825	October	130	puds
	November	101-1/2	
	December	107	
1826	January	114	
	February	221	
	March	107	
	April	79-1/2	
	Total	860	puds

This fish goes first to the hospital and then to the garrison and to officials. The garrison receives eight puds per day.

On holidays the garrison receives one-half pound of meat per man. Altogether, including that issued to families, six to seven puds of meat are given out each day at the Company's expense.

The Company also produces potatoes; the amount produced in gardens in 1825 totaled 150 barrels. These are used primarily to feed the sick and the school children each day; the garrison receives six to eight barrels per month during the winter, beginning in November.

When the Aleuts return from their hunt in August, they go along rivers where fish come in and take all they need for themselves. When the weather is calm

---

*In case there is a shortage of barrels, fish is salted in chests or bins which are lined with cloth. One such bin is 15-2/12 feet long, 5-10/12 feet wide and 6-8/12 feet high and will hold 891,000 cubic inches; figuring 231 cubic inches to the gallon, this would equal 3,860 gallons, or 1,158 vedros [pails] by Russian measurement.

in winter they sail in the strait to fish for cod, halibut, turbot, and perch,
which they take in whatever numbers they need for their own use, plus as much as
half again more to sell to other persons. There have been times when there was
a shortage of fish and the Company supplied the Aleuts with food.

Sea lions are taken rarely and cannot be included as part of the list of food
supplies, although their meat is eagerly consumed. Whenever a whale washes
ashore, this delicacy is added to the Aleut diet because they are extraordinarily
fond of the fat of this creature.

Among other similar food items they get from the islands are salted and dried
whale and sea lion meat and oil. Whale oil comes from Unalaska, and from Kodiak
come iukola, berries and whale oil, but not in any great amount.

Oil is used primarily for lamps; about 30 barrels is used each year. Only whale
oil is used for lighting in the barracks, in the Aleut huts, aboard ships and in
private dwellings. Also, it is given to the Aleuts for food and to be used in
greasing the baidarkas, because without it, they would soon wear out. It is used
in the flour mill in place of grease. It is also used in large amounts in the
tannery and by the caulkers. Six to seven pounds are issued to a barracks, to
be used for three lamps to give light during the winter nights. The same amount
is issued to other living quarters. When there is a shortage of oil, they have
to buy it from the Kolosh; it sometimes costs as much as ten rubles per pud. If
they do not have any, then animal fat must be used in the lamps.

It is possible to extract oil from herring in the springtime if the catch is
large; if necessary, this can be used for exchange. It is also used for food;
it does not have an unpleasant odor, and it is pure. One man can try out about
three vedros [pails] in one day using three kettles.

Hunting Methods

In the section on the sea otter hunt near Sitka it was pointed out that even
during the time of Baranov's administration there was a gradual decline in the
sea otter catch. After he was replaced, Chief Manager Hagemeister, on the basis
of the agreement concluded between Baranov and the Americans, made a similar
agreement with [Camille de] Roquefeuil, captain of the French ship Bordelais.
On April 20, 1818, Roquefeuil left the harbor bound for Kodiak where he was to
take on however many baidarkas would be needed and proceed to the strait. On
June 15 the Bordelais returned to Sitka with the sad news that after they had
reached the strait and set up camp on one of the islands there had been an out-
break of hostilities with the Kolosh. This had occurred at a place which the
Americans call by its Kolosh name, "Nepada;" it is located in the Prince of Wales
archipelago in a bay south of Cape Pole. While the Aleuts who had gathered
together on shore were resting, the Kolosh began to fire on them from the forest.
They killed 20 Aleut men and three women; 12 escaped by running into the water
and swimming in spite of being wounded. Captain Roquefeuil, who was walking on
shore, threw off his clothes and ran into the water and swam to the ship. They
also fired on him, but he managed to reach his destination safely. After this
experience, they had no further contact with foreigners as far as hunting was
concerned, but they sent hunting parties to the strait in 1819, 1820 and 1821
under cover of well armed sailing vessels. But they met with fierce Kolosh resistance everywhere they went, and at all times.

The table below indicates when, where and in what number baidarkas were used for hunting, and what was taken. It should be noted that in Prince Frederick's Sound, where in earlier years sea otters had been taken in such great quantity that in 1805 300 baidarkas took 1,645 pelts, the hunting party now found that they could take very few. And when our baidarkas went out after sea otter, several boatloads of Kolosh went there and killed sea otter with firearms. There were frequent skirmishes. One baidarka was captured by the Kolosh, but thanks to the intervention of the leader, it was returned.

YEAR	SHIP WITH HUNTING PARTY	LEADER AND HEAD OF THE PARTY	PLACE OF HUNT	NO. OF BAIDARKAS	NO. OF PELTS
1818	Finlandia	Young & Eremin	Frederick's Sound and vicinity	100	416 large 30 medium
	Platov	Likhachev			
1819	Finlandia	Young & Tarakanov	Cross-Sound & Near Island	80	296 large 18 small
	Baranov	Tumanin			
1820	Fortuna	Tumanin & Eremin	Near Island Chatham Strait	80	205
1821	Chirikov	Young & Eremin	In Sound	100	104
	Fortuna	Tumanin & Dorofiev	Near Island		47
1822	Rumiantsev	Pometilov & Molvistov	Yakutat Bay	60	323
	Fortuna	Ingestrom	Lituya Bay		
1823	Riurik	V.S. Khromchenko & Nosov	Yakutat Bay	90	362
	Fortuna	Ingestrom	Lituya Bay		
1824	Golovnin	Young & Nosov	Yakutat Bay	55	247
	Fortuna	Pometilov	Lituya Bay		
1825	Riurik	Khromchenko & Nosov	Yakutat Bay	85	460
	Fortuna	Pometilov	Lituya Bay		

The number of sea otters taken by each baidarka varied; experienced and lucky hunters sometimes took as many as 10 to 13, while less fortunate hunters got only one, or sometimes none. The following table shows the results of the hunt along the Northwest Coast over a period of three years.

[Number of pelts taken per baidarka]

	1-3	3-5	5-8	8-11	11-14
1823, number of baidarkas	36	32	19	7	3
1824, number of baidarkas	11	18	16	6	3
1825, number of baidarkas	13	20	32	14	5

Method Of Trade

Earlier fur companies knew no other method of trade but barter; islanders exchanged their pelts for goods brought aboard ships. Baranov began to trade with American and English sea captains because there was a shortage of provisions and of supplies for the hunters and the Aleuts. Baranov's successors continued these ties even when trade in the colonies was prohibited, and they had to carry on trade in adjoining areas. Rezanov opened trade in California, and Kuskov continued it to a degree, but after that it was necessary to establish permanent relations with that region. Baranov had hoped to occupy several of the Sandwich Islands. His commissioner, Dr. Scheffer, began this venture quite successfully, but it ended in failure. After Baranov was replaced there were opportunities to trade with these islands, and salt and foreign goods were acquired there. Trade with the Kolosh was a special kind of transaction that required particular goods to obtain furs. Russian and foreign goods were primarily used to provision people throughout the colonies. I will submit a detailed report on all of these kinds of trade in subsequent chapters.

After Baranov was replaced, some of these foreign relationships were indirectly transferred to his successors, for he had debts to some, and the payments were transferred; and in other cases some persons who had not sold him their goods had left them to be safely stored in the warehouses here. Nearly all goods were purchased from them, and it was thus that trade was established, and was carried on as follows:

NAMES OF SHIPS AND CAPTAINS, AND SUM OF GOODS PURCHASED, IN PIASTRES   PAYMENT

1818

Thomas Meek, captain of ship Eagle, goods   2,346   1,211 fur seals, @ 1-3/4

Roquefeuil, captain of French ship Bordelais
626 fanegas of wheat
775 arobs of tallow
Various other goods   5,514.6   Payment was covered by various accounts

1819

Ship Brutus, Captain Pei
[David Nye], goods   4,917.83   2,700 fur seals, @ 1-3/4

Brig Brutus, armed, for
5,000 fur seals   5,000 fur seals

Thomas Meek, captain of
Eagle, goods   1,789.97   605 fur seals, @ 1-3/4; balance
                                               on account

[Henry] Gyzelaar, [brig]
Clarion, goods   2,288.60   1,308 fur seals, @ 1-3/4

[James] Bennett, ship
Volunteer, goods   380.90   Paid in Russian goods

Tell, of Clarion, 239
puds of lump sugar   1,863.53   671 fur seals, @ 1-3/4; balance
                                               in Russian goods

Davis, in Sandwich Islands:
aboard Brutus, goods
purchased by Schmidt   1,285.90   Credit transferred to Thomas
                                               Meek

1820

Bennett, Clarion, goods   302.80   Paid in Russian goods

[William J.] Pigot, brig
Pedlar, goods for 2,620
fur seals   2,620 fur seals

Andrew Blanchard, brig
Thaddeus, goods for 7,801
fur seals   7,801 fur seals

1821

Thomas Meek, brig Arab   5,156 fur seals, @ 1-3/4, paid
In accordance with an agreement   for goods from Boston cash:
made with him in 1819, he
supplied from Boston:
Goods @   7,528.24 piastres   Piastres   1,500   rubles
Credit   1,491.96   Chervonets   500
Cash   3,685.11   Goods and
For Chief   12,939.31   transfers   728.53
Manager   234   piastres   Credit   690.58

1822

Captain Clark, ship
Sultan, goods   898.83   483 fur seals, @ 1-3/4
                                              54 piastres

Captain John Meek, brig
Pedlar, goods   7,775.98   4,361 fur seals, @ 1-3/4
                                              144-1/4 piastres

Captain Thomas Meek,
brig Arab
Brought from Canton:
By agreement of 1821, goods
at a 50% markup   9,622.89   800 river otters, 1st quality)
Additional purchases 1,043.30   800 river otters, 2nd quality)@ 4
Account of Chief Manager 821.30   800 river otters, 3rd quality)
Credit 1821   690.58   21,177.77   4,739 fur seals, @ 1.75
                                              Russian goods @ 3,274

Captain Stevens, brig
Pearl, goods   680.75   373 fur seals, @ 1.75
                                              piastres 28

This brig was in port at the time when the sloop Apollon arrived carrying an
order prohibiting foreign trade in the colonies. After that, a shortage of goods
forced us to trade with them in the Sandwich Islands and in California, where the
following exchanges took place.

NAME OF SHIP AND CAPTAIN, AND SUM PAID FOR GOODS	PIASTRES	PAYMENT

In California in 1823

Captain [George] Newell,
ship Mentor, goods   13,991.8   2,995 fur seals, @ 1.75
                                              credit   8,749.83

The Englishman, Hartwell,
trading in California
Goods   1,443
Wheat   4,600   6,043   3,276 fur seals, @ 1.75
                                              goods at   310

1824

Newell, from Mentor in
Bodega, goods   8,866.15   5,000 fur seals, @ 1-3/4

In Monterey, goods   3,150   Piastres   116
                                              500 fur seals on credit
                                              1,823 fur seals, @ 1-3/4
                                              1,800 fur seals, @ 1-3/8
Money in piastres   1,190   700 fur seals   1.70

Elwell [supercargo], from schooner Washington, goods	812.25	500 fur seals	1.75
In Sandwich Islands in 1824, from Meek, goods*	34,203.17	4,428 fur seals	1.75
		12,825 fur seals	1.75
		500 river beavers	4
Brig Arab...11,000 fur seals		11,000 fur seals	

In New Arkhangel in 1825

[Andrew] Blanchard, brig Lapwing			
goods, account 1	11,605.89		24,235 fur seals, @ 1.75
goods, account 2	15,657.66		
goods, account 3	1,244.50		
Brig Lapwing	14,000		
Bill for provisions	87.25	43,655	
Wells, on ship Parfian, goods	1,212.30	603 fur seals	1.75
		piastres 157	

According to these figures it is apparent that from 1818 to 1826 trade with foreigners amounted to 205,652.50 piastres, or, figuring one piastre as equal to five rubles, the total would be 1,028,262.50 rubles. This sum included 109,479 fur seals, 2,900 river beavers, 2,000 piastres and 500 chervonets. In addition three substantial ships were purchased from foreigners: Brutus, Arab and Lapwing, which were renamed Golovnin, Baikal and Okhotsk. During this entire period the price for fur seals remained constant, even during the time when they sold in Canton for between 1 ruble 35 kopecks and one ruble 50 kopecks. It was then agreed that it was better to accept higher prices on purchased goods than to lower the price on goods sold. A high price in Canton is from two piastres to three piastres 20 centavos. Thomas Min [sic Meek?] supplied needed goods from Boston and Canton at a 50% markup over the regular price. Goods most recently purchased from Blanchard were sold at an additional 10%.

On goods purchased from foreigners, prices underwent a 10-15% markup, but not all goods would bear such a markup. Some prices had to be lowered in order to make them equal to existing prices; thus it averaged out in such a way that the Company always made a profit.

Trade With California

Captain Hagemeister, commanding the ship Kutuzov, stopped at Fort Ross in September, 1817, en route to Sitka, and on the advice of Kuskov, he visited

---

*Meek brought the brig Arab to New Arkhangel under the flag of the Russian American Company, taking on fur seals here and departing aboard the brig Riurik, having agreed to take on salt, which will be explained in detail in the chapter on trade in the Sandwich Islands.

Fort San Francisco to ask the Governor to release several Aleut hunting parties who had been apprehended by the Spanish, and to request permission to trade. [Governor] de Solá did not come personally to the port, but in response to the demand, sent two Aleuts who reported that the others had been sent far away [held captive in the Presidio]; but he did give permission to trade.

The following year Captain Hagemeister sailed from Sitka to California and met with the Governor in person. From then on every year our ships engaged in trade, through which the following quantities of various California goods were received:

PLACES, AND SHIPS THAT SECURED PROVISIONS	WHEAT, FANEGAS	BARLEY FANEGAS	PEAS & BEANS FANEGAS	FLOUR IN SACKS	TALLOW AND MONTEKA IN AROBS	DRIED MEAT AROBS
1817 San Francisco, Kutuzov	358	256	109	180	203	-
1818 Monterey & Santa Cruz, Kutuzov	3,140	500	904	114	1,083	540
1820 Monterey & Santa Cruz, brig Buldakov	1,376	250	163	242	390	260
1821 San Francisco, brig Golovnin	737	-	24	-	263	-
1821 Monterey, ship Kutuzov Captain Dokhtorov	1,160	300	306-1/2	-	480	729
1821 San Francisco, brig Buldakov	1,880	-	-	15	258	-
1822 Monterey, brig Volga	129	280	25	-	4	-
1822 Monterey, brig Buldakov	1,026	200	152	163	318	180
1822 Santa Cruz, brig Volga	520	-	120	-	6	-
1823 Monterey & Santa Cruz, brig Riurik	742	115	86	101	188	170
1824 Monterey, brig Baikal	1,317	400	-	-	510	-
1824 D [?sic] & Santa Cruz, brig Kiakhta	1,316	-	25	-	92-1/2	181

1824	San Pedro, brig <u>Buldakov</u>	1,885	-	-	-	140	-
1825	Monterey & San Francisco, <u>Kiakhta</u>	1,510	-	39	-	258	-
1825	San Pedro and San Francisco, brig <u>Baikal</u>	530-1/2	6	-	-	22	-

In addition to these supplies, we occasionally received rawhide from California, sometimes soap and salt, and always live steers, both for food for the crew and to make salt beef on Sitka. The amount of salt varied from 200 to 300 puds per year. Prices and supplies in California varied. During the first years we were almost the only ones who could sell goods; but when the constitutional King of Spain opened all ports of America to foreign trade, after 1821 American and English ships came every year with goods to trade, and whaling boats came for fresh supplies. From that time on we were forced to sell our goods at much lower prices, and to buy supplies at higher prices. Wheat from California was exported only to Peru, which was at that time still under royal authority, and to Chile, a rich neighboring region which had become a republic. But subsequently there was a mutual exchange of goods.

The Americans and English bought steer hides, montan wax and tallow. They shipped hides to America and England, and sent the wax and tallow along the coast of Mexico and Peru. Their profit on hides is about 200%, but they sometimes sell the tallow and wax at a loss.

In California transactions are carried on in <u>reals</u>. There are eight reals in one piastre. If an item costs one piastre and one real, or one piastre and four reals, they usually say the price is nine or twelve reals, and so on, up to 24 reals. Beyond that they count in piastres. A <u>fanega</u> is a measure [1.5 bushels] which, depending on the quality of grain, contains three and a half to four puds [126-144 pounds]. According to Hagemeister, we generally consider a fanega of wheat here to be three puds 30 pounds. Barley--three puds; peas and beans--four puds. One <u>arob</u> equals one-fourth of a <u>quintal</u>, and contains 24 Spanish or 28-1/2 Russian pounds. Tallow and montan wax are purchased in sacks which generally contain half an arob, although many weigh more.

Trade is transacted in California in the following manner. When one arrives in port one must present to the port authority a manifesto in which the name of the ship is indicated, her tonnage, from where she has come, to whom she belongs, the names of the captain and the supercargo, the number of crew members and of guns. One presents the ship's passport and verification of the tonnage. A statement as to the size of the cargo is required. Formerly an indication of the value of the cargo was required, but at present this matter is handled simply.

To indicate when and at what price our commodities were sold, the following table is appended.

	1818 Kutuzov	1820 Buldakov	1821 Buldakov	1822 Buldakov	1823 Riurik	1824 Kiakhta	1825 Kiakhta
	piastres						
Iron, quintal	16	13	16	12	-	12	-
Iron kettles, quintal	18	-	18	18	16	16	16
Steel, quintal	40	40	40	24	-	-	-
Wax candles, quintal	120	120	100	100	100	-	120
Loaf sugar, quintal	22	-	30	-	-	-	-
Sugar candy, quintal	-	40	-	40	-	-	-
Granulated sugar, quintal	-	28	30	30	-	24	40
White wax, quintal	-	80	75	-	-	-	-
Virginia tobacco, quintal	80	80	76	60	56	-	prohibited
Millet, quintal	-	12	16	14	12	-	12
Shot, quintal	-	30	24	24	20	24	30
Rope, quintal	28	17	-	-	16	16	18
Lead							
Brick tea, pound	2	-	-	-	-	-	-
Dry tea, pound	-	-	-	-	-	-	2
Coffee, pound	-	12	-	-	-	-	-
Brass samovar, pound	1	1	1	-	1	1.2	1
Pepper, pound	-	-	4	-	-	6	4
Sealing wax, pound	-	-	2.2	-	-	-	-
Thread	-	-	2	-	-	5	-
Silk	-	-	-	16	-	16	16
Linen, wide, piece	1.50	1	1.2	-	6	-	-
Good quality calico	2	1.4	1.4	-	-	1	1
Medium quality calico	-	-	1.2	1	1	6	6
Bengal calico, piece	15	12	10	-	8	9	-
Grey linen, piece	50	48	45	50	42	35	40
Heavy sailcloth, piece	38	25	35	-	30	32	-
White Kiakhta cotton	4	-	4	4	-	3.2	3
Blue Canton cotton	3.4	4	-	3.4	3.4	2.4	-
Unbleached cotton	-	2.4	2	-	2.4	3	-
Fine wool, vara	-	-	12	12	-	-	12
Wool, 6 bundles	6.4	8.4	7	-	6	-	6
Flannelette, vara	1.4	2	2.4	-	1.6	-	1.6

Frieze, vara	-	-	-	3.2	2.6	3.4	2.4
Velveteen, vara	2.4	3.4	3	-	3.4	2.4	2.4
Common flannel, vara	1	-	-	-	-	-	1.2
Double flannel, vara	-	-	2.4	-	-	-	1.6
Men's cotton hose, dozen	30	-	-	-	24	18	1.6
Women's, dozen	-	-	-	15	-	-	1.2
Fur hats	6	6	-	6	6	-	-
Axes, each	2.4	1.4	2	-	-	-	2.4
Flat files, dozen	9	8	5.4	9	-	-	-
Yellow crockery	4	-	5	-	3.4	3.4	-
Needles, 1,000	3	4	-	-	-	-	-
Spanish spades	-	2	2	2	2	2	2.4
Ticking, vara	-	-	.7	.6	-	-	.5

Only such goods are indicated here as were exchanged in small amounts. All manner of small goods are shipped to California, especially white calico, all kinds of clothing, haberdashery, glass and crockery, carpenters' tools, metal-workers' tools, sewing supplies, etc.

It has been previously noted that during the first years of our relations with this region we were the only foreigners who were able to sell goods openly, and therefore we had great advantages. Americans and English smuggled goods along the entire coast of the Spanish possessions in America. In 1817 the ship Kutuzov unloaded goods in San Francisco which by St. Petersburg prices were valued at 3,706 rubles 80 kopecks. In Spanish prices, this came to 2,641.50 piastres. Considering one piastre to be worth five rubles 35 kopecks, this equals 14,132 rubles 37 kopecks. Consequently, the profit was 254%. In 1818 the ship Kutuzov unloaded goods in Monterey which were valued by Sitka prices at 36,719 rubles 40 kopecks. For these goods they received 17,221.50 piastres. Again, considering that one piastre is worth five rubles 35 kopecks, this means 92,735.52 rubles, or a 150% profit. In 1820 in Monterey the Buldakov exchanged goods valued by Sitka prices at 21,444 rubles for supplies valued at 8,995.25 piastres; at the exchange rate of five rubles for one piastre, this equaled 44,976.25 rubles for a profit on this occasion of 110%. The profit in sub-sequent transactions varied from 35% to 70%. The fact is that goods which are in great demand are sold even now at more than 100% profit, but others which are readily available from the Americans and the English, do not bring as high a profit as they should. The reason for this is that goods are bought for cash with which supplies are then procured. In a permit in 1823, prices were set based on former years, and the Governor announced that we could buy wheat in exchange for goods for four piastres per fanega if we bought on credit, or for three piastres if we paid cash.

Permission has been given from the Presidium for goods to be sold aboard the ships as well as on shore. Sometimes an overseer was appointed to be on shore to record all goods unloaded and purchased, but generally they trusted us to inform them after the sale as to the amount of goods sold and the prices paid.

As trade increased, duties also gradually increased. Prior to 1817 we paid no duty. Beginning in 1818 a 7-1/2% duty was assessed on goods sold, and 12-1/2% on food supplies. In 1820 the duty on goods sold went up to 12%, but the duty on purchased goods remained the same. In later years, in accordance with the Constitution of the Republic of Mexico, the duty on sold goods went up to 25%, and there was a moorage charge levied of two and one-half piastres per ton. Before the Constitution was approved, there was a 6% duty on purchased goods, but this duty was later lowered. The 25% duty on goods sold is figured in this way: if the total value of goods sold is 4,677 piastres, they deduct a 12-1/2% import tax, which amounts to 564.4 piastres; the remainder is 4,112.4 piastres, from which 25%, or 1,028.50 piastres, is deducted.*

One pays three piastres for one fanega of wheat; this is three puds and 30 pounds, so one pud costs four rubles. But if one takes into account the laws on duties to be paid, and the cost of other expensive supplies to be purchased, then one pud of wheat actually costs four rubles 80 kopecks; beans and peas cost the same, and barley costs four rubles.

Trade with California is conducted because of the necessity for supplying the colonies with foodstuffs, not for commercial profit; nonetheless, expenses for maintenance of the crew, etc. must nearly always be deducted from the various transactions. For example, in 1825, goods worth 29,060 rubles were sold to the Spaniards from the brig Kiakhta; from that sale, we purchased supplies at local prices, which, converted into rubles amounted to 29,803 rubles. In this transaction, the profit on goods sold was 18,422 rubles, and the profit from the purchased supplies was 4,931.50 rubles; other transactions brought a profit of 1,776 rubles, so that the total profit was 25,030 rubles and 55 kopecks. If one deducts from this amount the loss of goods, duties on the ship at two and one-half piastres per ton, duties for goods sold at 25%, for a total of 8,044 rubles, the profit remaining was 16,986 rubles and 44 kopecks. Supplying the crew with food for five and one-half months, plus several gifts to officials and other expenses came to 3,903 rubles 64 kopecks; deducted from the total, the profit remaining was 13,082 rubles 80 kopecks, which can pay the salary of the crew and in some manner pay for the ship's cargo.

This example, however, cannot be considered typical, for it all depends on the kind of transaction, the quantity of goods sold, and the time necessary for the voyage.

Trade With The Sandwich Islands

After Dr. Scheffer was expelled, the islanders feared that the Russians would take revenge.** [Carl Johan] Schmidt sailed there in 1819 aboard the brig Brutus which had been purchased from [David] Nye. He went to purchase needed provisions, and if the opportunity arose, to meet the King of the island of Atuwaya [Hawaii], Tomara [Kamehameha I] in order to find out how he felt about the Russians. Schmidt carried out the first part of his instructions; he reached the island of

-----

*Measures are in quintals. One quintal equals four arobs. One arob equals 25 Spanish pounds. 89 Spanish pounds equals 100 Russian pounds. Linear measures are in varas. 84 varas equal 100 Russian arshins.

**For a fuller account of the Hawaiian episode, see Okun, chapter VII, and Pierce, Russia's Hawaiian Adventure, 1815-1817. -- Ed.

Hawaii, landed, and met King Kamehameha who said, among other things, that although the items which the doctor had given him were still intact, he was willing to pay for them. He said that he had eight bolts of frieze, four bolts of blue wool, 80 axes, 10 flagons of powder, a schooner with arms and sails, two cast iron cannon and two bronze cannon. The king agreed to pay 200 pikols of the best sandalwood for these items, on the condition that he be paid 15 barrels of English powder in exchange for the maintenance of Company personnel. After that time our ships had no contact with the islanders until 1823 when we sent Etolin* there aboard Golovnin because we had a shortage of provisions. Etolin had bought the brig Arab from Meek, along with its cargo; he had come to Sitka with both ships, as noted earlier. Meek and his crew had to be taken to the islands, and so the brig Riurik was sent for that purpose, and Meek agreed to load it with salt in the Sandwich Islands. A similar agreement was made in 1825 with Blanchard, who sold his brig Lapwing and was taken aboard it to the Sandwich Islands.

Below is the list of goods purchased through Meek and Blanchard.

1824 Received on brig Riurik

1,000 cwt. salt @	1.75 piastres	
217 gallons rum	1.50	2,000 fur seals
133 gallons cognac	2.00	300 Spanish piastres
1,270 English pounds sea biscuits	8.00 [sic?]	
500 English pounds sperm candles	.45	
18 barrels tar	8.00	
39 barrels coconut oil	3.04	

Total   3,086 piastres

It is possible to procure produce from the Sandwich Islands such as salt, coconut oil, rum, taro root and jute rope, very useful for outfitting ships.

1825 Received on brig Lapwing

1,160 cwt. salt	1.75	2,030 piastres	1,223 fur seals @ 1.75
378 English pounds sugar candy	12	72	90.10 piastres
Various small goods		128.36	

Many travelers who heap immoderate praise on old Kamehameha, King of the Sandwich Islands, rashly suggest that he was an educated man and had sailed to Canton and along the shores of northwest America. The fact of the matter is that when the Americans learned that sandalwood, which is plentiful in the

------

*Arvid Adolph Etholen, Russianized to Adolf Karlovich Etolin, b. 1799 Helsingfors, Finland. In 1818 sailed with Vasilii M. Golovnin's expedition to Sitka, where he met Baranov. Advanced in rank and commanded several R.A.K. ships. Made Chief Manager, 1840-1845. Retired as Rear Admiral; d. 1876.

islands, can be sold at a profit in Canton, they returned to the islands to buy
it. As long as the islanders did not know its value, they sold it for practically
nothing. But when the merchants began to compete against each other, they raised
the price to eight piastres per pikol. In Canton this was sold for no more than
ten piastres. Whaling ships which had returned to hunt sea otter along the
shores of Japan often had to put in at these islands for supplies.

The English, Americans and the Spaniard, Marini, who had settled on these islands,
and had the king's trust, impressed on him the value of cash, and taught him
about goods. On their advice he would usually accept only piastres for the wood.
But if this was not possible, he would take goods such as calico, etc; and he
traded for 14 sailing vessels, the largest of which was a brig of 200 tons. He
used these ships to establish contact only with other islands in the Sandwich
Islands group. It is true that the Europeans who were close to the king advised
him to send a cargo of wood to Canton on a ship under his own flag. In 1818 an
American, Adams, sailed there aboard the brig Forester. When he arrived there and
sold his cargo, his profit was barely enough to pay the duties which had been
imposed under the laws of that country. Meanwhile, the ship needed repairs, and
in order to have the repairs made and to provide for the crew, the captain had to
borrow a substantial sum of money on the king's account from Americans he knew
there; and he returned in debt. This venture completely negated the king's
desire to trade. The king never sent his ships to Sitka, but he had relations
with Baranov through American acquaintances, and they sent one another gifts until
Dr. Scheffer's expedition ruined the relationship.

When the old king died, 300,000 piastres remained, which his son and successor
appropriated and spent; he then took the remaining 80,000 piastres and went to
England, where he subsequently died.*

This king was called Rio-Rio [Liholiho] or Tome-mea [Kamehameha] the Second. He
was succeeded by his 12-year old brother, Kaiki-ora [Kauikeaouli]; an elderly
minister, Kari-maku, and the queen mother [Kaahumanu] declared themselves regents.
In 1825, when Kari-maku was ill, every chieftain ruled according to his own will.
English missionaries also serve as members of the council and have a great
influence on affairs. The Spaniard, Marini, managed to gain a position of
special trust, and he is consulted for advice. When news was received of the
death of Liholiho, the islanders planned an uprising, but the governing authorities took measures to prevent it; they confiscated all weapons and ammunition,
and as a result the dissidents failed and had to be satisfied with destroying a
few drinking houses.

There was also an uprising on the island of Hawaii on behalf of the dead king
Kamehameha's son, but the leaders were seized and exiled to Oahu, and were
replaced by other persons, so that the insurrection came to an end. Kamehameha's
son lives in freedom on Oahu, but they supervise his activities very closely.

Debts which the dead king Liholiho had accumulated by purchasing whole shiploads
of goods and ships from Americans in exchange for sandalwood were still out-
standing in 1825. Kari-maku has only now promised to liquidate them, but to date
has paid very little. Many creditors left their agents on the islands to collect
the debts, and they receive some small part of the payment. But it is generally

*See Alfred Frankenstein, "The Royal Visitors," Oregon Historical Quarterly, LXIV
(March, 1963), 5-32.

acknowledged today that Americans reap no profit from trade with the islanders. In 1824 they had a good many stores there, with goods, but by 1825 only one store remained. They had no permanent trade, and sold as best they could.

Trade With The Kolosh

After Baranov was replaced, trade with the Kolosh continued as before, except that pay for furs was only one-half or two-thirds of the price agreed upon in the general contract. At that time the Americans were paying five or six large blankets, along with treacle, sea biscuits and groats; we could not pay that amount because the price would have doubled, and sometimes because we did not have enough goods. As a result our trade was always modest. Finally the Chief Manager, Matvei Ivanovich Muraviev, in accordance with the intent of the Governing Board, sent a directive, No. 388, to the New Arkhangel office on October 14, 1825:

1) Trade with the Kolosh should be based on the quantity and quality of goods stored in the local warehouse.

2) This trade should be directed not only for Company profit, but also so that we may establish friendship with the Kolosh and so that they will have a friendly attitude toward the Russians.

3) The office may decide to pay goods worth 100 to 150 rubles for sea otter pelts, or perhaps even more, depending on the quality of the pelts.

Payment for other sea animal pelts may be increased in relation to sea otter pelts, but I would consider it necessary to issue a new regulation regarding land animals. However, if it should be necessary for the Company's benefit, the Chief Manager may increase the payment somewhat.

On the basis of this regulation, trade began in 1826. How much exchange there had been prior to that may be seen from the following table.

Kind of fur	1818	1819	1820	1821	1822	1823	1824	1825	Total
Prime & yearling sea otters	54	54	27	21	20	24	16	22	236
Sea otter cubs	27	33	17	2	3	1	11	-	94
Prime sea otter tails	95	62	42	16	13	15	38	1	282
Yearling sea otter tails	21	37	7	9	1	5	1	2	83
River beavers, various sorts	265	147	115	41	39	177	198	74	1,058
River otters	262	242	137	75	48	120	187	63	1,134
Black-brown fox	17	17	8	4	-	8	6	11	71
Cross-fox	20	29	12	3	2	5	3	7	81
Red fox	6	8	3	-	1	-	1	4	25
Mink, all sorts	1,807	1,302	842	272	137	433	602	165	5,560
Sables, in tippets, all sorts	62	73	166	1	85	76	133	27	633

Black bears, various	40	36	30	20	20	26	24	34	230
Brown bears, various	3	1	-	3	-	2	-	-	9
Wolverines	1	2	1	-	2	6	-	-	12
Lynx	1	24	-	-	-	-	6	-	31
Muskrats	-	2	11	2	-	-	5	-	20
Various sea animals	2	3	1	-	-	2	-	2	10
Wolves	-	-	-	2	-	-	-	-	2
Squirrels	-	17	12	-	-	-	-	-	29
Seal skins	-	95	86	7	-	-	-	-	188
Beaver castoreum*	-	-	-	-	3#	5 3/4#	-	1 1/2#	10 1/4#

Over a period of eight years, according to official prices, the total goods exchanged with the Kolosh amounted to 29,987 rubles and 30 kopecks. Payment for these goods is indicated in a special statement below.

STATEMENT REGARDING PAYMENT FOR FURS ACQUIRED FROM THE KOLOSH

1821	March	1 sea otter	1 copper cylinder [?]	25 r
			40 sea lion whiskers	1.20
		1 sea otter	2 large blankets	24
	April	1 sea otter	2-1/2 arshins frieze	22
		1 sea otter	1 case razors	39
		1 sea otter tail	1 cast iron utensil	2
		1 river otter	10 ermine	6
		1 river otter	3-1/2 arshins cloth	6
		1 yearling river otter	1 axe	3
		3 yearling river otters	10 arshins calico	12.50
1822	January	2 river beavers	6-1/2 arshins cloth	11.20
		1 river beaver	10 ermine	6
		10 mink	1 mirror	1.65
	March	2 black bears	1 cast iron kettle, 25#	6.25
		3 black-brown bears	3 large blankets	36
	November	1 sea otter	1 piece copper	21
		1 sea otter	3 puiaks [?], 15	
			3 arshins frieze, 26.40	41.40
[1823 or 1824]				
	June	1 yearling sea otter	1 blanket	12
	August	1 black-brown fox	1 blanket	12
		2 river beavers	2 axes	6
		1 river beaver	10 ermines	6
		2 river otter	10 arshins calico	12.50
		1 medium black bear	5 arshins cloth	8.50
1825	August	1 river beaver	10 ermines	6
		2 large black bears	2 large blankets	
		4 medium black bears	20 arshins heavy linen	
		8 mink	1 pound Virginia tobacco	

---

*For an interesting discussion on preparation and uses of castoreum, see Charles E. Hanson, "Castoreum", The Museum of the Fur Trade Quarterly, v. 8 (Spring, 1972), pp. 1-5. -- Ed.

In addition to these furs, the Kolosh supplied tsukli, the familiar pelts of marmots from the Charlotte Islands, which are very much liked by the native inhabitants of North America. The Kolosh receive about 30 rubles per 100 of these pelts.

Factors which have hindered us to the present time from expanding our trade with the Kolosh are:

1) Without the approval of the Governing Board we could not pay prices to compete with those paid by the Americans, in order to attract them to us. Today we are paying at the rate of seven medium-size blankets per 15 rubles, but sometimes even more.

2) Americans carry on trade in the straits; this is gradually decreasing. According to their own accounts they have three or four ships plying the straits, which take on as many as 500 sea otter pelts per ship. They pay six large blankets, plus various supplies equal to two blankets. According to Hammet, these payments, plus the heavy expense of upkeep for the crew are responsible for the decline of trade. Americans pay from 10% to 30% for insurance on the ship and cargo, depending on the time of the voyage. The captain and supercargo receive from 2% to 5% of the transaction. A sailor receives a monthly wage of 12 piastres, and a daily ration of one and one-quarter pounds of sea biscuits, one pound of meat and a glass of rum. They receive coffee and tea in the morning and evening. Every sailor receives the equivalent of 200 piastres per year in wages.

Because of these circumstances there is reason to hope that they will soon completely stop trading along this coast, and it is probable that within the next ten years they will no longer visit this region.

3) Because of occasional shortages, the Company sometimes barters with the Kolosh for halibut, whale oil and seal oil, and in springtime, for tree bark to cover the stables, kazhims [communal living quarters], and other buildings which cannot be covered with boards since there is no lumber mill. In exchange for these items the Kolosh receive tobacco, cast iron kettles, axes, trade beads, pigments, Flemish cloth, calico and other things. The supply of fish would ease the food problem for the Company, if the promyshlenniks and creoles and their wives and daughters who live at the Company's expense, and there are many Kolosh women among them, would follow this simple rule: to pay moderate prices for fish. But they often pay without any good sense. In addition to these necessary items, in spring the Kolosh supply sea gull and other bird eggs, as well as ducks, geese, grey-hens, roots, herbs and berries in the summer, and in winter, mutton, crabs, shellfish and other crustaceans. They also supply handmade goods such as hats, blankets, masks, pipes and other things, for which they receive from the promyshlenniks, creoles, Aleuts and their wives all the goods and items which are sold from the warehouse, including large amounts of potatoes, and even flour and other grain products. This is most detrimental; the well-being of the Company and of society demand that this be eliminated as much as possible immediately. A promyshlennik will often exchange an item that cost two rubles for a bowl of berries; then he goes into debt. The Kolosh exchange everything they buy from American sailors, even weapons, which sometimes are of fine workmanship.

In addition to these dealings, the Kolosh have found yet another profit which
they consider necessary for their manner of living. Many of them bring their
slaves and young girls and invite the Russians to use them. The owner takes
everything that the girl receives. And this new branch of their industry also
brings them every possession the promyshlenniks have. Officials of the Company
are involved in these relations, as well as many visitors who have come to the
colonies aboard ships from Europe. Many promyshlenniks have lost everything
trying to dress their notorious lovers. Others have tried to run to us. They
spread disease everywhere to a great degree. This is also an evil, but a
necessary one if we are to avoid the sinful unnatural acts which have been
remarked, and which would otherwise result from the shortage of women.

It is important to realize the harm which is caused by these contacts. Were it
not for this, on the one hand we would have a considerable amount of goods and
other items in reserve, which service personnel and Aleuts buy as necessities
and often give away for absolutely nothing; and on the other hand the purchase
of furs would increase. The Kolosh say that when they are given the same amount
for a fish as for a fox, then they will most likely catch the former rather than
wander in the forest hunting for the latter.

Domestic Trade

Under this heading is included the supplying of necessities to all inhabitants
in the colonies. The following warehouses have been built in New Arkhangel:
1) A fur warehouse, where pelts are collected from various places and shipped
to Russia and other destinations. 2) A warehouse for Russian and foreign goods,
that is goods brought from Russia or purchased from foreigners. These goods are
stored and distributed to offices and departments and are offered for sale in
the stores. 3) A warehouse for building materials, where all materials for
construction and fitting out of ships and other harbor projects are received
and stored and distributed. 4) A general distribution warehouse where provisions
are given out, and where all hunting equipment such as lavtaks, kamleis, etc.
are stored. This is also the building where exchange with the Kolosh takes
place, and where Aleuts are paid for their hunt. 5) The trading store, which
receives goods and supplies in bulk every month from the packing house, and
sells them for cash to all officials, service personnel and Aleuts. For the
information of each office a price list is prepared and signed by the Chief
Manager and is posted on the wall of the store. Every purchaser knows the
price of the goods and under no circumstances can the official appropriate one
kopeck for his own use.

Following is the price list for 1825.

Item	Weight	Rubles
Loaf sugar	1#	1.50
Good white granulated sugar	1#	1.20
Brown sugar	1#	.60
Rock candy	1#	1.25
Molasses	1#	.40
Millet	1#	.40

Cheap black tea	1#	8
Dry tea	1#	4
Brick tea	1#	3
Rum, cognac and gin	Eighth	5
Cider vinegar	Eighth	3
Wine vinegar	Eighth	1.50
Boston ground cornmeal	pud	15
Wheat flour	pud	5
Peas	pud	4.80
Groats	pud	6
English bacon	pud	13
California and Kodiak bacon	pud	6
Yakut butter	pud	36
Kodiak and Russian butter	pud	20
Kazan soap	pud	30
Circassian tobacco	pound	1.50
Virginia tobacco	pound	1.25
Thread	pound	6
Rawhide	pound	2
Soles for shoes	pound	1.60
Cedar nuts	pound	1
Hops	pound	1.50
Pepper	pound	1.50
California mustard	pound	.50
Coffee	pound	2
Shot	pound	.50
Powder	pound	1.50
Copper ware	pound	3
Chinese Kiakhta cloth, large	piece	9
Chinese Canton cloth, large	piece	10
Large American blanket	piece	17
Small American blanket	piece	11.50
Large English blanket	piece	18
Medium English blanket	piece	14
Frieze, good quality	arshin	8
Frieze, medium quality	arshin	6
Frieze, kalmuk	arshin	6
English calico, good quality	arshin	3
English calico, medium quality	arshin	2.50
Russian calico	arshin	2.25
Good English wool	arshin	36
Dutch wool	arshin	25
Ordinary wool	arshin	10
Wool for sailors' uniforms	arshin	8.60
Wool for soldier' uniforms	arshin	5
Wool	arshin	1.50
Calico	piece	40
Bengal, for lining pockets	piece	2
Men's cotton stockings	pair	5
Women's cotton stockings	pair	3
Knit stockings	pair	2

Woolen stockings	pair	2
Leggings	pair	.60
Striped ticking	arshin	1.20
Heavy blue ticking	arshin	.50
Flemish cloth	piece	75
Sailcloth	piece	50

In order to indicate the quantity of goods sold in the store in New Arkhangel, appended is a list of total sales, by month, for two years.

1824		1825	
January	10,857.39	January	19,729.65
February	11,745.08	February	13,164.44
March	17,984.66	March	15,999.20
April	14,377.20	April	16,102.61
May	19,881.80	May	24,349.30
June	11,328.07	June	11,457.35
July	6,356.18	July	947.08
August	11,971.35	August	14,537.43
September	12,024.51	September	18,728.80
October	13,261.66	October	20,212.78
November	12,360.24	November	13,481.96
December	13,361.77	December	13,062.58
Total	155,509.91	Total	181.773.18

At the beginning of each year promyshlenniks receive a lump sum of 50 rubles to outfit themselves, and after that, 15 to 20 rubles per month. When the boats set out, they are supplied for a three or four month period, and therefore there is a larger sale of goods at that time. There were plenty of goods in 1825, and as a result the total sum for goods sold is larger. It should also be noted that at that time a naval sloop, the Predpriiatie was here from February to September, and the ship Elena, from August to November. Their officers and crew also bought goods from the store.

Building The Settlement

A headland which juts out into the sea and hangs over the coast is called a kekur in the parlance of the Siberian promyshlenniks. On such a kekur, composed of an outcrop of native rock, and rising 77 feet above the water, there is a flat area about 60 sazhens in diameter where the New Arkhangel fortress was built. At present it has three towers and a battery of 30 cannon, from three to six pound calibre, and a two-story building which houses the Chief Manager. Below this there are barracks accommodating 40 workers. Below the cliff on a slope on the shore side, there are warehouses, barracks and other quarters, which will be described later. These form the middle fortress.

Buildings

When Baranov was relieved of his duties, all buildings were in a state of desuetude. The Chief Manager's headquarters, barracks and others were kept up only by means of constant repair, until new ones could be built, which was done in the following order.

1818 During the administration of L. A. Hagemeister	Tower No. 1, two stories, octagonal, with eight cannon.
1819 During the administration of S. I. Ianovskii	1) Tower No. 2, two stories, octagonal, with eight cannon.
1820	2) Harbor facility on shore. 3) Windmill.
1821 to 1826 During the administration of M. I. Muraviev	1) Home for the Chief Manager in the upper fortress, eight sazhens [56 feet] long, with a guardroom and kitchen below. Above the gate is a billiards room, and there are two rooms on the mezzanine. 2) Tower No. 3, in the upper fortress, dimensions the same as those above, with six cannon. 3) A battery toward the sea, with eight cannon. 4) A lower barracks, divided by a corridor into three chambers (with a mezzanine on each side); these rooms can accommodate up to 80 men; it is nine sazhens [63 feet] long, and there are three rooms in the upper part for officials. 5) A building nine sazhens long, two stories, which has quarters for the priest, the doctor, two rooms for officials, an office, a pharmacy and an infirmary. 6) A house for the office administrator. 7) Bathhouse for officials. 8) Bathhouse for the garrison. 9) Rope walk. 10) Bakery. 11) A new harbor on new pilings to replace the one that had been consumed by worms. 12) Three stairways to the upper fortress, and a reviewing stand. 13) An arsenal, two stories, for small weapons. 14) A gate and a wall to the middle fort from the barracks to the priest's quarters, with a battery of two cannon.

One of the octagonal bastions from the fort at New Arkhangel remains
standing, a historic relic, long after palisaded wall has gone. Circa
1880's or 1890's. (OHS photo collections.)

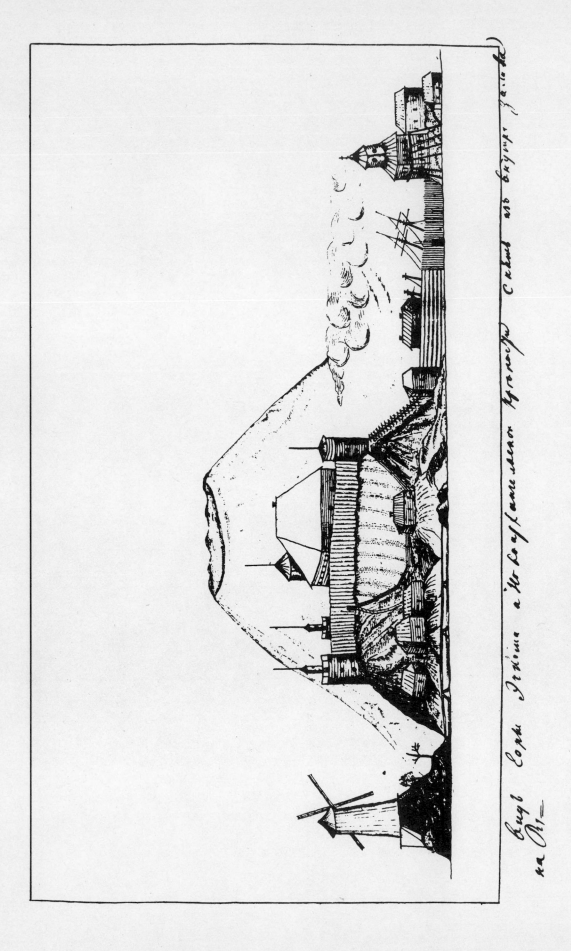

Вид Горы Эджина и Новоархангельской крепости. Снят из вхощу залива
на ост=

This spare drawing of Mount Edgecumbe and the fortress of New Arkhangel has never been published before. Although unsigned, it is probably the work of a member of the L. A. Hagemeister expedition which sailed around the world aboard the Russian Imperial Navy sloop-of-war Krotkii, 1828-1831. The seldom mentioned windmill was constructed in 1820. (From the K.T. Khlebnikov archive.)

The Siberian ostrog was the prototype for fortifications in Russian America. This hitherto unpublished view by contemporary Soviet artist Viktor V. Astaltsev shows octagonal watchtower and palisaded fence typical of Russian American Company's outposts in Alaska. Severe shortage of manpower forced the Company to use even young lads and invalids to man watchtowers on Sitka Island to prevent surprise attacks by hostile Tlingits.

"Sitka Island," by I.G. Voznesenskii, an exceptionally fine drawing
showing the central portion of New Arkhangel in detail. In foreground
are Russian homes and shops with boardwalk approaches to bridge muddy
roadways. The large imposing structure in the background is the home
and office of the Chief Administrator. Octagonal lighthouse atop sent
out a beam 34 meters above sea level, visible for a great distance. To
the right is the beautiful Cathedral of St. Michael the Archangel, twice
reconstructed. Octagonal watchtower on left is a reminder of the omnipresent danger of attack by the Tlingits, but off-duty one could use the
billiards room of the Chief Administrator's office. (Archive MAE AN
SSSR.)

"Sitka Island: log huts or dwellings of the Kolosh near the port of
New Arkhangel," by I.G. Voznesenskii, 1843 or 1844. The Tlingit settlement was confined to an area outside the palisade. Windowless huts on
the left are separated from the Russian settlement by path leading up
from the sea and by the high fortified wall at right. Two-story bastion
in right background afforded a vantage point for armed watchmen who
constantly surveyed the activity of the fierce Tlingits. The Indians
were allowed to trade inside the town during the day but had to leave at
four in the afternoon when gates were locked for the night. Inside the
palisade the second building back from the shore is the colonial school
for boys where both Russians and creoles were taught the fundamentals of
navigation. (Archive MAE AN SSSR.)

"Sitka: Little and Big Iablochnye Islands," by I.G. Voznesenskii, 1843
or 1844. Six Tlingits stoically endure the rainstorm as they propel
their dugout craft between islands in the bay. The canoe is typical of
fine Tlingit workmanship, embellished with open eyes and other ornamen-
tation. The clothing and adornment of the four men and two women are
carefully shown, including the labrets inserted through the lower lip.
(Archive MAE AN SSSR.)

"The funeral of a Kolosh toion," by I.G. Voznesenskii, 1844, an exceed-
ingly important ethnographic drawing made inside a large Tlingit
dwelling. It depicts the funeral ceremony of a toion of the Wolf clan.
The body of the dead toion, who was killed by his brother, is wrapped
in a ceremonial blanket and occupies the center of the raised platform.
A complete description of the ceremony and of all the Voznesenskii
drawings may be found in E. E. Blomkvist, "A Russian Scientific
Expedition to California and Alaska, 1839-1849: The Drawings of I.G.
Voznesenskii," translated by Basil Dmytryshyn and E.A.P. Crownhart-
Vaughan, in Oregon Historical Quarterly, LXXIII (June, 1972), pp. 101-
70. (Archive MAE AN SSSR.)

New Arkhangel: a view of the rear of the Cathedral of St. Michael the
Archangel, 1891. The orthodox crosses, with a second slanting
crossbar signifying the broken bones of Christ, are clearly visible
against the sky. (OHS photo collections.)

Left page, above: Busy scene of the fur warehouse at New Arkhangel
(circa 1830's) with Mount Edgecumbe in the background and possibly
Captain Lutke's ship Seniavin in the bay. Of special note are the tin
roofs, which would serve well in salt air location. The ravens were
omnipresent in New Arkhangel and in Northwest Coast Indian mythology.
(Fedor P. Lutke, Voyage autour du Monde...)

Left page, below: A later photograph of what may possibly be the same
warehouse, now renovated and covered over (1887), but serving the
same general though less exotic trade. (OHS photo collections.)

"Inhabitants of Norton Bay," by I.G. Voznesenskii, 1843. The natives
near the Redoubt of St. Michael were the friendly Unaligmut Eskimos.
Company men who lived in the remote redoubt carried on a brisk trade
with these Eskimos, bartering Russian manufactured goods and staples
for berries, fish, game and native handicrafts. Examples of these
decorative and useful pieces can be seen in the rich collections of
the Museum of Anthropology and Ethnography in Leningrad. (Archive
MAE AN SSSR.)

"Redoubt of St. Michael in Norton Sound," by I.G. Voznesenskii, 1843.
This distant Russian outpost was founded in 1833 on the eastern shore
of St. Michael Island, 60 miles northeast of the mouth of the Yukon
River. The drawing portrays the rectangular fort with a 12-foot high
palisade surmounted by a chevaux des frises of sharpened poles.
Hexagonal watchtowers are placed at opposite corners to survey both
land and sea approaches. Within the palisade are barracks, offices,
warehouses, an arsenal, bathhouse and kitchen. Lumber for all
structures had to be brought from New Arkhangel or sawed from driftwood.
The garden in the left foreground produced only vegetables that matured
in a short, intense growing season. (Archive MAE AN SSSR.)

Main street of New Arkhangel. The flag unfurls in front of the Sitka Trading Company and Saint Michael's Cathedral dominates the central portion of this circa 1880 photograph. No longer is the town enclosed by palisades and bastions. Native traders display their goods to tourists from a ship in the harbor, and one hopes that a few of those fine baskets found their way into museum collections. The trading company building shows strong Russian architectural influence, but there is already a New England flavor in the shuttered white house on the left surrounded by a neat picket fence. (OHS photo collections.)

At present a large warehouse 18 sazhens long is being built which will house various departments to provide storage for goods and supplies, and room for shops.

Some of the old buildings may still hold up for a time, but others are on the verge of total collapse. These include:

In the middle fortress: a general warehouse and a retail store.

Inside the enclosure: carpentry shops, blacksmith's shop, quarters for the carpenters, a metalworking shop, the general kitchen, the stable, three communal dwellings for Aleuts, the carpentry shed and the saw shed.

Outside the palisade: the church, a cottage that has served as a school and as living quarters for the teacher.

Because of the shortage of living quarters for the Company, we have purchased small private homes from the prikashchik Sungurov and from the serviceman Stepanov.

In addition to Company buildings, as many as 20 small private dwellings are located outside the fort down along the shore.

Workshops

In the review of the population of New Arkhangel, all the master craftsmen who are there were named. It is now appropriate to examine the nature of their crafts.

1) Blacksmiths work at three forges. One or sometimes two handle only projects connected with shipbuilding and the repair of sailing ships, which always needs to be done, but especially in spring at the time they are being outfitted. One man works exclusively making new axes and repairing old ones; this is his main and constant work. If time permits they also make plowshares for the California trade, especially designed to be used there to work the land. These can be sold at a 200% profit.

2) Metalworkers work in two shops. One repairs and cleans weapons from the arsenal, and the other repairs instruments used in the port and does various jobs for ships, such as making and repairing locks, etc. Because there are always large jobs to be done, there is seldom time to make anything new.

3) Coppersmiths have three shops. Two of these make new kitchen utensils of copper and tin, such as kettles, drinking cups, teapots and coffeepots, siphons, funnels and other utensils; part of these are used for trade with California and with the savages of North America, as well as to supply other colonies, because utensils are not supplied from Russia. One shop is occupied exclusively with small fittings for ships; additionally, they sometimes cast pins and hinges for the ships' rudders, and bells up to five puds in weight. Small bells are used for boats and large ones for trade with California.

Creole apprentices work in the blacksmith and metalwork shops, but so far none has advanced to become a master smith. Master coppersmiths in foundries and in the brass workshops are all creoles. They have studied here under master smiths, and they are well versed in their crafts.

4) Coopers have constant work preparing barrels for the ships, and making new small kegs and tanks and other ship equipment. Barrels are needed in large numbers to transport grain to the colonies, and therefore the main work is in repairing old ones that have broken on voyages, and there is seldom time to make new ones.

5) Woodworkers are constantly busy with such ship jobs as making new blocks and capstans, the repair of old ones and other necessary jobs. They occasionally make new ships' pumps, etc.

6) Boatwrights make rowing boats for the harbor and for sailing vessels. They build fine barks, whaleboats, gigs and skiffs of various sizes.*

7) Ropemakers make line and ropes, out of twine and other substances. They make loglines out of white flax, sounding lines, marline and other varieties. They also are constantly kept busy.

8) Candlemakers make tallow candles from California tallow, which requires 120 puds per year, because of the great need for lighting the officials' living quarters, as well as the need for candles aboard ships. For each voyage, each ship uses from two to four puds, depending on the time. From September to May, officials receive 30 candles per month; from May to September, 15.** Sometimes when there is need they make soap from California tallow.

9) The painter and his assistants work constantly making paint and boiled oil from coconut and linseed. Sailing vessels have to be painted every year, not so much for appearance as to prevent them from rotting in the constant rain. Every two or three years the iron roofs on the home of the Chief Manager and on the barracks are oiled. All dwellings are coated with a compound made of chalk or yellow ochre every year to prevent them from rotting.

One of the masters works to distill turpentine spirits from turpentine; this is used in great amounts to make oil paints.

One man paints flag poles, for the ships and the colony use from six to ten flag poles each year.

10) Stone masons work all the time making and repairing stonework in the homes. Bricks are brought from Kodiak and sometimes from Russia. The clay here is insufficient and of poor quality, and can be obtained only with considerable difficulty in a few places near the settlements.

---

*The master craftsmen of all kinds give the harbor master, or in his absence, the Office Administrator, a detailed account of all their work at the end of each month; these are entered into a special record book which is sent every month to the Chief Manager.

**In 1825 the ships used 31 puds; 84-1/2 puds of tallow were used in the fortress, in the barracks and in the living quarters of the officials; the Chief Manager used four puds of spermaceti and seven puds of wax. Prices for candles were as follows: made in Sitka, 25 rubles; made in St. Petersburg, 30 rubles; in Okhotsk, 40 rubles; spermaceti, 88 rubles; wax, 120 rubles per pud. Total up to 4,300 rubles.

Occupations

Occupations in the fortress and at the harbor are as follows:

1) Carpentry for boat and home construction. After Baranov was recalled only one cutter was built in Sitka, the Baranov; but the retimbering and sparring of ships requires the services of ten or twelve or more good carpenters and joiners every year. From ten to 20 carpenters and joiners are busy building new homes and repairing old ones.

2) Cutting, hauling and floating logs for the construction of ships and homes also represents a major occupation. All trees suitable for lumber have been felled in the vicinity; they must now be cut in areas from 50 to 200 sazhens from shore, which is very difficult. In the fall 20 men are sent out for one or two months to cut trees. In one day two men can cut as many as five trees, making logs from six to 12 sazhens long and from six to ten vershoks thick [one vershok = 1.75 inches]. They prepare from 300 to 400 such logs; when all have been prepared, 40 or 50 men are sent out to bring them to the shore. The shore line is quite irregular, hilly, and covered with fallen trees, which makes it extremely difficult to snake the lumber out. They cannot drag more than ten such logs to the shore on some days, but usually they manage from ten to fifteen. Bad weather makes this more difficult. By May all the timber is brought to the harbor. Generally they use rowboats to tow, each one towing from ten to 16 logs; but sometimes they tie 30 or 40 logs into a raft, and pull with two or three boats. If there are not enough Russians, the Aleuts help to row.

In addition to fir lumber, they use thorn apple, straight for decking rowboats and curved pieces for the frame. Fir roots are used for gussets and in other ways for ships.

In addition to lumber for local needs, nearly every year some construction lumber is prepared for Unalaska and the Pribylov Islands, and at present also for the Andreanovskii Islands. Every year keels and framing for baidarkas are also made. They make stretchers, drying frames and pelt forms for the fox and polar fox hunt, barrel staves and special clubs for killing sea lions.

3) A constant and arduous job is that of cutting wood and making charcoal. The wood is laid in a pile 10 to 16 sazhens in circumference. This is then covered over with dirt and set on fire. The burning goes on for as long as 15 days, and this yields from 70 to 150 baskets of charcoal, depending on the size of the pile. The charcoal is used by blacksmiths, metalworkers and coppersmiths, each of whom use from five to eight baskets per day. In spring when ships are being outfitted for sailing, charcoal is used to smoke out the rats from the ships. Thus barely is one pile used up when wood must be cut for the next one. One distinguished visitor to the colony remarked wittily that work here involves making axes to cut trees to make charcoal, which is used to make axes.

4) The thorn apple tree is cut for firewood, because it is softer and thorny. The wood burns noisily. The best wood for firewood, and the most appropriate for use in living quarters, comes from fir branches; they are full of resin, burn cleanly and provide more warmth. In winter two or three large barge loads of firewood are delivered to the harbor every week; it is used both for heating barracks and living quarters, and for baking and drying bread and sea biscuits. When ships are outfitted for a voyage, each gets a sufficient quantity of firewood.

It is important, if there is time enough, to peel off the bark, and not to load green wood, for experience has shown that it soon begins to rot, and this then affects the goods which are being transported aboard the ship.

5) In the spring the Company pays certain Aleuts one ruble per day to work in the gardens. They plant some 20 barrels of potatoes, and harvest about 150 barrels. In addition to potatoes they grow turnips, salad greens and cabbage; also cucumbers, which will only ripen in a hot bed.

6) In summer the most difficult work is making hay. This starts in mid-July, and if the summer is wet, it goes on until October. It often happens that the cut grass lies out in the rain and spoils. Very infrequently they succeed in cutting enough hay to feed ten head of cattle. It is left in place until fall or winter, and is transported dry by boat. The narrow strait where the hay is located often freezes over, and it is difficult to transport it until the rains break up the ice.

Vessels And Communications

Seaworthy sailing vessels in 1825 were as follows:

Good	Baikal, built in America	230 tons
	Golovnin, built in America	140
	Okhotsk, built in America	180
	Riurik, built in Finland	180
Moderately good	Volga, built in California	140
	Kiakhta, built in California	180
	Fortuna, built in Mexico	60
	Baranov, built on Sitka	30
Unreliable	Buldakov, built in California	200
	Konstantin, built in Okhotsk	80

Total: 10 ships

Unseaworthy	Otkrytie
	Chirikov
	Rumiantsev
	Platov

In that year the following voyages were made:

During the first period:

May	To Okhotsk Brig Volga	1
	With hunting parties Riurik and Fortuna	2
	To Kushagan Konstantin	1
June	To Sandwich Islands Okhotsk	1
	Around the colonies Baikal	1
July	To Nuchen [Nuchek?] Baranov	1
	To Unalaska with lumber Buldakov	1

Total 8

During the second period, to California for wheat;*

September	<u>Kiakhta</u> and <u>Baikal</u>	2
	To Kodiak with Aleuts <u>Riurik</u>	1
Total		3

Proficiency in building ships was acquired in the colonies, but experience has shown that it is more advantageous to buy ships from the Americans for the following reasons:

1) QUALITY. All ships purchased from them are of superior quality and are suitable for all purposes. They sail well, handle easily, and have a shallow draft.

Of the ships constructed in Russia, as far as quality goes, the <u>Rumiantsev</u> and <u>Volga</u> were good, but they did not have other advantages.

2) DURABILITY. The brig <u>Golovnin</u>, purchased from the Americans in 1819 and not new at that time, was in constant use until 1825, and only then, after six years, was it necessary to retimber it. All ships purchased from them were made of solid American oak reinforced with copper bottoms. Of the ships built in Russia, the <u>Rumiantsev</u>, which went into use in 1819, barely lasted until 1822, and then after a brief trip to Yakutat was discovered to be completely useless and unseaworthy. The brig <u>Buldakov</u>, built in 1820, was used until 1825, at which time it was likewise withdrawn from service. Of the ships built on Sitka, the <u>Chirikov</u> was in use from 1809 until 1824, with repeated repairs. It is likely that the forest on Sitka is well suited for construction. However, it has already been cut in the nearby areas, and now must be hauled over long distances with twice the difficulty and effort. This takes a great amount of time and many workers, who are occupied with the necessary work of building settlements. One must give credit to the common carpenter who built two ships on Sitka and later four ships at Fort Ross. But one must also acknowledge the fact that any person boarding these ships for a stormy passage cannot have full confidence in an individual who has no understanding of the art of shipbuilding.

3) COST. The cost of ships purchased from the Americans was as follows: <u>Brutus</u>, 5,000 fur seal pelts; <u>Arab</u>, 11,000; <u>Lapwing</u>, 8,000. The going price per pelt, in Russian money, was eight rubles 75 kopecks; thus the first cost 43,750 rubles; the second, 96,250 rubles; and the third, 70,000 rubles. <u>Brutus</u> was even then eight years old and less capacious, and the tackle and sails had to be replaced after two or three years. <u>Arab</u> was of better quality, had a larger capacity, was four years old, and had better equipment. If one subtracts from the purchase price 11,250 rubles for rowboats, cannon and other items, then she was fully equipped at 85,000 rubles. The brig <u>Lapwing</u> was two years old and all of her equipment was new; subtracting rowboats and cannon, priced at 10,000 rubles, the ship was then worth 60,000 rubles.

―――――――

*Every time ships were sent out, the rats were smoked out with charcoal, an absolutely essential precaution. If the smoking is badly done, or if after the smoking, rats come back on the ship and multiply during the trip, much cargo is lost.

80

Ships that were built at Fort Ross used from 30,000 to 40,000 rubles worth of materials, excluding payment for work; but when one averages it all out, even then the price of those ships was higher than the price of the one purchased.

For example, if the costs were:

Materials	35,000 rubles
30 craftsmen, working for one and one-half years, at an average wage of 400 rubles per year each	18,000
Bonuses to masters	5,000
Total	58,000 rubles

The consideration that persons who live in an area must earn their living somehow was the only reason shipbuilding attempts were considered. However, when it was found that California oak soon rots and is quite unsuitable for ship construction, the decision was made to terminate this activity, and people were put to work in agricultural occupations instead.

The Lake Redoubt

A settlement called the Lake Redoubt was built about twelve miles from the fort near a waterfall that originates in the lake. Fishing was the main reason for building it. Because there is a waterfall in the river, fish traps have been built and fish are taken there. At present the following structures comprise the Lake Redoubt:

1) A home for the administrator of the redoubt and barracks for persons associated with it; this is surrounded by a stockade for defense purposes. It is protected by a small tower with eight weapons, but this tower is outside the stockade.

2) A special barracks for promyshlenniks, outside the fort, with six rooms.

3) A mill, built initially with one wheel for grinding flour. An oak crusher is attached to it.

4) The flour mill was built in 1825, with two grindstones. Inside storage bins for wheat have been built; they can hold up to 1,500 fanegas of wheat.

5) A tannery to make leather uppers and soles for boots. Every year they tan from 100 to 150 hides from California steers.

6) A fish building, for which they have built a weir and a fish pond where the fish come in.

There are always between 25 and 30 men at the redoubt.

In the mountains beyond the lake which is near the redoubt, the men cut granite for grindstones. The lake is surrounded by mountains covered with dense forest where they cut construction timber and float it to the settlement. The settlement is located amidst snow-covered peaks at the end of a narrow bay. Entry from the sea and from New Arkhangel is blocked by rocks, and a sailing vessel can navigate there only with great difficulty. There is no good anchorage in the bay; the water is deep everywhere and there is a rocky bottom.

Five or six miles from the redoubt there is a hot spring where two small structures have been erected. The water flows into a basin where persons who come to use the water can lie in it.

Capital Goods Handled In New Arkhangel

The New Arkhangel office, as chief headquarters of the colonial administration, handles more important capital goods than do other offices in the colonies. Let us present two examples of capital handled during the year 1825, at the time Chief Manager Muraviev was replaced.

As of January 1, 1825, the total of cash and goods was	2,164,921.10 rubles
During the course of the year goods were supplied aboard the ship Elena from Russia, and from the Okhotsk transport, which were valued at	873,242.00
From colonial offices and departments transmitted to the New Arkhangel office	193,928.51
Profit from transactions with foreigners from the imposition of taxes on Russian goods and on the fur trade	470,493.43
Debts of officials and service personnel to the office as of January 1826	107,481.26
Total	3,810,066.30
Of this capital, the office owed at the beginning of 1825, to officials and service personnel	133,985.99
Transferred for furs to the Governing Board and to the Okhotsk office	330,484.03
Transferred to colonial offices for goods and translated into capital	427,875.22
Commercial disbursement for the year	403,368.80
Remaining capital, as of January, 1826	2,514,351.56
Total	3,810.065.60

In the course of that year capital listed under the Atkhinsk department from
the Okhotsk office was transferred to New Arkhangel in the amount of 172,869
rubles; that whole department [Atkhinsk] was incorporated into the colonial
administration, and thus the available capital increased.

In previous years, capital, both income and expenditure, of the office were as
follows:

YEAR	CAPITAL HANDLED	PROFIT FROM PRODUCTION	EXPENDITURES FOR PRODUCTION
1818	2,833,555.59	184,420.59	152,851.19
1819	2,009,769.13	113,275.73	204,935.98
1820	3,257,212.52	487,274.52	358,433.98
1821	3,479,107.49	188,889.28	321,447.49
1822	3,305,411.51	256,938.74	355,496.96
1823	2,865,946.76	79,287.81	366,668.02
1824	3,037,446.21	571,001.96	396,682.18
1825	3,810,066.30	470,493.43	403,368.80

One may note here a more than double return on expenditures. But one must also
note that: 1) During the first two years there were fewer officials here who
received substantial salaries, and fewer promyshlenniks, while the creoles
received small wages. 2) Sailing vessels were entered at the purchase price and
capital spent for their upkeep increased; subsequently depreciation and ships
that were not seaworthy were excluded, as noted below. 3) Home construction
was entered at the purchase price; after a house collapsed it was entered at a
loss. 4) During the first year promyshlenniks received a salary of 300 rubles
(but an additional 50 rubles were included in subsequent years) and there were
no bonuses.

In regard to the profit, it must be noted that this was quite large when there
were transactions with foreigners, and when Russian goods from St. Petersburg
were brought in, for they bore a 30% markup. But it is obvious that in the
colonies the profit from hunting cannot exceed 100,000 rubles.

Capital goods at the beginning and end of 1825 were as follows:

Cash in Spanish piastres at the going rate of exchange,
and colonial currency — 53,456.89 rubles

Furs, Russian and foreign goods, materials and supplies — 1,118,245.48

Weapons and equipment in the arsenal — 129,547.90

Seagoing, sailing and rowing vessels — 489,828.69

Accounts receivable from officials, hunters and Aleuts — 165,653.32

Church properties — 14,315.04

Household immovable property, furnishings, library,
pharmacy, etc. — 116,671.55

At the Lake Redoubt	25,160.42
Charged to commissioners	52,041.81
Total	2,164,921.10

In January, 1826:

Cash	22,704.11
Furs, Russian and foreign goods, materials and supplies	1,224,577.75
Weapons and equipment in the arsenal	140,637.27
Seagoing, sailing and rowing vessels	623,337.68
Accounts receivable from officials, hunters and others	180,487.95
Church property	18,133.05
Household immovable property, furnishings, library, pharmacy, etc.	122,626.41
At the Lake Redoubt	29,484.74
Charged to commissioners	152,362.60
Total	2,514,351.56

A Note On Currency

In order to handle financial transactions in the colonies, the Governing Board supplies scrip in denominations of ten, five and one ruble, and 50 and 25 kopecks. The first issue in 1817 was 12,000 rubles. Subsequently, as a result of a report that these notes were worn out, another 30,000 rubles were issued in 1822.* The earlier issued notes were exchanged and sent back, and the new issue was sent to all the colonies and is used by both Russians and Aleuts.

The colonial administration has always kept some Spanish piastres in the cashier's office in case it was not possible to get wheat in California in exchange for goods. In January 1825 the cashier had 7,591 piastres. Piastres were sometimes received from California and from foreign trade; sometimes they were exchanged for goods from the crews of naval vessels. Sometimes they came from officers to be given to the Governing Board, but not in any great amount. Klachkov, from the ship Riurik, left 3,647 piastres behind.

When ships were sent to California each year, 1,000 or 2,000 piastres were provided and they were instructed to keep them so that if necessary they could be used either to purchase wheat or to pay duties.

---

*Of that sum 6,000 was sent to Kodiak, 3,000 to Unalaska and Fort Ross.

Volume Of Chief Commodities And Their Consumption

As of January 1826 there was a large quantity of Russian and foreign goods in the warehouses which had been brought in during 1825 from St. Petersburg and from England aboard the ship Elena, and a full ship's cargo was purchased from the American Blanchard. In that year [1826] the amount of trade goods in the colonies was as follows:

English woolens
154 arshins @   36 rubles
316 arshins   20 to 26
1,533 arshins   10 to 20
2,018 arshins   6 to 10
1,260 arshins   5

2,095 arshins woolen cloth
5,900 arshins kalmun cloth
3,183 arshins various friezes
3,965 arshins large blankets, 14 rubles and up
1,532 arshins small blankets
1,329 bolts Chinese cotton
3,358 arshins various calicos
284 bolts calico, kolenkor
1,907 arshins calico, mitkal
2,837 bolts various fabrics
1,286 pairs stockings
23-1/2 puds thread
55,808 arshins various linens
42,160 arshins ticking and sheeting
240 puds yarn
67 puds various teas
35 puds wax candles
92 puds loaf sugar
1,358 puds granulated sugar
206 puds treacle
199 puds millet
104 puds butter
288 puds cherkassian tobacco
911 vedros rum, cognac, arak and gin
35-1/4 vedros vinegar
344 puds sheet copper
1,200 puds lead
200 puds shot
940 puds iron nails
170 puds copper nails
2,900 puds new anchors
2,973 puds wheat
552 puds barley
3,525 puds cable and rope
320 puds [? shkhimushgaru]
7,780 puds iron

96 puds tin
442 puds chalk
167 puds spades
50 shtoffs [1 shtoff = 1.2 litres] turpentine
30 puds coconut oil
27 puds olive oil
1,100 sheets tin
265 puds sheet iron
A substantial number of tools for various workshops, etc.

Shore and port taxes of 10%, 12% and 15% over and above the purchase price are imposed on goods purchased from the Governing Board and received from ships. And above this, as previously noted, a 30% distribution tax is imposed. Consequently taxes of 40% to 45% over and above the prices paid in Russia are imposed on goods. In such a case the goods are distributed on the basis of need, quality and quantity. Goods are divided into three categories: 1) Those assigned to the Company for its needs such as seafaring, business and local expenses. 2) Those destined to supply officials and service personnel of the Company. 3) Those assigned for trade with the Spaniards, Americans and the savages. Consequently the markup should be as follows:

1) Goods which will not be used in any way, but represent an essential capital investment, such as firearms, must be kept at a set price. Because of the climate, they must be replaced from time to time. They bring no profit, and in fact, represent a loss.

2) Luxury goods which cannot be sold immediately should be marked up 25% to 30%.

3) Materials and tools for shipbuilding and home construction bear a markup of 40% to 45%.

4) Goods to be sold to the promyshlenniks and Aleuts, such as tobacco, linen sheeting, hides, soap, blankets, stockings and similar items should bear the same markup.

5) Goods which are in no way necessities, but are available for purchase, such as glassware and faience, mirrors, woolens, calicos and other such items, all fall into the category of goods which are marked up 50%, 60% or 70%, depending on the quality, quantity, and use to which they will be put.

Goods which can be traded in California for profit, or for hard cash, or in exchange for provisions, are kept separate and are not sold in the colonies unless absolutely necessary. The most important of these are:

Glassware of medium quality
Pottery and porcelain of medium quality
Sittsy and mitkal calico
Narrow Flemish white goods
White goods and other yardage
Blue and scarlet woolens
Cast iron utensils

The colonial offices send in their requests to the New Arkhangel office every year, and the administrator of that office fills their orders on the basis of the available amount of goods stored in the warehouses. His decision is submitted to the Chief Manager for approval, and upon the latter's approval, the requests are filled. Requests are made once a year in Unalaska, Ross, Atkha, Fort Aleksandrov, and the Northern Islands Department; consequently they are supplied with enough goods to last for a year. Supplies go out to Kodiak two or three times a year, and so the supply list sent to that office is never the same.

If it sometimes happens that no requests are received, then goods and materials are sent out according to orders from earlier years and on the basis of the latest reports from that particular place; this can be done with few mistakes.

Sailing Vessels

Chief Manager Muraviev, in an instruction from the New Arkhangel office, number 22, of March 30, 1821, gave orders to deduct 10% to 15% from the accounts of ships for materials used to repair the ships, depending on the time involved and the value of the ship.

Obviously ships depreciate as they grow older. When they are no longer seaworthy they should be deducted from capital, except for materials which may be salvaged.

Rezanov, in his instructions to Baranov, declared that the lifespan of a ship built from dry lumber is twelve years, or eight years if built from green lumber. At the end of these periods of time, they are to be revalued. If a ship is wrecked, it should be entered as an annual capital loss. He ordered that ships in bad condition be sent to Unalaska and other places where there are no forests so that the lumber can be used in some other way to be counted as capital.

The New Arkhangel office takes an annual inventory of ships; it adds to the capital value of each ship materials [used to repair it] no matter where they came from. At the end of the year the office receives information from the captains, on the basis of which the value of the ship is established. (Materials which were used [for other purposes] are deducted, while any that were used to repair the ship are added to its value.)

As an example, we present the appraised value of ships in 1825.

Brig Golovnin, from original price	10%	6,672.10
Brig Buldakov, unreliable condition	30%	14,702.70
Brig Volga	10%	4,140.62
Schooner Chirikov, assigned to be dismantled	50%	10,219.38
Schooner Fortuna	10%	2,913.93
Sloop Konstantin	15%	2,556.59
Cutter Baranov	10%	1,563.84
Brig Riurik	10%	8,651.52
Brig Kiakhta	10%	4,772.00
Brig Baikal	5%	4,794.68
Otkrytie, in desuetude	25%	7,254.05
Rumiantsev, to be dismantled		1,916.24
Various rowboats		1,619.98
Total		71,777.54

Excluding depreciation, sailing vessels represented the following capital:

Brig <u>Golovnin</u>

With weapons, supplies, lifeboats	71,911.13
Navigational instruments	821.00
Firearms and cannon	2,356.78

Total   75,088.91

Brig <u>Buldakov</u>	41,426.20
Brig <u>Volga</u>	49,328.81
Brig <u>Riurik</u>	77,863.69
Brig <u>Kiakhta</u>	52,268.05
Brig <u>Baikal</u>	101,771.40
Brig <u>Okhotsk</u>	93,431.23
Schooner <u>Chirikov</u>	14,206.19
Schooner <u>Fortuna</u>	31,417.56
Sloop <u>Konstantin</u>	18,846.29
Cutter <u>Baranov</u>	22,758.95
Ship <u>Otkrytie</u>	31,970.95
Hull of ship <u>Amethyst</u>	1,046.16
Rowboats in port	10,666.86
Navigational instruments	1,236.43

Total   548,238.77

Of these, <u>Chirikov</u> and <u>Konstantin</u> were designated to be dismantled and sent to Unalaska; <u>Otkrytie</u> is unseaworthy; <u>Buldakov</u> is used for storing wheat.

A Note On Debts

Promyshlenniks who come from Russia usually owe debts amounting from 400 to 700 rubles. Some of them try to pay off their debts during the course of their seven-year stay. Generally, however, there are very few such persons; most, through negligence, give no thought to their credit, and manage in various ways to become indebted; and consequently their pay is quite insignificant. As an indication of this, there is the fact that of 400 persons on salary, their debts as of January, 1826, amounted to 150,585.45 rubles. Aleuts owed 11,723.46 rubles, and debts collectible in California amounted to 18,178.95 rubles. The Aleut debts are of long standing, dating back to the time of Baranov; there is probably no hope of receiving any compensation because of the insignificant number of furs taken at the present time.

Many officials and promyshlenniks have received advances from the Company; [in 1826] this amounted to 70,528 rubles. Some officials who have a credit balance with the Company transfer that balance to a savings account or to a bank. The Governing Board receives requests to deposit a sum of money and to issue receipts in their name for the capital which has been deposited.

NUMBER OF PERSONS WHO HAVE COME TO THE COLONIES, AND THEIR DEBTS

	No. of men	Debts in rubles
1819		
Aboard Chirikov		
Officials	3	
Promyshlenniks	35	30,164.32
1820		
From Okhotsk aboard Rumiantsev		
Officials	4	
Promyshlenniks	62	45,729.91
Aboard ship Borodino		
Officials	6	
Promyshlenniks	19	8,868.50
1821		
From Okhotsk aboard Konstantin	21	16,682.35
Aboard Rumiantsev	20	14,996.57
From St. Petersburg aboard Kutuzov		
Officials and promyshlenniks	28	27,829.36
1822		
From Okhotsk aboard Chirikov		
Promyshlenniks	50	2,843.80
Aboard Riurik		
Officials	7	
Sailors	30	10,900.00
1823		
From Okhotsk aboard Chirikov and Konstantin		
Clergy and officials	3	
Promyshlenniks	33	3,680.23
1824		
From Okhotsk aboard Volga		
Clergy	1	
Promyshlenniks	11	8,438.21
1825		
Aboard Elena		
Officials	2	
Sailors	3	2,959.94
From Okhotsk aboard Volga		
Officials	5	
Promyshlenniks	44	47,391.49
TOTAL	387	243,484.68 [sic]

NUMBER OF PERSONS WHO HAVE DEPARTED FROM THE COLONIES
AND THE PAYMENTS THEY HAVE RECEIVED

	No. of men	Payment, in rubles
1818		
To Okhotsk aboard schooner Chirikov		
Officials	2	
Sailors	7	
Promyshlenniks	23	2,400.27
Aboard Suvorov		
Promyshlenniks	3	1,486.20
Aboard Kutuzov		
Officials	2	
Promyshlenniks	4	
Creoles	9	6,132.45
1819		
To Okhotsk aboard Rumiantsev		
Promyshlenniks	19	9,029.74
1820		
Aboard Konstantin and Finlandia		
Officials and promyshlenniks	25	6,357.54
1821		
To Okhotsk aboard Rumiantsev		
Officials	2	
Promyshlenniks	25	13,040.40
Aboard Borodino		
Officials	2	
Promyshlenniks	14	4,147.93
1822		
Aboard Chirikov		
Officials and promyshlenniks	3	71,542.87 [sic]
Aboard Konstantin		
Officials and promyshlenniks	15	71,542.87 [sic]
From Kodiak	16	11,381.06
Aboard Kutuzov		
Officials	4	
Promyshlenniks	3	2,886.96
1823		
To Okhotsk aboard Chirikov		
Officials	4	
Promyshlenniks	14	10,469.25

1824		
To Okhotsk aboard Volga		
Promyshlenniks	17	8,563.46
Aboard a cruiser		
Officials	1	499.59
1825		
To Okhotsk aboard Volga		
Clergy	1	
Promyshlenniks	15	6,984.82
Aboard Elena		
Officials and service personnel	10	
Sailors	7	9,602.81
Aboard Predpriiatie		
Sailors	20	8,399.92
1826		
Aboard brig Okhotsk		
Officials and promyshlenniks	23	9,114.91
TOTAL	291 [sic]	182,040.18

Note: the payment indicated does not include the transfer of money from various officials to the Governing Board for deposit in banks, a situation explained above. Many older promyshlenniks who had served as prikashchiks here had debts which were sent on to the Governing Board; it was impossible to settle these accounts, which amounted to debts in excess of 30,000 rubles. Furthermore, according to reports of Chief Managers, the Governing Board was unable to collect debts from various officials and promyshlenniks which amounted to some 25,000 rubles. Some debts were cancelled for reasons of charity, others because of long service, and some because the debtors were reduced to poverty. In all honesty it must be noted that not every commercial organization can afford to cancel such debts, if there is a hope of receiving satisfaction.

A Note On Domestic Buildings

In regard to domestic buildings in the colonies, Rezanov instructed Baranov to appraise all Company structures, and to prepare a new inventory indicating the price of lumber, payment for labor and the cost of equipment used. The lifespan of wooden structures was set at twelve years; for the first three years they were to be appraised at actual cost; for the second three years at 12% less; for the third at 40% less; and for the fourth, 60% less. In the case of buildings that last longer than the estimated twelve years, when they are torn down, salvable materials are to be saved and the rest entered as a loss.

It has been remarked that all buildings which Baranov left were in bad condition and worthless. But in order to keep the records, everything was subsequently appraised and entered as capital, and was then written off as new buildings were built to replace them. Appraisal of new buildings included the cost of material and the approximate cost of labor; this established the general value of the building. In new construction emphasis was placed on building with squared beams rather than with rough logs. In order to prevent rot from setting in, new roofs are put on each year and they are either painted or coated with a special compound to seal the wood. Chalk or yellow ochre is used as a pigment.

Depreciation is constantly being figured. On new buildings it amounts to 10% to 15%, and on older ones, 25% to 50%.

In 1826 capital consisted of the following:

New:	The dwelling of the Chief Manager and its furnishings	24,259.38
	Bathhouse	1,130.25
	House for the office administrator	2,508.55
Outbuilding for the office, infirmary and quarters		10,000.00
Barracks with living quarters on the mezzanine		9,977.43
Arsenal		1,500.00
Three watch towers		4,606.45
Rope-walk		641.50
Flour mill		3,481.00
Kitchen gardens		991.80
Harbor and docks		3,323.28
Bathhouse for the garrison		1,464.28
Three homes, purchased for living quarters		4,262.00
Old buildings and various additions, inclusive		17,788.26
TOTAL		90,187.25 [sic]

Depreciation on the structures completed in 1825, according to the above, amounted to 10,385.19 rubles.

If one were to make a more exact account of work, for example, cutting, hauling and delivering lumber, making axes, preparing charcoal, and all the labor in which persons are employed, and if this were then added to construction costs, the figure would have to be increased by at least 100%. But in such instances the capital of the colony would be increased without benefit; this would result in increasing the value of immovable property, and losing the actual capital.

A Note On The Library And Instruments

The library on Sitka consists of more than 1,200 books, valued at some 7,500 rubles. More than 600 of these are in Russian, about 300 in French, 130 in German, 35 in English, 30 in Latin and the rest in Swedish, Dutch, Spanish and Italian. This collection was begun in St. Petersburg at the time when preparations were being made for the first around-the-world expedition. Active Chancellor Nikolai Petrovich Rezanov, who was to travel with it as plenipotentiary of the Company, even then wished to use every means possible to bring civilization to this far distant land. He explained this to wealthy individuals who were concerned with the well-being of the nation. They responded by sending him a number of volumes in various languages. Rezanov sent these to the Governing Board which had them richly bound and shipped them to the colonies for the library. These generous individuals included Metropolitan Amvrosii, Count Nikolai

Petrovich Rumiantsev, Count Pavel Aleksandrovich Stroganov, Admiral Pavel
Vasilevich Chichagov, Minister of Justice Ivan Ivanovich Dmitriev, Nikolai
Nikolaevich Novosiltsov, Aleksei Nikolaevich Olenin, Egor Borisovich Fuchs,
Senator Ivan Semenovich Zakharov, and others.

When the first expedition set out, filled with high aspirations, it was said
that the Russians were to be compared to Columbus, da Gama and Cook, and the
names of those great men were compared to our voyagers. It is remarkable to
see letters to Nikolai Petrovich Rezanov and to sense the zeal with which
distinguished persons were imbued by the setting out of this expedition. I
must include extracts giving personal expressions of enthusiasm.

(Ivan Ivanovich Dmitriev, Moscow, April 3, 1803.)

"I have undertaken the task you gave me and have fulfilled it in part. M. M.
Kheraskov has already sent two volumes of epic works, Cadmus, Harmonius and
Polydor. I shall send them to you by post tomorrow. Karamzin also wished to
send some. When I came on my name in your letter, I actually blushed and
thought, what shall I send along with these others? What shall my contribution
be to this bit of capital Russian venture? At last, partly out of selfishness
but actually out of admiration for you, I have decided to send my Fables and
Stories. Let your Americans learn Russian language from these before they
attempt to study rhetoric and piety."

(Egor Borisovich Fuchs.)

"Soon, my dear friend, from the granite shores of the clear Neva we shall watch
how you and your brave companions board your ship and sail the oceans; soon you
will be gone from sight. Then, for the last time you will hear the heartfelt
farewells of your fellow countrymen. Soon you will be in strange seas. Allow
me, my dear friend, to regard your bravery, and if I may say so, your daring
enterprise, and fully support your adventure, which inspires me to say,
'Columbus by his bravery acquired half the world.' Russia has her own Columbus,
Cook, and La Perouse. From the first canoe of the Peter The First, I turn to a
ship sailing to America! I have long witnessed how the Russians, led by the
invincible Suvorov on the battlefields of Caesar and Hannibal, have defeated
their enemies, overcome all dangers, and died for their fatherland. Now once
again, during the reign of our gentle humanitarian Sovereign, desiring peace and
security, Russians seek a new kind of danger.

"What nation can compare with our fatherland in the rapid advancement of
learning? Only at the beginning of the last century was this notable nation
awakened from its sleep to a political existence by the creative inspiration
of Peter the Great; from the lullaby of its youth, to its adolescence and
maturity; so that now it competes with ancient civilized nations, and even
transcends them. All of this has been accomplished in one century. Now, at
the outset of the present reign, the radiant Aurora from the throne of the
Sovereign spreads throughout the entire Empire, foretelling to us the golden
age of Astrei; hasten, famed son of the fatherland, to fulfill the will of your
Great Sovereign, to immortalize his name and reign. The name of Rus will be
known among the savage peoples. Carry to them the work of the immortal fore-
fathers of our land, of the creators of our prosperity, of the achievements and
greatness they have wrought; show them the image of the hero, Suvorov. All
this I wish to entrust to you.

"The savage has a soul, pride of learning and of art, feels the beneficence of heavenly light, and therefore should be able to comprehend the achievements of great men.

"And, finally, when you return to your beloved fatherland and bring us the treasures of India, and new wealth for science, art and trade, then will you receive the gratitude of the Sovereign, the astonishment of your compatriots, and a pure recompense in your heart. History immortalizes those who place the well-being of the nation above all dangers, above every sacrifice."

(Pavel Aleksandrovich Stroganov.)

"I am sending the book I offered to Your Excellency for the library which you plan to establish in our American settlements. It is with a special satisfaction that I take the opportunity at this time to express my cordial esteem of this project with this small token gift."

(Nikolai Nikolaevich Novosiltsov.)

"As you set out to travel around the world, in accordance with the decree of His Imperial Majesty, Your Excellency's purpose is not only to observe unique aspects of far distant lands, but to make certain observations pertaining to political relations of the Empire, and to obtain knowledge of nature for benefit to mankind. The Imperial Academy of Sciences will play a vital and active part in such important undertakings. In these circumstances we wish to cooperate as much as possible as a benefactor of government, especially in reference to your humanitarian intention to disseminate the seeds of learning among peoples separated from Europe and thus from learning; we have decided to select certain classical books and atlases, listed in the attached inventory, which will be sent to your Excellency with the same purpose with which, according to your request, the Imperial Academy of Art provided you with various objects of art. Your devotion to the commonwealth convinces the Academy of Sciences that these will not go unused, and may serve to educate people who do not have in their own land the means to rise above the condition of ignorance. They will thus benefit from the whole value of your gift, and the brief sojourn among them by Russian travelers, marked by your generosity, will remain in the memory of future generations."

(Count Nikolai Petrovich Rumiantsev.)

"I have discussed with the Throne the development and organization of our trade with America, and have also felt that Orthodoxy and education should be the first gifts which an educated man should share with the regions of the New World.

"Accordingly, I am sending with Your Excellency to Kodiak sacramental vessels to serve as an offering to commemorate Our Savior Himself; we wish that the holy edifices of that land should serve as an example of our church, of God, and of the Tsar.

"I am sending the works of the Free Economic Society, hoping that this insight into our thought will benefit those inhabitants in teaching them the facts regarding agriculture and economy which our trade will attract to them.

"I am also sending textbooks on the Russian language, as a testimony that Russia not only does not endanger, but on the contrary, actively encourages the education of America.

"Likewise, the books which Your Excellency has already received from me should be placed there permanently. Unfortunately not all of them are in our language, because of a shortage of translations, but I thought it would be better to send to the New World everything necessary for education, regardless of language.

"These are sincere feelings, which I delegate to you, my dear sir, to deliver there as a token gift from me for the glory of our fatherland. It is with some pride that I visualize a time in the future when the youth of that region will become educated and will realize that in the age of Aleksandr in Russia, they thought about education in America. As an indication of my sincerity, I gladly reveal to you that I have no selfish motives and that I wish you every success in this endeavor."

(From the reply of Nikolai Petrovich Rezanov to His Excellency.)

"I should like to mention here how fortuitous trade is when it resides in such capable hands, but I shall not dwell upon this. This freedom will belong to future generations. For my part, I can not find anything in my soul except to reveal to Your Excellency that when with God's help I reach Kodiak, I shall place there, in eternal memory, the gifts which you have so generously entrusted to me, as well as your splendid letter to me and this inadequate response concerning my strong convictions. Let future generations know your concern for this land, and may my pride be successful, that they may understand the value of my devotion."

Count Aleksandr Sergeevich Stroganov sent various portraits, drawings and maps from the Academy of Arts for the colony. The Minister of Naval Forces, Pavel Vasilevich Chichagov sent plans of various ships; and His Eminence, Metropolitan Amvrosii sent books for church services. The wishes of noted benefactors are being carried out. Many of the small boys who are being educated here have used and are still using these materials supplied because of their concern. Many of them have developed an inclination for drawing, and two of them, with no instruction but only using pictures, have shown marked success in drawing portraits which bear a striking resemblance to the subject.*

In the museum there are many mathematical, physical and other instruments, of rich English work. In addition, all ships are supplied with sextants, octants and binoculars; chronometers and semichronometers are kept here for coastal use, as well as a theodolite, a circular instrument which is the work of Trouton. There are also an astrolabe and a very precise Jurgenson pendulum; also telescopes, fine binoculars, a large microscope, an electricity machine, natural and artificial magnets, barometers, thermometers, charts, maps, atlases and the like. The instruments which are kept in the museum represent a capital of 12,500 rubles, not including those which are used on voyages.

------

*Khlebnikov himself sent a number of books to this library after his return to Russia. Clarence L. Andrews describes the library more fully in "The Historical Russian Library of Alaska", Pacific Northwest Quarterly, XXIX (April, 1938), pp. 201-204. -- Ed.

A Note On The Pharmacy And The Infirmary

The Governing Board sent a medical official to the colonies in 1820, and since
then it supplies drugs and medications every year. Officials are selected and
replaced constantly. Ever since 1825 three good rooms have been set aside for
the pharmacy and the medical personnel who work there. Medications are kept
in jars in orderly fashion, and of course in quantity and quality do not take a
second place to any good pharmacy in any uezd town. Surgical and anatomical
instruments are of excellent workmanship. The doctor now has four creole boys
studying medicine, anatomy and surgery with him.

The infirmary, which is next to the pharmacy, has a separate room with eight beds
for seriously ill persons. Others live in their own quarters and come to receive
medicine in the morning.

The infirmary is maintained from capital set aside for the benefit of the
indigent; that is, capital which comes from deducting one-half percent from
profits, according to an administrative decree from the Company, dated March 29,
1802; this capital is transferred from the Governing Board to the New Arkhangel
office. In addition, some capital comes from various articles not entered as
capital of the colony. At present, in accordance with instructions from the
Chief Manager, it has been decreed that five percent be deducted from the proceeds
of auctions held when officials depart from the colonies; it has also been
stipulated that furs which officials and promyshlenniks have held secretly, over
and above those which are their legitimate property in accordance with the
official Imperial decree, be confiscated, and their value be transferred to
capital for this use.

The sick who are kept in the infirmary at doctor's orders receive fresh food, tea
and sugar without cost, provided by the Company. Nothing is deducted from their
pay for medication.

It is to be hoped that of those persons given a scientific education by the
Company, several young men may succeed in learning how to heal, so that infir-
maries could be constructed in other departments for the good of all.

A Note On The Arsenal

The capital which the arsenal represents, as of January 1, 1826, consisted of
140,600 rubles; but this sum does not include the artillery pieces with which
sailing vessels and outposts are equipped. That is listed separately in each
account. The arsenal inventory includes weapons in the fortress and those in
reserve, which are kept in good condition, clean, and are stored in a two-story
tower especially built for that purpose. These are guarded bv a special supervisor who has an assistant.

Principal items in this capital are:

49 guns and caronades, cast iron	16,300 rubles
15 falconets	925
28 brass guns, various calibre	16,221

43 muskets, various sizes	1,315
1,368 military weapons, various sorts	40,963
34 hunting weapons, guns	1,166
53 carbines	1,895
291 pistols	3,837
205 rifles	7,381
95 rifles with bayonets	3,730
Sabers, broadswords, cannon balls, cartridges and various artillery equipment	35,235
Powder	10,064
4 fire pumps and other fire equipment	1,585
TOTAL	140,617 rubles

The cast iron caronades are between 12 and 24 pound calibre; the cannon are from three to six; brass cannon on field carriages are of various calibres. Exotic weapons provided by the Governing Board include: two Persian rifles with bayonets, one of which cost 450 rubles; one Damascene saber inlaid with precious stones valued at 560 rubles; one Persian yataghan in silver, 210 rubles; one Dalmatian saber, 112 rubles; one pair of Persian pistols, silver, 300 rubles; and one rifle inlaid with gold, 150 rubles. Military weapons are mostly of French or English manufacture, and they are very good. Rockets and flares are made here every year and are quite good; they are made in whatever amount is necessary for annual use. They are used chiefly for signaling during the time ships sail at night. Every year they also make powder and ammunition for guns. Between 3,000 and 5,000 cartridges for guns and pistols are used each year. 35 to 40 puds of powder are used each year for signaling and saluting.

Remarks On The Lake Redoubt

We have earlier discussed the construction of the Lake Redoubt, which took a considerable amount of capital. Buildings at the redoubt consist of:

Two barracks and the fort	7,000 rubles
The old millhouse and millstones	2,000
Tannery	500
Fish processing building and harbor	3,108
New millhouse	6,267
Total for buildings	19,875 rubles
Instruments	2,187
Artillery pieces	6,067
Total, for all	28,129 rubles

Persons stationed at the redoubt include masters, that is, smiths, carpenters, woodcutters, stonemasons and others. Preparing logs, and other work, is done by all in turn. Sometimes ten or fifteen men are sent there from the harbor during the winter.

Remarks On Commercial Expenses

Expenditures, not including trade expenditures, consist most frequently of debts from which are excluded salaries for officials and promyshlenniks in accordance with general agreement. Nearly all expenses are designated, except for certain insignificant items; however even these are always authorized by the Chief Manager.

A detailed account of expenditures for 1825 is as follows:

LIVING EXPENSES

Workers: land and sea provisions, portion of rum, etc.	50,439.01 rubles
Officials: sea provisions and candles; clergy: usual provisions	6,390.35
Aleuts: outfitting for hunting expeditions, provisions, payment for various work	3,897.35
Various items pertaining to general living expenses	1,829.90
Salt for preserving fish at Lake Redoubt	2,847.89
TOTAL	65,404.50

SALARIES AND BONUSES

40 officials and service personnel on contract	113,589.24
290 promyshlenniks, including bonuses	91,585.84
37 government sailors	8,672.02
87 creoles and Aleuts	23,976.47
Bonuses, in addition to those noted above	2,864.50
TOTAL	240,687.07

DEPRECIATION

In the fortress, on old buildings	10,385.19
In the port, on ships, for expenses	73,007.07
Buildings at the Lake Redoubt	1,500.00
TOTAL	84,892.26
Expenditures at the harbor, in workshops, and in the fortress for the arsenal, and for domestic purposes	9,800.43
Normal loss of goods in warehouse	2,644.64
SUBTOTAL	12,445.07
GRAND TOTAL	403,428.90

Advantages Of The Location On Sitka

"There are no advantages without disadvantages," says the adage. This certainly applies to the settlement on the island of Sitka. This contradiction is

difficult to argue with until such fortuitous time as it may at last be possible
to pacify the native inhabitants. Local advantages, compared with other colonies,
are as follows:

Landmarks From The Sea, Channel And Docks

Mount Edgecumbe, which juts out into the sea as a headland, is a very fine and
unmistakable landmark for all sea voyagers, even those who have never seen it
before. To have a true landmark when one approaches the coast during a storm is
a great aid to seamen. Once Mount Edgecumbe is sighted and one reaches the
channel with the aid of bearings on Lazarev Island and Biorka, a direct point
opens on the right compass North to the lighthouse beacon, and even in the worst
storms, all the rocks are on the side of this course. While there are many rocks
in the bay, they are all above water and have been correctly described from the
beginning by navigator Vasiliev, and subsequently by the experienced officers
of the sloop Predpriiatie. Underwater rocks are also noted on the maps. It is
true that persons who have been accustomed to sailing into convenient foreign
ports do not like to enter Sitka Bay. But it is better than any other bay in
the colonies and consequently is the most useful. Entry can be made in three
ways: two to the east, and one to the west of the port. The dock is safe and
convenient. It can accommodate more than twenty ships between the bay and the
fort. The depth is from five to nine sazhens during low tide. The bottom is
silt in some places and small rock with shellfish in others. At the east dock
the bottom is silt, and the depth is from six to twelve sazhens. The docks are
protected from the sea by islands. When strong winds blow from the southeast
and northwest, there is considerable wave action, but very seldom are boats cast
up on the shore. Ships depart during the winter to southern latitudes, and
sometimes to Kodiak. The dock sometimes is iced over.

High Tides

Tidewaters at the time of new and full moons usually reach fourteen feet; and if
the wind is blowing from the sea, sixteen or seventeen feet. According to
observations made by officers on the sloop Predpriiatie, the applicable time is
30 minutes.

The advantage of the high water is that it provides an excellent opportunity to
examine and repair vessels without difficulty or danger. A ship is offloaded
of its cargo and brought close to shore at high tide; then it is allowed to dry
and is examined. If a large amount of repair is necessary, or retimbering,
then it is placed on blocks and a dry dock is built to repair it. Small repairs
are carried out at both waters, and the ship is then put in anchorage.

Timber For Construction

The abundance of fine timber for construction purposes is a great advantage.
In addition to use locally for ships and building, there could be an important
trade in timber and lumber in the Sandwich Islands, along the coast of
California and all the way to Mexico. This branch of trade has not entered

into our economy, and therefore no one has paid attention to it. If a lumber mill could be built at the Lake Redoubt, then hopefully a good source of income could be opened up. The forest near the fort has already been used for construction. Those buildings that were built by Baranov are already in a state of collapse, or soon will be. Consequently a second period of construction will or should follow. Every year from 300 to 500 logs are cut from the forest, and if one had kept count from the beginning of the settlement, that is from 1804, taking 400 as a yearly average, then the total logs cut for Company needs during the last twenty years is 8,000. If one adds to this trees cut for firewood, charcoal, ship construction and home building for private individuals, then the number is much larger, and it would be no exaggeration to say that 20,000 trees have been cut during the past twenty years. Although the rugged shores are covered with trees as thickly as wild animals are covered with fur, the closest ones have been the ones first cut, and over a period of time this has been a growing problem. Nonetheless, they can be used for a century without the supply becoming exhausted.

Good Crop Of Potatoes

Potatoes grow better on Sitka than anywhere else in the colonies. Some of the seed came from Siberia and some from California. The potatoes have an especially good flavor and are nourishing. The soil is rocky and is usually fertilized with seaweed, or, as they say here, sea cabbage. In better locations the crop brings a twelve to fourteenfold harvest; in poor places, from six to eightfold. Thousands of barrels, or almost four thousand puds of potatoes are harvested. All land around the fortress has been put into gardens. Considering the demand for this crop, one could say that it is replacing bread, and contributes greatly to health when eaten with salted fish. When there is a good harvest the price per barrel is ten, or more usually fifteen rubles per barrel. American seamen and government ships sometimes buy as much as 100 barrels from the inhabitants. All of this together represents a local advantage.

Taking Fish, Mountain Rams; Introduction Of Swine And Poultry

A well-built fish pond near the settlement supplies a sufficient amount of salt-water fish each year, and the ever present annual herring catch are also advantages not offered by other locations. In winter the Aleuts take their baidarkas to catch halibut, cod, perch and other fish; those not needed for their personal consumption are sold to the Russians. Perch bring 50 kopecks each, and halibut, depending on their size, up to three rubles. It is no exaggeration to state that they receive some 1,000 rubles for fish during the winter.

The hunt for mountain rams by the Aleuts deserves notice. The hunt begins in November and continues until May. It is impossible to determine the exact number taken, but in a good year they take at least 200 head. This hunt provides good meat for the officials, and a profit for the Aleuts who receive from ten to fifteen rubles for one ram. This hunt makes it possible to have fresh meat quite inexpensively throughout the entire winter. A ram weighs about two puds when it is fat.

Swine and poultry have also been introduced here in large number. Swine that are fed on fish and shellfish have a bad flavor, but those fed on grain and potatoes are quite delicious. The price for small piglets is from five to seven rubles; larger pigs weighing from five to six puds sell for 60 to 80 rubles. Chickens usually cost four or five rubles, and eggs are from three and one-half to five rubles for ten. Both pigs and chickens can be bought from the local inhabitants at all times of the year.

Trade With Foreigners

In commenting on the occupying of Sitka, I stated that trade with foreigners does not comprise a real advantage, because they are able to sell their goods everywhere. But this actually refers only to those who have cargoes. Some ships come into Sitka from the Sound who have only a small part of their cargo left; they may have been trading with the natives, and they would have little to gain by going far off [to sell the rest of their goods.] There have been times when ships came here from the Sandwich Islands and even from Boston, and no goods were bought from them, either because they were too expensive or because they were not needed; but neither example should influence us. One would hope that ships will come every year from Boston, Canton or the Sandwich Islands, stop here, and then go on to California and all the way to Chile to sell their goods. The extraordinary activity of the Americans is quite phenomenal. They go directly from Boston to Sitka, then stop for three to five days in the Sandwich Islands for repairs and provisions. Such a voyage takes from 140 to 160 days.

Local Disadvantages In New Arkhangel

Disadvantages can be divided into two categories: permanent disadvantages, that is, those that exist all the time; and indirect disadvantages, that is those that result. The latter can be further divided into two categories:

1) In case of war with European powers, the fort could not withstand a blockade. Some persons maintain that England and the United States have no need to send warships to the northwest coast of America to carry out a destructive raid on a fortress in Norfolk Sound, that such an effort would not be fruitful in relation to the ships involved. But such powers would not send squadrons from Europe or North America, but would rather send here only such ships which already cruise along the shores of Peru, Chile and Mexico in great numbers; this might even include the fleet of the East India Company. There would be many privateers who would encourage and assist them. Such persons believe that our Company's fur trade is the only means of existence for this society and this colony. They maintain that they would find an abundance of furs here, and commodities and materials, and that they would know how to double their money. All it takes is the appearance of a hostile ship, and we are surrounded from the other near side by ever more dangerous enemies and are caught between two fires. Every enemy utilizes treason, and obviously would not pass up an opportunity to make an alliance with the Kolosh. So, having no hope of repelling from the sea, the only thing left to do would be to surrender the fortress to the civilized enemy, hoping for satisfactory terms, rather than to allow it to be destroyed and then giving over the garrison into the hands of the barbarian peoples.

If for some reason an insufficient supply of grain should come in from California, then the colony would be in danger of famine. Obviously in the winter potatoes and local produce may supplement, but this is insufficient. It is not possible to secure an abundance of fish or iukola. Salt fish, even if it were to be preserved, does not provide adequate sustenance without grain, and (as happened when there were shortages during Baranov's administration) people are forced to buy goods with their monthly allowances and trade them to the Kolosh for fish. If the main colony were to be located on Kodiak, then in similar times of shortage, their diet could be supplemented with fresh perch, dried fish, sarana and berries.

From the time the native inhabitants, the Kolosh, were defeated during the second raid on this fort, they have become our deadly enemies. At present the colonial administration takes measures to bring about cordiality and rapprochement and pacification, and these keep them from open hostility. But their hearts are filled with vengeance, they seethe with open animosity, and await only an opportune time to strike. At the present time their leaders, overwhelmed by our kindness, emphasize the fact that they intend no trouble. But at the first even slight disagreement between them and the promyshlenniks or Aleuts, they seize their knives and with a ferocity native only to such barbarians wait for the moment trouble will be initiated by us. They are clever enough never to openly initiate action, although several times it has happened that they armed themselves after the smallest incident, hid behind trees and bushes, and awaited action. Peaceful negotiations with their toions usually end in savage viciousness. Of course it would be easy to keep them in pacification near the fort by means of arms. But to kill several hundred of them would be to instill a tribal vengeance into several thousand men, who could easily seize isolated groups of our men out on hunting expeditions or those who are in rowboats going out for lumber or fish.

Every year their chiefs make plans for attacking the fort. One bold man to prove his daring sneaked inside the enclosure one dark and stormy night, went into the shallow water behind the old ship Amethyst, and stole some admiralty possessions and took them as a trophy to his fellow tribesmen.

They contend that we have taken the areas where their ancestors lived, and that we have deprived them of all the advantages of hunting, and use the best fishing places. On the other hand we maintain that we have provided them with the opportunity to trade and make a profit, that we supply them with items they need, and that we show them how to plant and use potatoes and the like.

But all these arguments are shot through with an overriding vengeance which is inherent among all uneducated people. Observers have noted that people who make their living by hunting do not willingly change their way of life, and nothing in the world will bring them to change their condition. To support such observations these persons cite numerous examples: the Kolosh are agile, strong, have great endurance and are therefore capable of all kinds of physical skills. They could have been excellent sailors. But there is no way to turn them away from their natural instincts. Some of their young persons have served us for several years, and have had good jobs and the usual maintenance; but then they become bored and leave.

Only one thing may change their attitudes in time: this may be the tie between the Russian men and the Kolosh women. The generation resulting from this liaison

may serve as a foundation for union. It is possible that the lure of our customs
may spread among them and become a habit. The departure of the Americans from
trade [with them] will also bring about closer ties between them and ourselves.
But above all we should hope that some day they will be enlightened by the light
of the Holy Word. The good stemming from this will resolve the problem more
effectively than all efforts of human thought. A wise and skillful priest who
would learn their language would be most helpful. Many of them have expressed
curiosity about God, agree that He exists, believe in the immortality of the
soul, and believe that one will be rewarded for good things done in this life
and punished for evil-doing. They seem to believe that God is omniscient and
omnipresent. This concept is sufficient to implant in them the holy truth of
our faith. We must proceed at their level of understanding.

A careful watch is kept near the fort as a precaution. There are two watches
aboard every ship, and on the larger ships there are three, who are replaced
regularly. There are two men at six posts in the fort. Two responsible men
make rounds each day to supervise the watches.* During the night one additional
person, usually the cook, assists in making rounds. In spring and summer they
begin at four in the morning, and at nine in the evening. The watch makes six
signal shots per hour during the night. Those who make rounds inspect all posts
and travel in boats.

Cannon are always loaded in the fort and on the ships, and they are inspected
each week. Persons who are sent into the forest or to the Lake Redoubt usually
travel with loaded guns. There are more Kolosh gathered here in spring when the
herring run starts; they come to collect roe in various places. At such a time
as many as 1,000 of them camp out near the fort, and sometimes the same number on
the nearby islands. There are fewer of them in summer, but it is not unusual for
500 to 600 of both sexes to be close to the fort itself. Baranov would not let
them live in the fort or even on the nearby islands, but he did allow them to
come to trade, in daytime only, and sent them off at night. Very rarely a few of
them receive permission to build huts alongside the fort and live there for a
time. Baranov's first successors permitted them to build cabins as well, but
those who came inside had their weapons confiscated and placed under the supervision of the nearest guard.

Chief Manager Muraviev permitted them to live near the fort. He believed that
if their goods and women and children lived under the cannon this would be good
leverage for security and that under this situation they would not be able to
carry out their secret plots.

Near the fort persons are assigned to posts with necessary weaponry. In the
summer of 1826, during the absence of the Chief Manager, this was the disposition
of men:

Upper fort, armed	29 men
Lower fort, with cannon	27
On longboat, with 6 cannon	21

---

*Those who make rounds in the morning report the number of sick persons in the
fort and the number of Kolosh who stayed overnight in the fort, listing men,
women and toions; they make an oral report about the number of Kolosh; the pass-
word is given them by the Chief Manager.

Tower No. 1, upper fort	12
Tower No. 2, upper fort	11
Tower No. 3, upper fort	11
Tower No. 4, within enclosure	3
Tower No. 5, within enclosure	3
North gate carronade	3
South gate carronade	3
At cannon aboard Amethyst	4
Manning fire fighting equipment	12
Parade ground, near elevated cannon	23
Aboard brig Buldakov	8
Aboard brig Kiakhta	10
Aboard cutter Baranov	6
Aboard ship Otkrytie	16
At weapon distribution center	2
At infirmary	4
Total	208

The above chart includes young lads, the sick and the infirm, and only a few of them are familiar with how to handle heavy weapons.

In regard to other precautionary measures, Chief Manager Ianovskii issued an order which has been often reissued up to the present time, most often in the absence of the Chief Manager. The order contained the following provisions:

If fire breaks out outside the fort at night, only those persons should go to fight it who are assigned to fire fighting equipment. The rest must not leave the fort without special orders.

If an attack is made on the fort during the day, the alarm must be given by beating drums, ringing bells and operating noisemakers. The watch in the fort must immediately run up a red flag with a scythe and everyone, no matter where he may be, as soon as he sees the red flag on top of the fort, must run to the fort as fast as possible. In the night, an alarm should be given by beating drums, ringing the bell, and using noisemakers.

If there is a fire, then only the bell should be rung, and the flag should not be raised.

Every officer must inspect his weapons often, to see that they are clean and the powder dry, flints and all equipment in readiness; he should remind every man assigned to him to have his weapons ready and to know his assigned place.

During an alarm watchmen should be in whatever post they are assigned to, except for those outside the fort; those men must run back inside the fort as quickly as possible.

If it should happen that those persons outside the fort cannot get inside immediately, they should try to sail by boat to the south gate. If they cannot reach the ships, they must defend themselves in their homes, making certain the doors are shut fast.

The inspector making rounds to check outposts should listen throughout the entire night from sundown to sunup, to detect whether any persons are hiding outside the

fort or in the forest or behind bushes. If they should see such a person,
they must immediately notify the watch so the alarm can be sounded.

When the alarm sounds, the sentry with the keys must post himself at the north
gate. When he identifies his own men he must let them into the fort.

Inspectors must frequently inspect the watch to make certain they have not
fallen asleep, and to make sure that they are keeping a sharp lookout. They
should also see that weapons are in order, especially in the towers, and that
everything is in readiness. If a weapon is to be loaded all during the week, it
should then be unloaded, cleaned and reloaded with a new charge. All watchmen
must be reminded that anyone who falls asleep on duty or fails to keep a careful
watch, especially anyone who leaves his assigned post, will be severely
punished. The watch should be subjected to even greater supervision if they
have failed to carry out their duties. Everyone knows that we have enemies who
watch every minute to see if we will make some mistake, and should that happen,
then we would all perish.

The fort is strongly guarded. Everyone relies on the guards. Inspectors and
watchmen must be attentive at all times.

Inspectors must check on any sort of commotion, quarrel or disorder; such persons
should be seized and put under guard, and an immediate report must be made to
the administrator of the office, detailing what has occurred during the watch.

Condition Of Aleuts Living On Sitka

In March the Aleuts commence preparations for making baidarkas. The Company
gives them plenty of lavtaks [hides], whale whiskers and sinews, always when
they are needed. In May they set out for their hunting aboard sailing vessels
and return at the beginning of August. Thus they are busy hunting for only
three months. In August and September they prepare fish for winter; then for the
next five months they spend most of their time idle and inactive, except for
those few who are at work hunting mountain sheep.

According to the population chart for New Arkhangel, it is evident that there
were 145 free Aleut males who live here at their own request. They sometimes
travel to Kodiak to visit families.

There are many persons on Sitka, and officials; military personnel visit there,
and not infrequently, foreign vessels. Aleuts sometimes receive vodka and other
luxury items in exchange for fish, wild game and mountain sheep, but since they
are badly addicted to strong drink, they often try to get it through various
illegitimate means, such as deceit and other low devices, which indicates how
they are corrupted. In addition to drinking hard liquor they also develop the
habit of drinking tea, and to have cultivated tastes in food; in short, all
those luxuries which only Russians have. Many of them have wives, and in accordance with the customs of their ancestors, women have two or three husbands. The
Aleut men leave them for several months, so they are free and obviously are not
idle, since there are four women to every man. As a result of this lewdness,
women are usually infected with venereal disease, with the result that they
presently suffer from infertility and contribute to the colony's small birth rate.

Children who are born here, along with the milk they are nourished with, pick up the bad habits of their fathers and mothers. As they grow up, they are exposed not to the natural upbringing of their ancestors, but to the shouts of sailors, the hammering of the craftsmen and the pranks of a noisy crowd, all of which have a strong influence on them as they mature.

In other colonies Aleuts wear bird skin parkas, which are warm, comfortable and attractive. But on Sitka they want to have clothes made not of regular soldier cloth, but from good frieze or fine wool. Many of them wear frockcoats and dress coats. Their wives were formerly delighted to have parkas of rodent fur and cotton kamleis, but here they all want a printed cotton dress, a shawl, etc. All of this represents a style of luxury which is harmful both to them and to the colony.

If the Aleuts were not living on Sitka, but were transferred to Kodiak, then at the beginning of fall they would be busy hunting foxes and river otter, and they would be useful both to themselves and to the Company. There would be no difference in transporting them aboard ships from either Kodiak or Sitka to hunt sea otter in places hunting parties are assigned to. At present there are not enough Aleuts living on Sitka so every year some are brought in from Kodiak and then taken back on 20 or 30 baidarkas [a distance of more than 600 miles].

There are 250 Aleuts on Sitka, with their wives and children. Their way of life demands twice as much as if they were living in their own environment. Moreover, the Aleuts and their women receive a good deal of money from the Russians by various means; having that money, they want such things as tea, sugar, syrup, millet, etc. They have become accustomed to these, and it would be injudicious to deny them their wishes. If they were to be dispersed to their own settlements, then in time perhaps they would abandon their present desires and be quite satisfied with local products.

The Impossibility Of Breeding Livestock

It is necessary to have some livestock at the main colony to resupply those traveling around the world on ships, and to provide milk for officials and for the ill. There are some eight head of cattle here for that purpose. But if one takes into account the amount of work, number of persons, and time and material, which are necessary to prepare hay, then this would amount to more than 100 rubles per head of cattle. Consequently, the maintenance of an animal in normal times is equal to the maintenance of a human. If there is no hay, cattle must be fed grain, and the expense is doubled. The damp cloudy weather rarely permits the gathering of dry hay. Frequently the cut grass rots completely from the constant rain, but both people and time were necessary to cut it. The very location does not permit keeping more than ten to twelve head of cattle, because only in three or four places in various bays are there meadows where grass may be cut for three or four small haystacks; most of the time these meadows are inundated when the tide comes in. Only at low tide may the grass be cut and carried to a higher elevation so it will not be swept out into the water.

The Damp Climate Is Deleterious To Ships And Buildings

Many ships and buildings are in a state of decay because of the climate, but if one were to compare this colony with others, obviously there would be no appreciable difference. On Kodiak where the climate is similar, buildings also quickly fall into desuetude. This disadvantage prevails in nearly all areas along the northwest coast of America. In reference to ships, they must be repainted carefully every year; this will preserve them rather well. Tackle and sails suffer the most damage.

Expenditures Not Connected With Hunting

Precautions against hostile neighbors force us to maintain an unnecessarily large garrison on Sitka; this means we have more persons than are actually needed, and this adds to the loss. The surplus is about 100 persons; their maintenance represents a loss. Maintaining 100 persons is a significant expense; what they consume could be used to supply 100 persons at some time in the future.

I am not suggesting here that the colony be transferred; there will be a discussion about this at a later time. I only note that if it were not for the hostile Kolosh, we would not have this loss, nor would there be those expenditures by Russians which were mentioned in the article on trade with the Kolosh. In later chapters comparing Sitka and Kodiak, we will list the comparative costs between Sitka and Kodiak.

II. FORT ROSS

Early Views On Settlement In Albion

In the first part of these observations, reasons were given for relations with California being established by American sailors for the purpose of obtaining sea otters. Subsequently Baranov sent ships for that purpose. But the idea of establishing settlements along the shores of New Albion originated with Nikolai Petrovich Rezanov. When he visited the fort of San Francisco in 1805, he found that the Spaniards had no settlements further to the north. He made this observation to Baranov, who sent the information to the Governing Board; the government then took the matter into consideration.

Rezanov was chiefly concerned with supplying the colony with grain, and he therefore emphasized that settling any place along the shore of Albion would assure the colony of all its needs. Baranov knew about the abundance of sea otters in California, and those two considerations together caused him to give the matter his attention.

Looking Over The Area

After Rezanov left the colony Baranov entered into an agreement with [Jonathan] Winship concerning the hunting of sea otters along the California coast; he sent with Winship his trusted lieutenant Slobodchikov, who was assigned to examine all areas and the number of sea otters. Slobodchikov went to Trinidad [Humboldt] Bay, Bodega [Sonoma] Bay, the island of Seros, then to the Sandwich Islands; he returned to Sitka the following year.

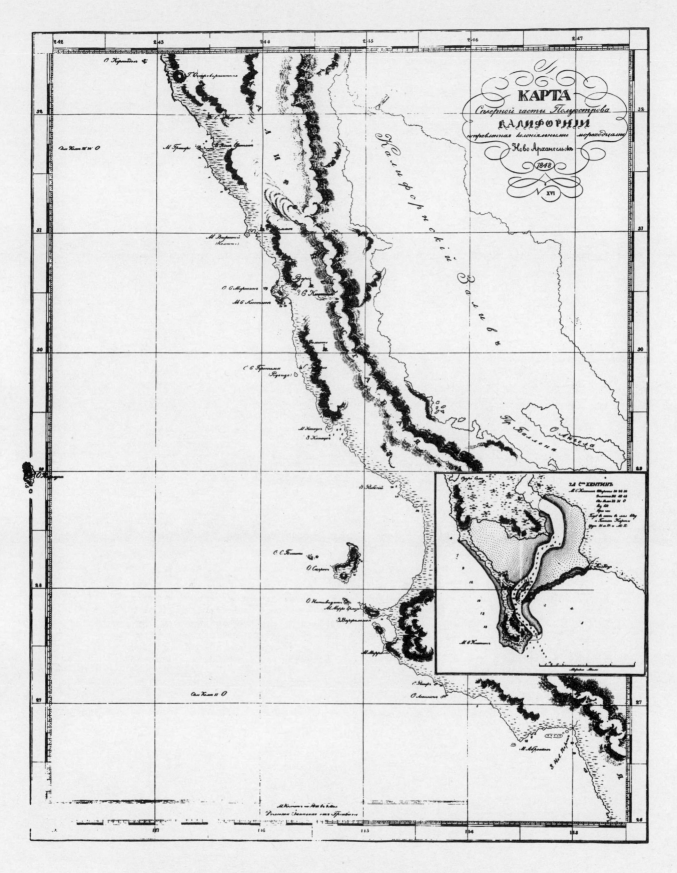

Map of northern part of peninsula of California, 1848. (Plate XVI of Tebenkov Atlas, cited in full with Sitka Bay map.) Khlebnikov favored extending Russian claims north from Ross along California coast, remarking that "the land from Fort Ross extending up the northwest coast of America all the way to the Columbia River is not occupied by any state..."

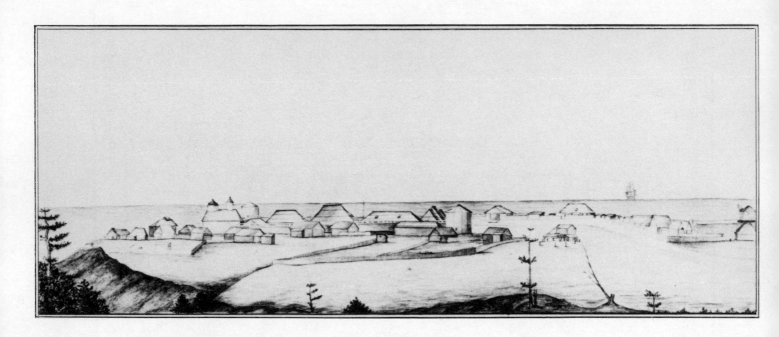

"Ross Settlement," by I.G. Voznesenskii, about 1840. The palisaded fort encloses chapel, administrative offices, barracks and officers' quarters as well as kitchen and storehouses. The bathhouse and stables are outside the fort, to the left. On the right are workshops and small dwellings for Aleut trappers, who had given up their traditional iurts in favor of Russian-style log cabins. This drawing was intended by the artist as a gift for the last manager of Ross, A. G. Rotchev. (Archive MAE AN SSSR.)

"Fort Ross," an unfinished sketch by I.G. Voznesenskii. The clearly
depicted high palisaded walls and octagonal shore bastions bear a
strong resemblance to the earlier traditional Siberian ostrogs. The
Orthodox chapel is visible on the right. The structure collapsed in
the 1906 earthquake, was rebuilt in 1915, burned to the ground in
1970-1971, and was again faithfully reconstructed according to the
original plans. It was dedicated in the spring of 1976 by a devoted
historian, His Grace, The Right Reverend Grigorii, Russian Orthodox
Bishop of Sitka and Alaska. (Archive MAE AN SSSR.)

"A view of the Chernykh ranch in northern California," by I.G. Voznesenskii, circa 1840. A year after this unique sketch was made, the Russians sold the Ross settlement and arranged for all the inhabitants to be resettled in New Arkhangel. Although farming was generally not a successful Russian venture at Ross, the Chernykh ranch was an exception. In the foreground one sees a fenced area for livestock; there were two hothouses; and the ranch produced grain, vegetables, fruits, and had a vineyard with 2,000 grapevines. (Archive MAE AN SSSR.)

Officers of Captain Belcher's surveying ship HMS Sulphur are given a tour of the busy harbor of Honolulu in the late 1830's, even then a popular provisioning port and a place to take on water and a cargo of sandalwood, as well as a tropical respite from the rigors of ocean travel. (From Sir Edward Belcher, Voyage around the World, 1836-1842.)

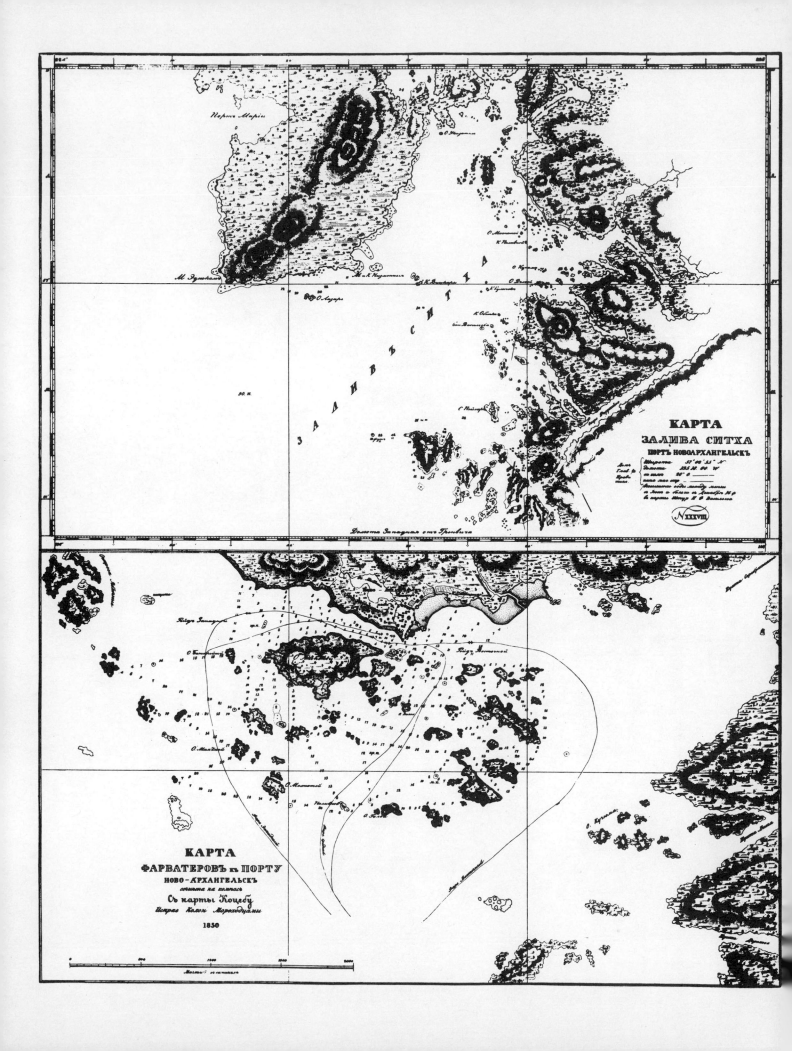

КАРТА
ЗАЛИВА СИТХА
ПОРТ НОВОАРХАНГЕЛЬСКЪ

N XXXVIII

КАРТА
ФАРВАТЕРОВЪ къ ПОРТУ
НОВО-АРХАНГЕЛЬСКЪ
сочинена на компасъ
Съ карты Коцебу
Исправ Колон Мореходцами
1850

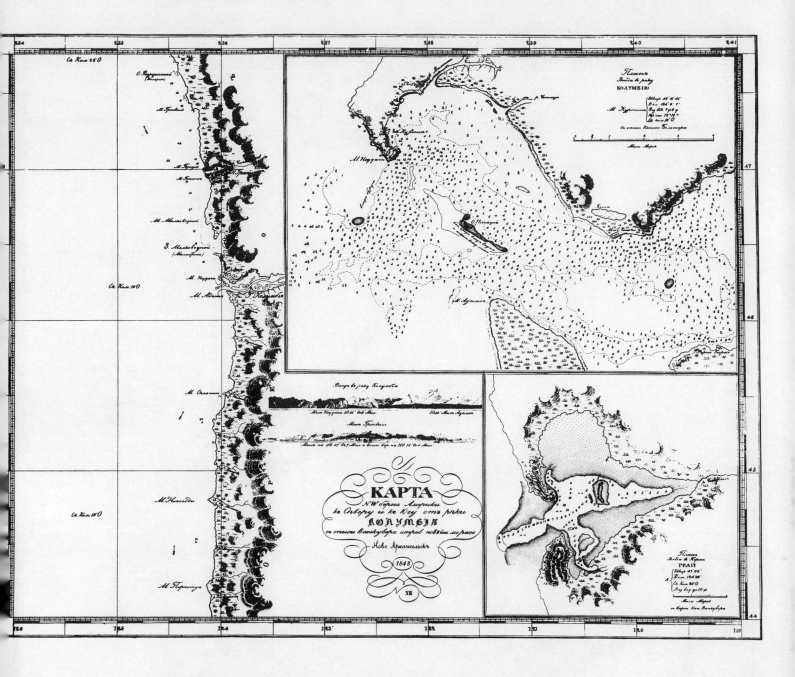

Above, map of the Northwest Coast of America, north and south of the
Columbia River, 1848 (Plate XII, Tebenkov Atlas), with plans of the
mouth of the river. Russian interest in this region continued, although
the 1808 expedition from New Arkhangel aboard the schooner Nikolai was
shipwrecked before a Russian post could be established on the Columbia
River.

On facing page (left), map of Sitka Bay, Port of New Arkhangel,
undated; and map of entrances to Port of New Arkhangel, 1850. (Plate
XXXVIII, Atlas severozapadnykh beregov Ameriki...[Atlas of the North-
western shores of America...], compiled by Capt. Mikhail D. Tebenkov,
St. Petersburg, 1852.) This superb atlas was the work of an Imperial
Russian naval officer who eventually became Chief Administrator of the
Russian American Company. His hydrographic maps utilize data collected
personally during his 25 years in the North Pacific, as well as material
amassed by other navigators. The copper plates for the atlas were
prepared under Tebenkov's direction by Captain Kadin, and were engraved
at New Arkhangel by a creole master craftsman, Kozma Terentev.

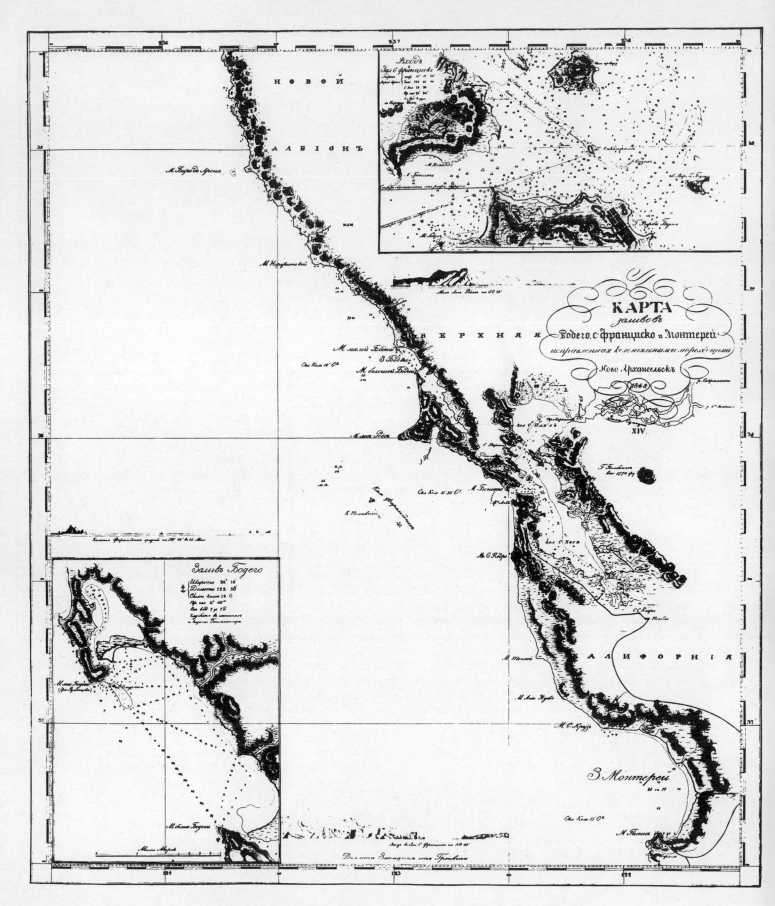

Map of the bays of Bodega, San Francisco and Monterey, 1848. (Plate XIV, Tebenkov _Atlas_.)

In 1808 Baranov sent two ships [from Sitka] with instructions to follow the coast to the Columbia River and to rendezvous in Gray's Harbor; from there they were to take part in the hunt together. The schooner Nikolai was shipwrecked, and Kuskov returned in October aboard the ship Kodiak under the command of navigator Petrov. They could not reach Gray's Harbor because of strong headwinds, and so went to Trinidad, reaching there on November 28. On December 28 they went on to Bodega where they took 1,453 large sea otter, 406 mediums and 491 small ones.

They left Bodega on August 28, and because of constant headwinds from the northwest, had to sail for 49 days, reaching Sitka on October 4.

On January 22, 1811, Kuskov was sent to Albion on the schooner Chirikov commanded by [Khristofor] Benzeman. They reached Bodega on February 21, but they did not find such an abundance of sea otters there as formerly; they therefore sent 22 baidarkas to San Francisco Bay. In that place they found a band of Aleuts under the supervision of Tarakanov, who had been left there by [William] Davis. They had 48 baidarkas. There was also a party who had been with Winship, under Losev's supervision, who had 68 baidarkas. Altogether the three groups had 140 baidarkas. Using the 22 baidarkas from Kuskov's group, in a three-month period the hunt took 1,160 prime sea otters and 78 yearlings.

At first the Spanish did not interfere, but later, for reasons no one knows, they became resentful; since they had no means of preventing the hunting excursions, they posted guards at all the springs along the bay where the Aleuts procured drinking water. Consequently the party was forced to leave. They departed from Bodega on June 20, stopped at the Farallon Islands, took on a supply of sea lion meat, and reached Sitka on July 28.

The Establishment Of A Settlement

Meanwhile Baranov had received permission from the Governing Board to establish a settlement there [California] in some location which would be satisfactory in regard to various considerations; he decided to entrust this expedition to his associate, Kuskov, who took 25* Russian workers and 40 baidarkas of Aleuts and left Sitka in November of 1811 aboard the schooner Chirikov.

Bodega Bay, or as it was called then, Port Rumiantsev, was considered inadvisable for a settlement because the surrounding area was completely devoid of forests; a more satisfactory location was found eighteen miles northwest of there, on the coast at the foot of a hill and near a river. The area around it was heavily forested.

In June, 1812, they built a log settlement in 38°33' [North] latitude and 123°15' West longitude. It was 110 feet above sea level. The fort was surrounded with a

------

*Svetlana G. Fedorova, Soviet ethnographer, has pointed out a discrepancy between a manuscript version held in the Leningrad Branch of the Institute of History (Arkhiv LOII AN SSSR, f.115, d.344, 1.198), which reads 25 men, and the 1861 published version (p. 138) which gives the number as 95. -- Ed.

fence which enclosed an almost square area of 42 by 49 sazhens. The fence was palisaded. The dwelling for the administrators, the barracks, warehouse, store-house, stable, kitchen, workshops, bathhouse, tannery, mill, barn and other service buildings were completed in 1814.

Hunting Sea Otter

Although the Aleuts were there for the primary purpose of hunting sea otters, they nonetheless took an indirect part in construction, helping to carry logs to the settlement, and they also helped in building.

Meanwhile, when time permitted, they went out in groups to hunt, but they could not go as far as San Francisco because of increased vigilance on the part of the Spaniards. Consequently the hunting area extended from Barro de Arena [Mendocino] to Drake's Bay. The numbers taken were as follows:

From 1812 to 1815	714 prime sea otters	163 yearlings
1815	114 "	39 "
1816	84 "	13 "
1817	44 "	11 "
1818	10 "	3 "
1819 (on Ilmen Island)	58 "	13 "
1820	16 "	6 "
1821	32 "	3 "
1822 and 1823	39 "	4 "

This indicates that the number of sea otters decreased within a short time after the settlement was established because of intrusions into their grounds. The Spanish in the port of San Francisco watched carefully in order to prevent them from entering by any means; in order to preserve friendship, they were forced to stay away from there, in spite of many temptations.

Unsuccessful Attempt To Hunt Near Trinidad

Kuskov tried to send a group of 38 baidarkas to Trinidad Bay in July, 1818; but even before they reached the bay this group encountered strong native resistance. They returned on September 11, having taken only eleven pelts.

The toion Somoilov who was in charge of this group made a detailed report to Kuskov, from which I am giving the most interesting parts.

After they had gone about 20 versts north past Cape Mendocino they encountered strong southeast winds. It was impossible to go further, so they anchored in a bay which they knew about which was located near there. As they entered the bay they suddenly encountered a multitude of boats, large and small, full of people armed with bows and arrows and long handled spears with stone heads. The Aleuts realized that the Indians had discovered their approach and had armed themselves; consequently they took measures for their own defense. They sailed into the bay to a large river which emptied from the north. The Indians pursued them in their boats and captured one baidarka. They managed to rip the top, but other Aleuts saw this and moved in and managed to free their companions and move rapidly to the river without further pursuit. At the mouth of the river the Aleuts found a large settlement with many persons of both sexes, and also many boats of various sizes. The Aleuts needed to get fresh water, so they moved up the river for about three versts, as far as tidewater.

When they returned they found that the Indians had blocked off not only the mouth of the river but the entire bay. The Aleuts moved their baidarkas together and moved ahead and broke through the line of boats. The Indians again took one baidarka but shortly thereafter had to let it go without harming it. Since the group could not sail out of the bay into the sea because of strong tides, they were forced to stay there. At the far end of the bay they found an elevated place where they disembarked and threw up a barricade hurriedly made from driftwood.

Before nightfall all the Indians from the settlement moved toward them in boats and on foot. The first ones came to shore, disembarked and joined those who were moving in on foot. They stopped about twenty sazhens away. The toion Somoilov gave his Aleuts arms and ordered them to prepare to repel but not to start firing.

The Indians shot a volley of arrows at them and the Aleuts responded with gunfire. But this did not frighten the savages off, and within half an hour they began to move again in strength. Finally the gunfire forced them to retreat to their settlement. The Aleuts went after them, but could not catch the Indians who were accustomed to running very swiftly. When they returned to the camp, they found 120 boats on shore, most of which were large and would hold from twelve to twenty men. They destroyed all of the boats. The continued strong winds from the sea and heavy waves prevented them from leaving, and they were forced to remain there for eleven days. During this time they reinforced their camp as much as possible. They were in desperate need of drinking water, so the entire group sailed into the river to get it. On this occasion they found only two old Indians in the settlement. Their iurts are large and are built from broad cedar planks, similar to those the Kolosh build. They saw another large settlement on the opposite side of the bay and concluded that many persons must live there. The Aleuts noticed that another large river emptied into the bay and paddled up it to look it over. They went up river about two versts in their baidarkas and found a treeless meadow where there was a very large Indian settlement. The Indians observed the group and immediately went to meet them in boats and on foot. The group returned from the river. The Indians chased after them and at the mouth of the river shot many arrows at them, but as before, no one was wounded.

According to Somoilov this bay is divided into two branches, the first to the northwest of Trinidad Bay and the second to the northeast. It is quite large in circumference. In addition to the two large rivers, three smaller ones empty into it. Both in the bay and in the rivers they noticed fish that surfaced such as sturgeon, salmon and others which were unknown to them, and many seals. The shores of the bay and the large rivers are covered with forests which could furnish building materials such as fir, cedar, alder and others, as in the region around Fort Ross. The meadow which extends to the northwest is not forested. The entrance from the sea is not very wide and has a sand bank, which they had not observed when they first stopped there in 1817.

Incidental Hunting In California

When ships from Sitka and Ross were sent to buy grain, they carried two
baidarkas for hunting purposes, and sometimes the hunt was successful. But
eventually the Californians began to be suspicious, and this kind of hunting
also came to a halt. Nevertheless by this means they took the following:

1822, brig Volga	10 prime sea otters	5 yearlings
1823, brig Buldakov	44 prime sea otters	2 yearlings
1823, brig Volga	30 prime sea otters	11 yearlings

Hunting Together With The Californians

Captain [Leontii A.] Hagemeister was the first to have ideas on this subject.
While he was aboard the ship Kutuzov at the port of San Francisco in 1817,
Don Pablo de Solá who was Governor then invited him to supply the government
of California with goods worth 30,000 piastres in order to provide local
military supplies and other needs for the mission. For this transaction he
was to receive cash from the treasury in Guadalajara. Captain Hagemeister
would not agree to this, but instead suggested that the Governor conclude an
agreement pertaining to a joint sea otter hunt, with each party taking half
the catch. He suggested that the share belonging to the Spanish government
should be given to the Company at the agreed price as payment for the debt.
The Governor could not agree to this without the approval of the Mexican
Viceroy, and consequently this proposal was not effected.

Subsequently Chief Manager Muraviev, every time he sent a ship to California,
instructed its captain to persuade the Californians to accept these terms, but
all of these attempts were for a long time fruitless.

The Agreement Concluded With Argüello

In 1823 after the departure of Governor de Solá, the California-born Captain
Don Luis Argüello became Governor. He concluded an agreement with the
administrator of the New Arkhangel office, with terms as follows:

1. Twenty to 25 baidarkas are to be sent to California under the supervision
of a capable man, with a similar person to be provided by the administration,
so that they may hunt wherever it will prove most profitable.

2. Sea otters thus taken shall be dried and divided into two equal shares for
distribution: one will go to the Russian American Company and the other to
the California administration. The government will appoint ten Indians to
help prepare the pelts.

3. The prepared pelts, before being divided up, shall be deposited for safe-
keeping with the Commander of the Port of San Francisco, or shall be sent to
Monterey. Each skin shall bear the official stamp of R.A.K.

4. The prepared pelts, as per above, will be divided into two equal parts;
since the Russian American Company according to law pays the Aleuts two

piastres for each prime sea otter and one piastre per small pelt, the Company shall assume the responsibility for making that payment for the duration of the terms of this agreement.

5. The hunt will last four months, from December 1, 1823 to March 31, 1824, at which time a new agreement will be concluded by mutual consent. During the course of the four months, the hunt will take place wherever the government designates.

6. Since baidarkas cannot be used in the water for more than three months without being repaired, if repair is necessary the Company reserves the option of re-placing them from New Arkhangel.

7. At the end of the four-month period, when hunting resumes on new terms, the government of California shall pay the Company, as its share, two piastres per prime sea otter and one piastre for each small pelt.

8. During the hunt the government agrees to supply the Aleuts with whatever provisions they happen to have on hand, half at its own expense, the other half on the account of the Company.

9. These terms shall be written in both Spanish and Russian, in two copies, one of which will go to the Company and the other to the Chief Commander and Governor, Don Luis Antonio Argüello. Neither the government of California nor the Company will violate the terms of this agreement prior to its expiration, but will preserve it inviolably in full force. Monterey, December 1, 1823.

When this agreement was concluded, the administrator of the New Arkhangel office contacted the Ross office, and a hunting party went out from there to San Francisco under the supervision of the prikashchik Dorofeev. The number of sea otters taken was as follows:

From November 1823 to January, 1824   455

The baidarkas were later sent to San Francisco for repairs. The following year, 1824, 10 baidarkas were sent from New Arkhangel aboard the brig Baikal to replace those at Fort Ross. Meanwhile baidarkas returned from Fort Ross and continued to hunt all the way down to Monterey. By March they had taken and given the government   386
and had a secret undeclared catch of   43

for a total of   429

These 405 declared pelts were divided into two shares of 202 pelts each. One pelt was given to the San Francisco commandant. In addition, 50 pelts were set aside for the Company, so that the Company had 252 pelts. Of that figure the pelts received were:

Government   193
Company   236

In June the catch was

Prime sea otters	146
Yearlings	29
Cubs	26
Total	201

On October 1,

Prime sea otters	133		
Yearlings	18		
Cubs	18		
		Government share	214
Total	169	Company	214

In San Pedro, taken by baidarkas
carried on Baikal

Prime sea otters	41
Yearlings	13
Cubs	4
Total	58

On the return voyage, until		Government share	68
September 14		Company	128
Prime sea otters	87		
Yearlings	16		
Cubs	33		
Total	136		

Sixty pelts were added to the Company's share.

The total catch was 1,508; according to the agreement the government of California received 677 and the Company 830, and one pelt went as a gift.

The Agreement Concluded With Herrera

In 1825 Commissioner Herrera who had just come to Monterey from Mexico concluded a similar agreement with the administrator of the New Arkhangel office, and the brig Baikal was sent to San Diego for hunting. But [Jose Maria] Echeandia, the Governor of California, would not give his approval and would not permit them to hunt under the agreement with Herrera. Taking the situation as it existed into consideration, that the ship had come specifically for that purpose **and** had brought the Aleuts who were to receive provisions, and that other expenses might accrue, permission was given to the captain, Benzeman, to begin hunting between the missions of San Luis Rey and Todos Santos.

The expedition began on November 26 [1825] with a group of twenty baidarkas, and by February 14, 1826, they had taken 468 sea otters of various sizes. Benzeman took into account his expenses and the payments to the Aleuts, which the governor refused to assume in accordance with the agreement with Herrera. Benzeman declared [only] 322 pelts, of which he gave half, or 161, to the government, and the Company kept 307.

In 1828 Chief Manager P. E. Chistiakov sent the ship Baikal to San Quentin for a load of salt, and ordered them to take six baidarkas from Fort Ross and ask the governor for permission to hunt in that bay. Shelekhov, the administrator of the office at Ross, could only provide two baidarkas, so although the governor did permit them to hunt, they had little success with only two baidarkas. They took only 63 pelts between December 1 and February 1, and declared only 39. Of this number half, or 19, went to the government; the Company kept 44.

Thus in the three periods indicated they took 2,039 pelts in California, gave 857 to the government of California, and kept 1,181 for the Company.

Trade With The Spaniards

The first trade with California was transacted at the time Rezanov visited the port of San Francisco aboard the ship Juno in May of 1806. At that time, during negotiations with the local government, a relatively small exchange took place with the mission at San Francisco, and the following supplies were acquired:

381 arrobas* 15 pounds	flour @ 1-1/2 - 2 piastres			581.06 piastres
797	lard and tallow	2		1,594
105	6	salt	2 reals	52.05
25		wool	3 piastres	75
26	14	jerky	1	26.04
671 fanegas**	wheat	2		1,342
117	barley	1-1/2		175.04
140	peas and beans	1-3/4		259.02
60	frijoles	2-1/2		150
14	garbanzos	3		42
11 large and medium sea otter pelts	5			55
For sacks and transport for grain				846.01
Various small goods				386.06
Total				5,587.25

---

*Arroba = 25.3 pounds. -- Ed.

**Fanega = 1.5 bushels -- Ed.

The Californians were paid for these items with Russian goods brought aboard the Juno, of which the most important went at the following prices:

Flemish cloth, per bolt	31 piastres
Sail cloth	25
Heavy woolen, per arshin	3
Cotton goods,	from 1 to 2
Needles, per 1,000	4
Boots of Siberian leather, pair	5
Tempered saws	15
Axes, each	1-1/2
Ticking, per arshin	1/2

The beginning of the settlement was established shortly thereafter. The local Spaniards were at first surprised to see these people, whom they had previously known only by hearsay and who lived in the stormy far off north, so close and so similar to themselves. All during the time the administration was corresponding with the Mexican Viceroy about the situation, the missionaries and other inhabitants became acquainted with their new neighbors and supplied them with livestock, grain and poultry, in defiance of their own government's prohibition of this very thing.

Several times after that officers came from the garrison at San Francisco, on order of the Viceroy, and asked Kuskov why he had settled there, and advised him to leave the region.

During 1815 Kuskov visited San Francisco aboard the schooner Chirikov, and Eliot aboard the brig Ilmen. Baranov sent the latter as supercargo for trade along the California coast. In that harbor the following goods were exchanged:

In June, 1815, Eliot exchanged:

713 fanegas wheat	@	2-1/2	1,782.50 piastres
4 fanegas peas		2	8
438 arrobas, 6 pounds jerky		1	438.25
97 arrobas, 4-1/2 pounds tallow		1-3/4	168.44
79 arrobas, 8 pounds flour		1-3/4	138.75
49 rawhides		1-1/2	24.50 [sic]
4 ounces 7 drachmas 45 grains gold		14 per oz.	69.50
8 sea otters			75

In August

531-3/4 fanegas wheat	2-1/2	1,344.37
226 fanegas, 1/2 pound tallow	1-3/4	396.38
Various goods		925.13
Total		5,371.82

Kuskov in July

431-3/4 fanegas wheat	2-1/2	1,079.37
25-1/2 fanegas flour	1-3/4	44.63
7 fanegas tallow	1-3/4	12.25
Other items		151.17
Total		1,287.42

They paid for all these supplies in goods, the most important of which were exchanged at the following prices:

Virginia tobacco	arroba	25.00 piastres
Granulated sugar		8.00
Chinese cotton	bolt	3.50
Iron kettle	arroba	5.00
Bengal calico	bolt	12.00
Cotton	yard	1.50
Pewter ware	pound	1.50
English yarn	pound	6.00
Coffee	pound	.50
Cotton stockings	dozen	36.00
Iron	cwt.	18.00
Sailcloth	bolt	33.00
Wax candles	arroba	30.00

This was the only exchange that Kuskov negotiated. He later visited the port of San Francisco at the invitation of Governor de Solá, when [Otto von] Kotsebue was there on the brig Riurik in 1816, but only for a discussion about removing the settlement. Kuskov wrote Baranov in regard to this and complained that the Spaniards had at various times captured groups of hunters, and that several Russians and Aleuts had been captured from Eliot's trade expedition (which also included baidarkas for hunting) and refused to release them. Early in 1817 Baranov sent Lieutenant [Iakov Ankievich] Podushkin aboard the schooner Chirikov to Governor de Solá, and he was politely received. Several Aleuts were released, and permission was given to exchange some supplies. The exchange was insignificant in quantity.

When Captain Hagemeister was in Monterey in 1818 the same Governor gave him permission to carry on trade. As a result of this, ships were sent from Sitka on a yearly basis to carry on a trade not related to the Ross settlement.

When Kuskov responded to all requests to remove the settlement by saying that he could not leave the area without permission of his administration, and would take defensive measures if attacked, Governor de Solá decided not to permit us to occupy areas north of San Francisco Bay; he founded two new missions, the first, San Rafael in 1819, and the second, San Francisco Solano, in 1824.

The missionaries needed various materials and tools to construct these buildings, and had constant intercourse with Fort Ross. The travel distance in good weather was only one day, so there were uninterrupted relations. Kuskov received livestock from them as well as various supplies which were transported from the mission in baidarkas.

After Kuskov was replaced, there were no special commercial transactions, but relations continued with the missions and with the port.

Subsequently the missionaries needed sailing vessels for transport along the vast San Francisco Bay and came to ask us to build ships for them. Consequently, in 1823 we sold them an old bark which had been built by Kuskov, for which Commandant Martinez paid 125 fanegas of wheat. In 1826 we built a bark for the San Francisco mission, equipped with sails, for which they paid 1,200 piastres; finally, in 1827 we built a bark for the San José mission, fully equipped, for 1,500 piastres.

We received supplies from them in payment for all of this construction; sometimes these were loaded aboard ships which had come from Sitka, and sometimes on those en route to Fort Ross.

Shipbuilding

Once the primary reason for establishing the settlement, that is, hunting sea otters, had been foiled, there was no real advantage in having the establishment. Baranov suggested that shipbuilding be undertaken there, maintaining that local oak would be particularly suitable for that purpose. The promyshlennik Grudinin, a carpenter who had earlier worked on ship construction on Sitka with the American, Lincoln, volunteered to undertake the building of ships. For a long time he mistakenly believed California lumber was suitable for that purpose, and he continued to build with it. The results showed him his error, and indicated that it should not be used in this way. It is possible that if oak were cut at the proper time and immersed in water for several months, it might achieve the necessary qualities, but this precaution was never tried out. For the most part the trees were cut and the lumber was used while still unseasoned. During the construction period in this mild climate the moisture caused the wood to rot, and the ship was launched just when the rot set in. After three or four years the changes of climate, of heat and moisture, caused the rot to increase in all the vital parts of the ship and there was no way to repair it by usual means. Thus not one of the four ships built there was used for more than six years. They were built in the following order:

1) The brig Rumiantsev. The keel was laid in 1816 and the ship launched in 1818. It had a displacement of 160 tons and cost 20,212.63 rubles, which included materials but not labor. This brig was under the command of Lieutenant de Livron in 1819, and was brought to Sitka and was in use until 1823, when it was declared unseaworthy because of the open rot in all parts.

2) The brig Buldakov. The keel was laid in 1819; it had a copper bottom and was launched in 1820; it had a displacement of 200 tons, and including materials, instruments and other expenditures, the cost came to 59,404.75 rubles. This amount includes bonuses of 500 rubles to the master builder and 2,000 rubles to the various craftsmen who built the ship; this was done in accordance with the decree of the Governing Board. In 1820 she sailed to Santa Barbara in California and was in use until 1826 when it was apparent that rot had set in. The ship was then stripped and placed in dry-dock where she was to replace the Otkrytie as a storage facility for wheat. Including payment for labor, that brig cost the Company 80,000 rubles.

3) In Kuskov's time oak trees were felled for lumber for a new ship, but there was no opportunity to bring it to the settlement during the time of his administration. Later, they examined the logs and found that all were rotten, so they were abandoned, and new trees were cut. In 1821 the keel was laid for the brig Volga, of about 160 tons. She was launched in 1822. Including equipment and materials the brig cost 36,186.54 rubles. Tumanin was appointed skipper. This brig was in use until 1827, when it was declared unseaworthy and was sent in 1828 to the island of Atkha to be used to store lumber.

4) The brig Kiakhta. The keel was laid in 1823 and she was launched in 1824. She was about 200 tons and cost 35,248.36 rubles. She was built of fir, but the keel and sternpost were oak. Tumanin was appointed captain. This brig made several trips to California, and one along the Aleutian Islands.

Experience demonstrated the unsuitability of this wood, and therefore they decided to halt shipbuilding; but so that people would not be idle, they concentrated on agriculture. Shipbuilding brought no real advantage except for a certain amount of esteem among our inactive neighbors, the California Spaniards. They were astounded at this activity, seeing the construction of four ships,* one after another, in addition to the construction of the settlement.

Agriculture

There are mountain slopes near Fort Ross, sometimes level areas, and sometimes hills and meadows; and not far from the sea, about a mile back, the forest begins and grows thick along the hills. Obviously the flat meadow areas are the best for agriculture, and the further from the sea they are, the better protected they are from fog. But, because of lack of experience, cultivation was first begun on the hillsides.

Kuskov began this, not because there was any shortage of persons knowledgeable about agriculture; but because of the labor necessary to begin, he cultivated only a small area. His successor, Schmidt, had been busy building ships throughout his administration; however as soon as that activity was concluded he expanded agriculture, and Shelekhov later developed it considerably. Not one piece of suitable land near the settlement was left uncultivated; and even some pieces of land as far as three versts distant were used.

-----

*Khlebnikov was obviously unaware of the extraordinary shipbuilding activity at the Spanish colonial shipyards such as San Blas. See Malcolm Hall Kenyon, Naval Construction and Repair at San Blas, Mexico, 1767-1797, unpublished Master's Thesis, Albuquerque, University of New Mexico, 1965 -- Ed.

The table below indicates the annual planting and harvest of grain at Fort Ross during the administrations of Kuskov, Schmidt and Shelekov.

	PLANTED				HARVESTED			
	Wheat		Barley		Wheat		Barley	
	Pud	Funt	Pud	Funt	Pud	Funt	Pud	Funt
Under Kuskov								
1815	5				8			
1816	14	14			48	23		
1817	15				8	7		
1818	29	10	9		106	30	46	3
1819	31	30	24		92	12	64	22
1820	41	8	1	30	173	20	11	20
1821	37	25	11	20	235	33	26	10
Total	174	7	46	10	673	5	148	15
Under Schmidt								
1822 Company	54	35	12	20	426	5	34	20
Private persons	57	20	8	20	418	24	97	
1823 Company	70	25	18	10	733	2	48	25
Private	114	17	15	30	1,118	14	88	37
1824 Company	103	15-1/2			927	18		
Private	217	7-1/2	33	15	1,200		350	
Total	617	37	88	15	4,823	23	619	2
Under Shelekhov								
1825 Company	201	39	39	17	1,815	8	198	
Private	240	30	64	20	1,830	20	356	33
1826 Company	428	18	27	35	2,000	29	86	30
Private	350	4	80	35	1,016	15	609	21
1827 Company	507		42	30	2,333	34	141	18
Private	259	13	143	26	953	13	574	18
1828 Company	644	26	107		4,421	20	508	4
Private	220	14	107	8	604	33	428	6
1829 Company	857	39			3,450	4		
Private	286	18			1,114	33		
Total	3,992	201	609	171	19,601	9	2,913	10

This table shows that the best harvest for wheat was in 1823, and the best for barley was 1824, yielding from ten to eleven-fold. However, according to private records, there was a fifteen-fold harvest on wheat and nineteen-fold on barley in those same years in more suitable areas.

It is difficult to estimate how much land was under cultivation because there were numerous small plots in various places, and some of these were square, others followed ravines, etc. But considering the fact that in England eight chetverts* of wheat, barley or rye are planted per one desiatina** of good land, and in Russia one plants twelve chetverts of wheat or rye, one can estimate the average planting at Fort Ross at ten chetverts per desiatina. A chetvert of good wheat contains 49 pounds, so consequently in 1828 865 puds of wheat and 215 puds of barley were planted, for a total of 1,080 puds, or 881-2/3 chetverts over 88 desiatinas, or 211,600 square sazhens.

The land is cultivated after the first rains of November and December, which is the way the Californians also do this. In some places the soil is good chernozem [black soil], in other places it is sandy, but it is equally fertile everywhere. The land is never fertilized, even though there is a substantial number of livestock. But the animals graze over large areas and it is obviously impossible to collect manure. All manner of implements are used for cultivation. There were workers from all parts of vast Russia in the settlement, and each one made tools according to his own liking. There were Finnish plows, Little Russian plows, Great Russian plows, Siberian plows, and California plows--and the plowshare is nothing but a heavy piece of iron. Oxen were used to pull the plows, and they also use horses to pull wooden plows. In hilly areas where it is not possible to use a plow with either a wooden or a metal plowshare, they employ Indians to break up the earth with spades.

Livestock

It was noted that when Kuskov became acquainted with the Californians, he secured several horses and horned cattle from the mission and from inhabitants of San Francisco, even though the government strictly prohibited this. The decision to increase the herds of livestock in order to supply the colony with meat could have been profitable, especially since there was always grass and hay to feed the animals; but when agriculture was expanded, it was difficult to graze livestock in the vicinity since the land was under cultivation and there were no grazing grounds near by. Consequently the livestock moved off into the hills; often they became lost, sometimes they fell from cliffs and were killed, sometimes Indians killed cows and calves, and sometimes livestock became separated from the herd and were killed by bears and wildcats. (During Kuskov's administration one huge bull came in all covered with blood, with pieces of flesh torn out, and his horns all gory, which indicated that he had inflicted considerable injury on his attacker.) As a result it was often not profitable to increase livestock production. Two Russians, Aleuts or Indians looked after the livestock. The bulls were exceptionally large. One which was delivered aboard the ship Kutuzov in 1817 yielded 23 puds of pure meat. Pigs which wander along the shore eat shellfish and their meat has a dreadful taste.

---

*Chetvert = 49 pounds. -- Ed.

**Desiatina = 2.7 acres. -- Ed.

The table below shows the number of animals at various times, their increase, loss by various means, and the amount consumed as food.

	Born				Died				Consumed as food				On hand			
	Cattle	Horses	Sheep	Pigs	Cattle	Horses	Sheep	Pigs	Cattle	Horses	Sheep	Pigs	Cattle	Horses	Sheep	Pigs
Under Kuskov September, 1817	-	-	-	-	-	-	-	-	-	-	-	-	61	10	161	not known
Turned over to Schmidt from Kuskov, October 26, 1821	-	-	-	-	-	-	-	-	-	-	-	-	149	21	698	159
October 26, 1821 to November 1822	Purchased 62	10	191	143	11	2	47	63	13	-	106	115	187	29	736	124
From October 1, 1823	-	-	-	-	27	-	90	-	-	-	-	-	213	46	842	81
To Schmidt's replacement September 1, 1824	-	-	-	-	-	-	-	-	-	-	-	-	195	83	580	46
September 1825	-	-	-	-	-	-	-	-	-	-	-	-	247	90	588	23
September 1826	96	67	301	50	12	4	9	4	18	-	305 (on Sitka)	11	315	153	575	58
September 1827	132	44	412	43	17	2	4	4	34	1	282 (on Sitka)	5	389	206	696	92
September 1828	137	37	213	23	38	6	8	4	38	-	340	17	450	237	555	100
September 1829	125	24	261	21	28	8	6	3	22	-	72	11	521	253	614	106

Sheep are sold for the most part as food in exchange for money; sometimes bulls are slaughtered and the meat is used for the garrison for holidays. Company ships which put in there generally receive one or two bulls and several sheep to replenish their supplies. In 1826 Sitka received 150; in 1828, 105; and in 1829, 200 puds of salt pork. They sometimes bought a few horses from the Spaniards to thresh grain. At present there are enough mares to give an annual increase of twenty colts.

Various Husbandry Pursuits

Various husbandry pursuits have obviously come into being as a result of building the settlement. A shortage of trained persons in various areas prevents these from being better carried out; but no matter what they have been to the present time, they should be noted, according to what has been done.

Livestock breeding and produce: insofar as fruit trees are concerned, Benzeman brought the first peach tree from San Francisco aboard the schooner Chirikov in 1814, and fruit was harvested from it in 1820.

In 1817 L. A. Hagemeister brought grape vines from Lima, and in 1818 peach trees from Monterey. In 1820 we sent 100 cuttings of apples, pears, cherries, peaches and bergamots aboard the brig Buldakov; these were small cuttings which produced their first fruit in 1828.

Roses were brought from San Francisco and castor wood from the Sandwich Islands. Sometimes the grapes are good; they were first harvested in 1823.

Melons, squash and pumpkins were planted by Kuskov, and in a good year 800 melons are harvested. Kuskov liked to garden and was very busy at it; he always had a surplus of beets, cabbage, turnips, radishes, lettuce, peas and beans. Radishes and turnips grow unusually large, but they are not flavorful. He supplied all the ships that put in here with vegetables, and he frequently pickled beets and cabbage and sent a large amount to Sitka. Potatoes were planted twice a year, but the harvest was no more than six or occasionally eightfold. Rodents destroy a great deal of garden produce by eating the greens the moment new shoots appear. The fruit harvest often depends on the weather. If the summer is sunny and fogs are infrequent, then the harvest will be plentiful; but if it is stormy from May to September and the sun seldom shines, fruit will not grow. A large amount of mustard grows in various places, sometimes from three to six puds will be harvested and sent to Sitka at an appraised value of twenty rubles per pud. It grows in the wild without any attention.

A by-product of stockraising: tallow. From livestock are procured tallow, hides, butter and wool. The amount of tallow is not large, because animals are not slaughtered when they are fat, as the Californians do purposely, but rather, whenever they are needed for food or to replenish ship provisions. Tallow amounts to ten to fifteen puds per year; it is used for candles and night lamps.

Butter was first produced during Shelekhov's administration, in the following amounts:

1825	68 puds	31 pounds
1826	68	31
1827	92	11
1828	101	20
1829	84	26

Of this amount approximately one third goes for the fort and for officials on incoming ships who ask to purchase it; two-thirds is sent to Sitka to be sold at 20 rubles per pud.

Local hides and those from California are tanned and dressed into leather for boots and soles. Sometimes these are of exceptionally fine quality and whatever is not needed for use here is sent to Sitka.

A substantial amount was sent in the following years:

1826	aboard Kiakhta		
1827	Kiakhta	66 tanned	
1828	Kiakhta	67 tanned	20 undressed skins
1829	Golovnin	90 tanned	

Prepared hides are appraised at fifteen rubles each. The master tanner is a Kodiak Aleut who learned his trade from a Russian. He also tans reindeer, elk, and wild goat hides as suede which is used to make the undergarments worn by workers.

The California sheep has a heavy pelt. Missionaries make blankets for the Indians from it, but we do not use it at all. Up to 50 puds of wool is collected each year. On the basis of the California experience, Schmidt wanted to make blankets, but there were no persons who could spin it into yarn, and there was no master to build a spinning wheel.

Locally produced goods: they extract a very fine resin from local pine; it is not difficult to extract twenty or more barrels of it.

They make a large amount of brick from a very fine clay, and frequently ship these to Sitka. The clay is found in various qualities.

Redwood is a very soft wood and is thus suitable for making barrels. There are always from 20 to 50 small barrels on hand in the settlement for salting meat, which is taken on board ships which come in from Sitka.

The Farallon Artel

The Farallon Islands are located opposite the port of San Francisco, about fifteen miles southwest of Drake's Head. When our ships first stopped there, they found a good many fur seals and many other seals. When the settlement was built, our people felt that it was necessary to occupy these islands. They are treeless, and have only a bit of grass; the largest of them is no more than three miles in circumference. They were created by volcanic action, which is obvious from their characteristic barrenness, and the lack of minerals. Persons who live there say that during storms the islands shake, and one can hear a kind of moaning noise against the breaking waves. The islands have no fresh water or driftwood, and consequently persons who stay there have a very hard time sustaining themselves. The following advantages caused us to occupy them.

From the beginning of occupation, that is from 1812 to 1815, over the period of six years during Kuskov's administration, 8,427 fur seals were taken there, an average of 1,200 to 1,500 each year. Later this gradually decreased, and in recent years not more than 200 to 300 pelts are taken there each year.

Some of the American captains said that prior to our occupation of those rocks, they had stopped there one fall and taken as many as 10,000 fur seals. These are smaller than those to be found on the Pribylov Islands; their fur is darker and coarser, and consequently they do not have the same value.

Every year up to 200 sea lions are killed for their hides, called lavtaks, their intestines and meat and fat. The lavtaks are used to make baidarkas in the settlement; the intestines are used for making kamleis, [waterproof garments] and as much as 100 or 150 puds of meat is salted; in addition, the Aleuts dry some 200 or 300 chunks of it. The fat is stored in small kegs and is used both as food for the Aleuts and for lighting purposes.

From 5,000 to 10,000 sea ducks are killed every year, but in 1828 50,000 were killed. They are dried and sent to the artel as food; some are also sent to the fort. In 1828 100 puds of meat was supplied from these. The skins of the birds are not used for any purpose, so once the feathers are plucked, the skins are discarded. In 1827 the artel supplied nine, and in 1828, eleven inflated bladders of feathers; each weighed 30 puds, at a value of twenty rubles per pud; they were sent to New Arkhangel. They collect a good many eggs from these ducks, which they use for themselves and send to the fort. One can get some idea of the abundance of these birds from the number taken in 1828.

There is one Russian administrator for the artel, and generally from six to ten men, both Aleuts and Indians. They live in earthen dugouts; they bring in water and wood by baidarka; they try to collect rain water in winter; and in order to save wood, they cook by burning sea lion bones which have been soaked in oil.

A baidarka is sent there five or six times a year to supply the artel with water, wood, barrels for oil and meat; and to bring back prepared provisions and lavtaks. The island where the artel lives is very rocky and there is always a strong tide. There is only one place where boats can land, and even that is quite dangerous; thus boats dock and embark with great difficulty and peril. Small transhipments are made in baidarkas, and two baidarkas are always left with the artel. If there is a wind, it takes the baidarkas a week or two or more to make the trip. It is always difficult to sail around Drake's Head in the open sea, and nearly impossible to return if there is a strong northwest wind. Consequently they have to wait in Drake's Head. The frequent dense fogs also add to the difficulty of bringing in supplies.

Climate And Location

The climate of New Albion does not differ from the climate of the areas of
northern California; it is quite temperate. There are two seasons of the year:
winter and summer. Winter begins in November or December, and is marked by
torrential rains and strong southeast and southwest winds which continue, with
intermittent periods of clear skies, until March or April. Sometimes there is
snow, which will remain several weeks on the mountains, but at lower elevations
and in areas close to the sea, the snow melts as soon as it touches the ground.
There are no frosts, but the cold in the morning can sometimes be quite
penetrating. But the extreme low seldom if ever reaches below the freezing
point. In summer the south winds stop and the wind comes from the northwest,
when there are usually hard storms. It often happens that one cannot see the
sun for two or three months, and the weather is quite cold. But these storms
reach only as far as the mountains close to the sea and do not go beyond them.
When one crosses the mountains, sometimes no more than one or two or three
versts from the shore, entirely different weather will be encountered. The sun
shines, the air is warm, the sky clear, and the climate is uniformly pleasant.
Storms linger in the foothills of the mountains like waves at sea.

The ridge of mountains parallels the shore along the entire peninsula of
California, and sometimes spreads appreciably inland. According to some
observers, these mountains form an integral part of the Andes.

When traveling east of Fort Ross for three days, we did not find any flat land.
In 1823 Schmidt and the prikashchik Dorofiev and some Aleuts took a baidarka
along the Slavianka [Russian] River which empties into the sea halfway between
Bodega Bay and the settlement; they went out about 100 versts from the fort.
Behind the mountains they found beautiful meadows covered with forests where
many Indians lived. From Bodega Bay along the Avacha River the meadows begin
near the sea, and the farther one goes the more fertile the soil is. North of
the Ross settlement the coastal mountains are forested, but south of the
settlement there are no forests; trees can be seen only on far off high
mountains; the hills close to the sea are treeless. One river, the Slavianka,
is of a good size and can take small rowing vessels. Its mouth is sometimes
choked with sand, at other times open. Almost everywhere in the mountains the
soil is chernozem; there are always springs of pure water. There is no water
on the sand hills.

Natural Resources

Every scientific observer knows that there are many new things in all parts of
the New World, but what is of interest to a scientist is of little import to
us, and consequently what we shall attempt to do is to comment here only on the
highlights, on things that have been most noticed.

<u>Wild life</u>. Among quadrupeds the most important are bears, lynx, ordinary wolves,
and small ones which the Spaniards call coyotes, small skunks that exude a very
vile odor, wildcats, elk, buffaloes, mountain goats, rams, rabbits, an abundance
of moles, small mice and other rodents; and although it happens rarely, nonetheless one does sometimes see close to the American settlements American lions
[puma] and amphibious animals such as river beavers and otters.

There are numerous snakes, lizards and frogs, and occasionally scorpions. There has been no incidence of snake bite. It seems that they are not poisonous, at least the Indians believe this to be true.

There are white eagles, all varieties of hawks, magpies, crows, woodpeckers, wild pigeons, condors and quite a few birds of the sparrow family. Some of these have beautiful feathers. There are huge flocks of blackbirds which the Spaniards call chanatas, which live near the grain fields and destroy the harvest. Ducks, numerous various kinds of woodcocks and geese come down from the north to spend the winter; there are also swans, cranes, herons, many grey and white pelicans, sea gulls, sea ducks, urils, albatross and loons.

Close to shore there are many whales which the Aleuts hunt. Kuskov said that they found a whale eighteen sazhens long, but they are usually smaller, from four to five sazhens. From this size one can obtain a pure oil, as much as twelve large barrels, that is, 30 to 36 vedros. Sea lions and sea elephants abound on the Farallons, and they also bask on various rocks along the coast. There are a few seals at present, and these are found only around the cape of Barro de Arena. Along the shore they angle for such fish as perch, mackerel; herring come in seasonally. They catch sturgeon in the Slavianka River when the channel is open.

Among shellfish there are blue crabs, other crabs, crawfish, and small turtles in the lakes beyond the mountains. In October, 1822, men sailing from the Farallons in baidarkas killed an unusually large sea turtle which had exceptionally delicious meat; but this does not happen often.

Vegetation. It has been noted that there is a forest near Fort Ross which is very dense as one goes north. There are such conifers as ordinary pine, fir, larch, silver fir, and bugbane, so called because it has a very sharp odor, similar to the smell of the insect that has that name. This tree appears to belong to the cypress family, and is similar to the Alaska cypress in Sitka. The chaga, or redwood, is a red pine distinguished by its softness; it is not very resinous but very moist, and it has a dark red color. The redwood is exceptionally tall and straight and unusually large in circumference. I measured one which was growing near the fort; the circumference was 33 feet, thus it was 11 feet in diameter.

Among deciduous trees, there are two kinds of oak, maple, elm, poplar, two kinds of alder, horse chestnuts, laurel, willow, purple willow, and some ten other varieties whose names are unknown. Our promyshlenniks call one of these a palm, but this is quite inaccurate. Many of these trees are heavy, hard and excellent for making furniture which will be varnished. The leaf of the laurel has a strong odor, much stronger than the East Indian variety.

Of the shrubs, there are currants, hazelnuts, raspberry, buckthorn and elderberry. The Indians sometimes collect a great many delicious nuts. There are sometimes blueberries and nagoonberries. There are many other varieties which are unknown to us, but which the Indians eat.

D. B. [probably Dr. Eduard Blaschke] records such medicinal plants as globularia and acnothera, and familiar herbs such as wormwood, wild mint, fern, scurvy grass, and sea onion. The onion-like root of one plant which grows on sand dunes near the sea can be used instead of soap; it gives a white foam, but it is injurious to white fabric and rapidly destroys it. But it is very good for cleaning decks and floors. Wild roses grow in many meadows. Horsetails grow more than a sazhen high in damp areas, and they are very firm and hard. There are also many kinds of reeds which grow.

Indians always eat wild rose haws, collecting them after the flower has finished blooming, and storing them. In fall they burn the grass and dig for edible roots. Acorns are a major food for both Indians and woodpeckers. These birds use their bills to peck holes in the bark of redwood trees; they put an acorn in each hole to save it for winter. One can see a whole tree studded with acorns. Often the Indians will gather in the cache of the birds after they have eaten their own supply.

Minerals. The mountains near the sea are almost all made up of granite and syenite; and there is much sandstone beneath the surface of the soil. The settlement uses some varieties of this for grindstones and whetstones. There is plenty of good soil in various places. At the mouth of the Slavianka River there are whole blocks of green rock with small bits of granite, and iron ore has been found in its upper reaches. On top of some of the mountains they have found obsidian, serpentine and hornstone. A pure iron-bearing sand is carried up on the sandy shores from the sea.

Suggestions For Improving The Settlement

If the settlement of Ross were to remain forever a possession of Russia, and were to be duly acknowledged by other governments, then it could become a permanent settlement and attention could be given to more important considerations. The first point of concern is to supply the colony with grain; the second, to protect the Company; we must seek less expensive and more satisfactory ways of achieving these. Agriculture can be established without any inordinate difficulty by the following means:

In regard to agriculture, we have already noted that there are no cultivated areas available around Fort Ross, and those that are already in use are hopeless because they are too close to the sea. Consequently, we should turn our attention to the meadows near Little Bodega Bay. There is meadowland there with rich arable soil and it is not too far from the port. It would be necessary to build a summer house about ten versts up the Avacha River where laborers could live, and where some livestock could be raised. The land could be worked there, as is now being done, by three Indians; these men sometimes appear voluntarily at work time in the spring. There should be a warehouse for storing grain in this settlement, and the grain should be shipped to Bodega Bay immediately after threshing either by ox cart or by carts drawn by mules. The distance is short and the road is quite good. A warehouse should be built in Bodega where grain would be stored while awaiting the arrival of ships to be loaded with the grain. Because of the proximity, the grain should be transferred by barge, and then be moved by rowboat from there through the mouth of the bay. There would be no difficulty in building a storehouse on top of a barge.

If one were to organize agriculture along the Avacha River, it would not be necessary to cultivate land near the fort. One could simply use part of the best land to supply the garrison. The rest, which is presently being used for agricultural purposes, should be set aside for livestock because it is so close. Barley could be planted in other areas, and one place could be used to grow mustard.

There should be from ten to twelve Russians in the settlement on the Avacha, but no elaborate equipment would be needed because there should be a permanent communication system established between that place and the fort, which would be used either once a week, or as necessary. One can make the round trip by land in one day. There should be guards at the Bodega warehouse, and a sloop or a boat for transfer at the mouth of the bay.

If one were to cultivate from 300 to 400 fanegas of wheat, that is, between 1,200 and 1,500 puds, then one could expect that the average harvest would be from 3,000 to 4,000 fanegas, or from 12,000 to 15,000 puds: that is, the annual need of the colony.

Meanwhile, as circumstances permit, one can purchase several hundred fanegas in California ports; then, one should also expect to obtain it less expensively, and without the imposition of additional fees, which at present are frequently added.

In addition to wheat, one could also cultivate along the Avacha a supply of corn, peas and hemp which the colony needs. This latter item is necessary for ship use, for making heavy rope, plummet and others, and it does not require any special effort. As we expanded the production of fruits and vegetables we could supply the colony with plenty of red beets, cabbage and cucumbers, all of which are very useful for seafaring and serve as antiscorbutics; squash can usually be preserved for a long time, and in winter are brought to Sitka in perfect condition.

Livestock. The colony has a special need for salted meat, especially for sea voyages, for tallow for candles, for hides for shoe soles and boot uppers and for fur. Consequently, if livestock production should be increased to 600 or 700 head, then considering an annual increase to be 20%, one could slaughter up to 100 head of cattle every year to be salted, as well as eaten fresh. If one considers this number to be average-sized livestock, not large, then using an average of six puds of meat per head, that would give 600 puds. The colony annually uses from 300 to 400 puds. Sheep should be increased to about 1,000, and pigs to 200; this could supply the Fort Ross garrison. Of the 600 cattle, one third could be milking cows which would each provide one pud of butter per year, thus 200 puds, which is enough to supply all the colonies, and monteka would never have to be purchased.

Forests. We might receive a substantial profit from the local forests. Redwood is very soft, splits easily and straight, and cuts into lumber which can be used very nicely in construction. A board three sazhens long and three inches thick can be sold for a piastre; one and one-fourth inches thick, for one-half piastre. A beam eight inches square will bring from three to four piastres in San Francisco and Monterey. Pine boards and beams bring double that. One can extract tar from pine without much difficulty; this has several times been done. Consequently this branch of our economy could cut by half the amount of commodities we must purchase for our needs.

Manufactured goods. When considering the improvement of the settlement, I have not taken into account any costs involved before gain or profit can accrue from manufacturing. I am suggesting only those things which can be accomplished with a minimum of effort. One master craftsman would immediately become a teacher for our exceptionally adaptable young creoles. All articles which I am suggesting are of local manufacture, and have been neglected to the present time.

Many village dwellers in Russia know how to clean wool and spin it into yarn, make cloth from it, knit stockings, etc. Blankets, which the Indians use, although they are also made in California, would be used instead of payment in other items for agricultural produce. It is also useful and necessary to make felt and hats. Felt could replace coverlets for beds which are presently made out of bear and elk skins and feather beds. Harness goods for horses are made out of felt. Hats, besides being used in the colonies, could be sold for profit in California. We receive one piastre for a Kolosh hat made of tree roots, and a wool hat could always be sold for at least that much. Blankets and saddle blankets for horses and felt can also be sold at a profit. One thousand sheep will produce 100 puds of wool; this amount would be sufficient for everything.

At the time the ship Kutuzov was sent out in 1816, the Governing Board considered sending a master craftsman to make glassware, a man who had been contracted and freed from the Aleksandrovsk glass factory. But it seems that family circumstances prevented him from coming. Before a master is brought out, it should be determined whether necessary materials can be obtained locally. It is true that a glass factory producing ware of a rather low quality would be very useful, and glassware could be distributed throughout California and even into the more distant provinces of the Mexican Republic. But this is a complex undertaking, and one which requires a number of persons and involves considerable effort and expenditure. Introducing a factory to make cooking ware and other crockery from a low grade clay would not be as complex an operation, and the technique is a familiar one to many persons. Clay of good quality is to be found in various places, and thus it would not be too difficult to introduce this operation. Simple pots are necessary for making local butter. At present wooden boxes are used, which cause the milk and cream to turn rancid and the butter is also thus bitter.

Earthenware could very well be used in the colonies to replace the pr ently used copper pots; frequently the tinning wears off, and the copper as everyone knows is rather poisonous, so there is evidence that the use of such utensils is unquestionably harmful. Not only can an experienced master make pots, he can also make plates, mugs, cups and other small goods which are needed everywhere; and because there are no simple ones, we have to buy expensive ones. Obviously there is real advantage in manufacturing all of these items.

At present only shoe soles and rawhide uppers are produced here. They do not know how to handle sheepskins, so they sell them. The preparation of these skins would help supply the colony with shoes. Local oak bark is very good. Elk and buffalo and wild goat hides can be made into suede and chamois. It is easy to introduce domesticated goat, and their hides can be used for manufacturing.

If slaughtering were to be done at an appropriate time for the meat to be salted, then a good deal of tallow would be available, and both candles and soap could be made from this. Ashes from local oak are excellent, and lime can be obtained from shellfish. Hopefully someone will discover limestone deposits if an attempt to do so is made; there is an abundance of it near by in the missions of San Francisco Solano and San Rafael.

Livestock horns are usually discarded, but one could easily make combs, powder horns, lamps and other things from them, which would be very useful and could be used for exchange purposes with our neighbors, as well as being used throughout the colonies. We sell simple horn combs to the Spaniards for 25 piastres per 100.

An Observation On The Russian American Company's Colony Known As Ross

Like the northwest coast of America, the Aleutian Islands belong to the Russian American Company; they are not suitable for agricultural purposes because of their extremely primitive condition and the lack of good arable soil. Perhaps livestock could be raised with some success on Kodiak. Because of the infertility of the soil, during the first years the Company was in existence it was so difficult to provision the colonies that nothing could be worse than returning to those times. Bread and sea provisions had to come from Irkutsk via Iakutsk and Okhotsk, at great expense; therefore they were always supplied in a quantity bordering on bare subsistence. The tremendous shortage of provisions was partly compensated by the exchange of fur seals for these items from foreign ships which put in to our colony. But this method, which was begun by Baranov, then Chief Manager of the colony, with foreigners, was neither reliable nor fully satisfactory. Thus it happened that in this severe climate where wholesome and plentiful food is necessary to maintain human life, neither land-based personnel and promyshlenniks nor sea voyagers had bread regularly; often they had to eat sea lion meat and fish. The same situation in regard to provisioning the colonies also existed when the late Rezanov came there as an ambassador from the Company with the first around-the-world Russian expedition. Shocked by such conditions among the service personnel of the Company, he did his best to end such a tragic shortage of the necessities of life. The late Baranov's intention was to establish a settlement on the shores of New Albion where no European power had yet laid formal claim. In order to satisfy himself that this was possible and feasible, Rezanov himself went to California, saw New Albion, and, excited by the climate of that country and convinced of success, wrote to the directors recommending the Baranov plan be carried out. The Governing Board of the Company, through the State Chancellor Count Rumiantsev, requested Imperial permission. His Excellency informed the Company in a directive dated December 1, 1808, that "His Imperial Majesty refuses at the present time to organize a settlement in Albion at government expense, but grants the administration [of the Company] permission to create such at its own expense, and hopes in any case to give such an enterprise Imperial support." On the basis of this Imperial permission to establish a settlement in New Albion, the Governing Board of the Company then drew up its own regulations. As a result, the late Councilor of Commerce Kuskov was sent from New Arkhangel by the Chief Manager of the Company, Baranov, on March 15, 1812, and founded a fort called Slaviansk or Ross on the shores of New Albion, at 38°40", slightly north of Port Rumiantsev or little Bodega Bay, in a place which the settlers called Mad-zhy-ny.

On this occasion, the well-behaved Indians of that area were completely free, and had no protection whatsoever from their Spanish neighbors. On the contrary, they were oppressed by the attacks of savages under the control of the Spaniards, and had a hostile attitude toward them. Because of this, the local Indians not only did not object to the presence of the Russians on the shores of New Albion, but expressed the desire to see them there in greater numbers, in order to make certain that they received protection from their hostile neighbors. One of the chief elders or toions, named Chu-Chu-Oan, who had owned the land which was taken to build the fort, voluntarily gave it up to the Russians in exchange for certain appropriate gifts. The Indians informed Captain Golovnin, who was then in the port of Rumiantsev aboard the sloop Kamchatka, that they were independent of the Spaniards, that they hated them, and that they wished the Russians to settle and live in their vicinity. One elder, Valenila, asked Golovnin to give him a Russian flag so he could show it as evidence of friendship and good will toward the Russians.

It is important to realize that the Spaniards regarded our settlement in an entirely different way. The government of California, in its dealings with the head of the Company, the late Kuskov, several times expressed dissatisfaction, and even insisted that he dismantle the settlement and leave. During the administration of the noted [Agustin de] Iturbide in Mexico, a special official came to the port of San Francisco and expressed a similar demand; however it was subsequently discovered he had no authority to do so. Several times the administration in Monterey resorted to hostile actions such as imprisoning our people. Finally in 1819 the Spanish Ambassador to our Court sent an official note to our minister concerning this problem. At the request of the Minister of Finance the Governing Board prepared an explanation, and the affair has remained unresolved from that time because of changing political circumstances. Meanwhile, the local California administration sees that the present developments give it a protective leverage by using her Russian neighbors. During a recent Indian uprising against the Spanish missions, the Company supplied weapons to the Spaniards, although we had a shortage of them ourselves, thus we demonstrated genuine assistance to them.

Considering the opposition of the California administration to our settlement in New Albion, which the Spanish Ambassador has reiterated, it should be noted that the Spanish had extended the right of Spain to control the entire coast of New Albion all the way to the straits of Juan de Fuca. That such a claim is unfounded is clearly evident, in the first place, by the testimony of the Indian tribes as to their independence, and moreover, that the authority of the Spanish never extended beyond the port of San Francisco; and secondly, that the government of the United States authorized itself to occupy the mouth of the Columbia River, a situation which we have just imitated for ourselves; and subsequently, the southern [sic] border of Louisiana was declared to lie at the 42nd parallel, that is, a full five degrees south of the straits of Juan de Fuca.

Regardless of the circumstances that followed the establishment of the Ross colony, the Company was not able to assume full legal possession; therefore in the course of twelve years no appropriate measures have been taken to strengthen it. This is the reason why the colony has never been used in the important manner originally intended, even up to the present time. Nevertheless, it has provided and continues to provide quite significant benefits, serving as an indispensable and useful means of supplying other colonies. Also, the abundance of oak and pine forests suitable for construction purposes made it possible to build several seaworthy ships there, in extreme cases, the construction of which was as advantageous to the Company as was their actual use.

The Ross colony presently consists of a small wooden fortress with seventeen small calibre cannon. Within the fortress there are the administrator's home, an office, barracks, a two-story warehouse and several other buildings. Those

who live in the fortress work at various jobs; all are in the Company service.
There are 50 persons in addition to the Aleuts who are periodically sent out on
sea otter hunts. Of the 38 promyshlenniks there, 12 are engaged in agricultural
pursuits, most by their own volition rather than by obligation. They plant
grain, about 200 puds of wheat and 40 puds of barley, although cultivation is
carried on without any great improvement of the soil, in fact, without any
systematic plowing; nonetheless the harvest is tenfold. The example of the
neighboring Spanish missions, who have a fortyfold harvest, indicates that if
agriculture were to be handled properly, we could expect this in Ross. The
climate is such that vegetables can be planted twice a year, and every kind of
vegetable and fruit can be grown there.

Ross [in the early 1830's] has the following number of livestock: 46 horses,
213 bulls and cows, 81 pigs and 842 sheep. The abundance of wild livestock, and
the oak forest, makes it easy to operate tanneries. Sheepherding alone, which
is so easily increased, would provide the Company with countless advantages.

Generally speaking, on the basis of this first experience, one can easily believe
that once agriculture in Ross is carried on properly, the Company could be fully
supplied with grain in all of its American colonies. One need only note that the
annual requirement of the colonies is no more than 10,000 puds of grain. If
measures were taken to double the harvest, then one can easily state that the
Ross colony could supply grain to Kamchatka and Okhotsk. The Company would then
be in a position to completely supply the government, which tries to rely on the
Iakuts to supply grain to the government, which is done with great difficulty.

In general, with the exception of those items supplied from Ross, the subsistence
needs of the colonies are obtained from foreigners. This is done in two ways:
from ships that come to New Arkhangel; or from California, in which case Company
ships are sent. It is obvious that these are not always reliable means. They
depend on the arrival of foreign ships, and on continued friendly relations with
the government of California. It is apparent that knowing the colony's needs,
the foreigners have the opportunity to increase prices, and the Company administration is forced to pay much more than is really necessary.

In addition to these, there is one other means of supply: around the world.
This depends, in the first place, on peaceful relations with all seafaring
powers; and secondly, on various circumstances connected with prolonged sea
voyages. Consequently this is never a reliable means. It was long ago shown
that the extraordinary expense involved in this means of supplying the colony
with grain is not at all to the colony's advantage.

All this leads directly to this conclusion: that if the Company should be forced
to dismantle the Ross colony, and if as a result of political circumstances, on
the one hand, mutual relations should change with California and with countries
whose ships visit our colonies; and on the other hand, should freedom of around-
the-world navigation be terminated, then our colonies would have only one means
of being supplied, through Okhotsk. Otherwise they would all be utterly
without supplies. Thus it is clear that the prosperity of the colony and of the
Company itself demands that the Ross colony not be abandoned. On the contrary,
all measures should be taken to strengthen it to such a degree that its agriculture could fully supply all the other colonies. In order to accomplish this,
it is necessary that the Company receives full authority to control that colony.

Recently the government recognized our inalienable right to occupy the Aleutian Islands and the northwestern shores of America which the Company has controlled for twenty years. This was approved by special conventions with Great Britain and the North American United States. It is imperative that the Mexican government recognize the right of the Company to control the Ross colony.

Several years ago the friendly relations between our Court and the Madrid government presented an opportune time to establish such a right firmly, but recent developments in South America have altered her political existence, and it appears that the new Mexican government is not very agreeable to Russia possessing an area so close to California. Therefore it is necessary to send to Mexico a commissioner from Russia who would consummate a convention with that government and who would secure forever the right to possess Fort Ross.

If he were sent to Mexico this would secure other benefits for the well-being of the colonies, because the Company, secure in its possession of Ross, could increase its economic activity. Additionally, such a commissioner should be authorized to secure for the Russian American Company the right to hunt sea otter along the shores of California, with some concessions to the local administration. In addition to substantial income which the Company could receive from this enterprise, the animals who live in its possessions would be left in peace, which would cause their increase.

Thus, having secured the right of control of the Ross colony, the government would thereby provide the Company with the opportunity to secure its desired objective, namely: the simultaneous guaranteed provisioning not only of its colonies, but also of Kamchatka and Okhotsk, where grain would be supplied for half the cost at which it is presently being supplied there.

An Observation On The Advantages Of The Ross Settlement

The soil on the islands and along the northwestern shores of the American mainland which belongs to the Russian American colonies is totally unproductive and unsuitable for either agriculture or livestock. This crucial situation forced the Russian American Company and the administration of the colonies to purchase provisions from foreigners or from Okhotsk in order to supply the colonies. Significant inconveniences were encountered in both circumstances; and since our colonies could not provide themselves with these necessities, they were dependent for this vital commodity on outside circumstances which could be neither foreseen nor controlled. They were in a most difficult position, and often required these necessities. Thus Baranov, the former Manager of the Russian American colonies, and Active Chancellor Rezanov, who was sent from the court of His Imperial Majesty to inspect the colonies, sought means to alleviate these disadvantages. They tried to persuade the Governing Board of the need to establish a settlement in New Albion on shores not hitherto claimed by any European power. The Governing Board understood the importance of this proposal and recognized the advantages which such a settlement would provide for the colonies in the future.

On the basis of provisionment they made a request through the State Chancellor Count Rumiantsev for Imperial permission to put their plan into effect. By a directive of December 1, 1809, His Eminence informed the Governing Board that

His Imperial Majesty at the present time declined to have the State Treasury support such a settlement in Albion, but did grant the Board the right to establish a colony there on its own, and assured them that they could expect Imperial protection in every instance. Using this Imperial permission, the Governing Board then instructed the Manager of the colony, Baranov, to undertake this task. As a result, Commercial Councilor Kuskov was sent from New Arkhangel, and on March 15, 1812, established in New Albion the settlement known as Ross as 38°34" northern latitude. The Russians found that this place was not occupied by any one at that time, and the indigenous inhabitants were at that time completely free. The coastline has never even been thoroughly mapped, although maritime explorers of several nations have sailed there. In addition to our right of original occupation, our title to this area is strengthened by the fact that we acquired it by purchase from the indigenous inhabitants, in a peaceful manner, and have occupied it for more than twenty years, which to date no one has challenged.

In spite of the present numerical insignificance of its population, this colony has supplied and continues to provide various important advantages for all of our North American colonies. Agriculture, orchardry and livestock production have all been useful in Ross, although rather insignificantly because of the shortage of personnel; but these have often been indispensable, and hopefully are becoming even more so, in provisioning the population of the barren islands of Sitka, Kodiak and others. The abundance and good quality of timber for construction purposes have given the colonial administration the means to build several vessels at Ross, at great benefit to the Company. In spite of all of this, the settlement is still far from being able to fully provision our colonies because of its present small population.

The Russian American colony receives necessary supplies from foreigners in two ways: either through purchase from foreigners who put in at New Arkhangel, or by purchase in California, which is done by sending Company ships there for that specific purpose. In both instances, especially the second, the cost of provisions is determined by the colonial administration, according to demand. Thus we are forced either to pay in cash at high prices, or to exchange our goods at low prices. The most harmful and dangerous aspect of this is the fact that if there were a crop failure in California, or should there arise some political situation either there or in the government of the North American states, our colonies would be quite bereft of provisions. One should not count on being supplied by around-the-world expeditions, because experience has already proved that this is very dangerous and unprofitable. The Russian American Company, seeking means to eliminate all these disadvantages, and thus to provide the colonies with necessities, and to end this dangerous dependence on foreigners, will find the only means of accomplishing this to be in strengthening its permanent agricultural activity in the Ross settlement.

The warm climate of that area, the fertile grazing lands for livestock, and the proven fertility of the soil which abundantly rewards man's slightest efforts, all give reason to hope that the colonies can be supplied in the future even with an insufficient number of personnel. Along with this advantage to the colonies there are related advantages for Kamchatka; within two years after agriculture is permanently established at Ross, it may be supplied with necessities of life, at a saving of both money and time for the Treasury. This would fulfill an often expressed desire of the government.

Moreover it will be possible to introduce shipyards and other business enterprises into Ross, so that the Company will be freed from the unnecessary expense of buying ships from foreigners; and this would in some degree strengthen our seafaring position in the Pacific Ocean.

In spite of this right which Russia has to own Ross and the important advantages which would accrue from its settlement, the Russian American Company cannot undertake any of this without knowing in advance whether this will receive Imperial and government approval.

Here it should be added that from the time the Ross settlement was first founded the Company has regularly sent ships to California carrying various commodities which the local Spaniards needed, and receiving in exchange for these, items which our colonies needed. These commercial and cordial relationships are based on mutual advantage. They grow broader and more important with every passing year. To strengthen these ties for the future, and to develop agriculture to benefit all the Russian colonies, it is both necessary and desirable that our control of the area on which the Fort Ross settlement is located be permanently approved. The favorable attitude of our local Spanish neighbor, and the cordial relations with the government in Madrid lead us to believe that we will encounter few problems at the present time.

The border of the Russian settlement around Ross, on the California side, judging by local circumstances, should be the Levantula River which empties into the greater Bodega Bay. Local authorities of both governments should determine the interior border after careful consideration. It would be advantageous to extend our possessions two degrees north along the coast.* All this would be profitable because the land from Fort Ross extending up the northwest coast of America all the way to the Columbia River is not occupied by any state; and except for Spain, no one even claims the land up to the forty-first parallel; and these claims are founded on quite nebulous rights. Such a determination of frontiers would eliminate any possible future conflicts that might arise in this matter. But above all, the Company would thus be enabled to boldly extend and improve its activities for the good of the colonies, as noted above, even as far as Kamchatka.

---

*Scholars looking for confirmation of Russian imperial and mercantile designs on the North Pacific and Northwest Coast littorals will be interested in this tangible indication of intention on the part of certain administrative officials of the Russian American Company who more than appreciated the richness and potential of the coastal bays and interiors even then being assayed by American expansionists. -- Ed.

Appendix 1

RUSSIAN SHIPS IN THE ANDRIANOVSKII, BERING AND
KOMANDORSKII ISLANDS AND THEIR FUR TAKE, 1746-1762

SHIP	CAPTAIN	Year	Sea otter	[?]	Seals
Kapiton	Sergeant [Emilian] Basov	1746	1,670	2,240	1,990
Evdokiia	[Mikhail] Nevodchikov	1747	320	-	-
Ioann	[Andrean] Tolstoi	1748	362	1,481	-
Perkun [I Zanat]	[Afanesii] Bakhov	1749	58	650	-
Ioann	Bakhov	1749	1,040	2,110	-
Petr	Sergeant Basov	1750	522	1,080	300
Simeon [I Anna]	Cossack Vorobiev	1752	820	1,900	7,010
Boris I Gleb	Nevodchikov	1753	1,920	-	-
Ioann		1754	790	7,044	2,222
Ioann	Kholodnikov	1755	1,600	-	-
Boris I Gleb	Druzhinin	1755	6	1,222	250
Eremei		1755	1,260	-	-
Ioann	A. Tolstoi	1755	1,644	82	-
Sv. Nikolai	Cossack [Kodion] Durnev	1757	3,117	-	10
Orit [?]	[Nikifor] Trapeznikov	1757	4,573	-	-
Ioann	[Ivan] Krasilnikov	1758	169	2,149	-
Petr I Pavel	Trapeznikov	1758	1,819	720	840
Kapiton	Merchant Tverena [?]	1758	990	-	-
Adrian I Nataliia	Cossack [Ignatii] Studentsov	1759	292	-	-
Petr I Pavel	A. Tolstoi	1759	5,360	1,813	-
Zakhari I Elizaveta	Andrei Serebrennikov	1761	2,444	-	-
Nikolai	Cherepanov	1762	1,750	530	-
Vladimir	Trapeznikov	1762	9,280	-	-
Petr I Pavel	[Dmitrii] Paikov	1763	1,485	-	-
Petr I Pavel	[Ivan] Rybinskii	1763	301	10	-
	Merchant Popov	1763	567	67	-

Appendix 2

RUSSIAN SHIPS AND THEIR FUR TAKE, 1762-1797

SHIP	CAPTAIN	YEAR	Sea otter	Black-brown fox	Cross fox	Red fox	Otter	Fur seal
Ulian	Glotov	1762	1,465	1,002	1,100	400	-	-
Gavriil		1762	390	2	39	349	18	-
Petr I Pavel	Delarov	1766	340	569	513	170	-	-
Nikolai		1766	143	61	130	7	-	-
Adrian I Nataliia		1766	1,867	393	561	420	70	-
Ioann Ustiuskii		1768	1,272	681	802	425	-	-
Pavel	Ocheredin	1770	600	960	1,018	10	-	-
Adrian		1770	1,107	996	1,419	593	-	-
Ioann Ustiuskii		1772	1,107	1,002	1,427	600	-	-
Prokopyi		1773	250	-	20	40	-	-
Pavel	Solovev	1775	1,904	1,493	2,115	1,278	86	-
Mikhail	Polutov	1777	3,627	431	1	198	-	1,430
Nikolai	Petushkov	1777	230	6	30	-	-	190
Vladimir	P. Zaikov	1779	4,421	549	1,090	1,204	92	1,725
Evpl [?]		1779	951	252	378	630	63	540
Pavel	Ismailov	1781	2,726	577	976	821	-	-
Nataliia	Bocharov	1782	270	45	70	-	-	-
Nikolai	Paikov	1785	2,073	395	729	1,930	930	-
Klement	Polutov	1785	1,129	612	743	445	427	61
Evpl [?]	Grigorii Korelkin	1785	1,130	196	395	1,309	3	394
Aleksei	Delarov	1786	882	73	220	1,276	147	2,352
Aleksandr Nevskii	Stepan Zaikov	1780?	1,830	674	1,124	1,417	-	-
Georgii Pobedonosets	Pribylov	1784	1,270	-	-	1,025	-	31,151
Zosmma I Savvatiia		1797	88	140	167	175	-	-

Appendix 3

THE CATCH OF FUR BEARING ANIMALS BY HUNTERS
UNDER THE JURISDICTION OF THE KODIAK OFFICE, 1803-1817

	1803	1804	1805	1806	1807 to 1811	1811	1812	1813	1814	1815	1816	1817
Sea otters,					unrecorded							
large	1,189	254	422	410		248 1/2	188	148	71	117	185	124
medium	227	110	98	55		24	28	53	38	24	37	37
small	185	42	62	40		11	8	16	12	9	3	12
Tails, large	1,161	252	401	390		234	183	247	170	117	179	132
medium	221	97	91	42		40	30	59	48	25	36	24
River beavers	1,575	2,172	2,463	3,262		2,576	2,681	1,961	2,093	1,525	3,051	3,849
River otters	470	506	374	488		202	368	606	423	223	464	849
Mainland fox,												
black-brown	29	21	17	52		17	21	17	6	13	84	86
cross	62	50	78	78		45	19	27	21	57	47	58
red	464	725	402	462		185	234	279	240		493	469
Island fox,												
black-brown	216	201	100	253		254	154	249	174		264	502 1/2
cross	363	255	156	390		352	189	382	248	8	304	680
red	207	156	128	254		264	166	271	180	10	294	510
Sables	515	474	485	783		329	540	575	1,556	1,346	757	1,228
Lynx	36	66	61	62		8	25	22	45	25	112	125
Wolves	1	7	2	1		9	9	4	10	8	3	9
Wolverines	52	52	39	46		48 1/2	62	65	48	38	67	58

Black bears	52	90	63	97	68	75 1/2	67	79	61	89	117
Red bears	8	22	26	39	44	21	6	9		5	
Minks	19	46	8	21	2					4	12
Castoreum	23 1/8	1-2 1/2	1-3	1-36	30 3/4	1-1	12	3		29 1/2	31
Ermines	666	199	84	351			136				
Muskrats	44	188									
Walrus tusks, puds	1-19					8 1/4					

Appendix 4

THE CATCH OF FUR BEARING ANIMALS BY HUNTERS
UNDER THE JURISDICTION OF THE KODIAK OFFICE, 1818-1830

Type of animal	1818 & 1819	1820	1821	1822	1823	1824	1825	1826	1827	1828	1829	1830
Sea otters,												
large	179	109	108	98	77	45	82	35	54	82	51	86
medium	8	18	14	12	8	13	8	3	14	20	13	9
small	12	11	7	7	9	8	12	6	9	13	6	16
Tails,												
large	169	108	106	94	72	42	80	30	56	82	50	85
Tails,												
medium	26	17	14	12	7	5	4	2	9	20	12	9
River												
beavers	3,982	2,805	3,709	3,661	4,838	2,876	3,687	3,296	3,261	3,053	3,032	4,081
River												
otters	320	480	523	476	559	492	551	730	467	714	576	576
Lynx	165	192	71	38	26	19	31	105	117	263	206	139
Wolverine	36	63	65	70	88	31	51	93	92	45	50	95
Black bears	118	107	200	95	120	56	104	93	127	136	118	100
Brown-black fox,												
mainland	49	37	46	72	80	44	58	52	81	71	51	52
Cross fox, mainland	78	50	68	86	108	57	83	73	138	64	63	58
Red fox, mainland	288	290	66	135	145	236	376	408	866	497	485	275
Black-brown fox, island	51	349	300	425	572	410	521	690	530	590	372	188
Cross fox, island	112	426	417	461	661	484	585	779	580	831	581	211
Red fox, island	84	295	273	262	383	287	502	485	360	550	422	200
Wolves	12	3	10	12	6 1/2	11	7	11	9	7	3	2

Sables	1,275	677	477	497	472	87	88	247	717	1,130	519	1,097
Castoreum, puds	1.20 puds	35 3/4 pounds	2.21 pud	2.24	4.7	1.36	2.26	628* pounds	1,075 pounds	1,026 pounds	1,180 pounds	1,813 pounds
Hares	105											
Muskrats	494	100	100	39							84	168
Ermines	22	69	42	7							45	10
Minks	14	7	8	26	28	19	41	14	35	52		65
Squirrels	100	13										69
Walrus tusks	4.14 puds	25 puds	11 pounds	4 1/2 puds	10 puds	1 pud	1.29 puds		1.36 puds	5 puds	26 puds	
Whalebone, puds	70		60 pieces								200 pieces	
Gopher	144	167	185	196	241	200	203			100	50	100
Brown bears	6											100

---

*The castoreum figures for 1826 on possibly refer to the number of pairs of dried castor glands. Six pairs of glands equal one pound. -- Ed.

Appendix 5

POPULATION OF PRIBYLOV ISLANDS IN 1825

	MALE		FEMALE		TOTAL
	Adult	Young	Adult	Young	
ST. GEORGE					
Russian	3	1	3	1	8
Creole	3	1	2	1	7
Aleut	29	13	23	16	81
TOTAL	35	15	28	18	96
ST. PAUL					
Russian	4	3	4	2	13
Creole	3	2	2	-	7
Aleut	36	23	27	22	108
TOTAL	45	28	33	24	130

Salaried personnel

Russian 7
Creole 6
Aleut 4

Apprentices

Aleut 59

TOTAL 76

Appendix 6

CENSUS OF NATIVES ON KODIAK ISLAND AND IN OTHER AREAS
UNDER THE JURISDICTION OF THAT OFFICE

Year	Kodiak Natives on Sitka		On Kodiak Island		In Alaska		Kenai Bay		Chugach Bay		Total
	M	F	M	F	M	F	M	F	M	F	
1792	-	-	3,027	2,669	439	375	83	93	209	204	7,109
1796	-	-	3,221	2,985	included in Kodiak no.		64	57	409	357	6,993
1800	-	-	2,750	2,714	119	90	1,207	1,171	367	347	8,765
1806	358	89	1,478	2,019	included in Kodiak no.		not recorded				3,926
1817, when Baranov was replaced	-	-	1,496	1,815	415	472	735	768	439	502	6,692

Appendix 7

CENSUS OF PERSONS UNDER THE JURISDICTION OF THE KODIAK OFFICE, AS OF JANUARY 1, 1825

	Adult		Minors	
	Màle	Female	Male	Female
Clergy	2			
Russian officials and promyshlenniks	68			
Retired promyshlenniks	5			
Non-salaried promyshlenniks	9			
Creole service personnel	31	96	76	74
Creoles freed from service	1	1		
Aleuts on salaries	9	6	5	3
Aleuts freed from service	12	5		
Total	137	108	81	77
Free Aleuts on Kodiak Island and nearby islands	883	1,110	442	344
On the shore	5	4	3	6
Total	1,025	1,122	527	427
Infants	527	427		
Total for Kodiak	1,552	1,649	in all, 3,201	
On Unalaska	36	34	15	13
In the Sutkhum artel by census of 1822	17	13	5	6
In Chugach Bay, Chugach	460	517	322	264
In Kenai Bay, Kenaits	383	418	253	245
Aleuts in Katmai settlement	43	46	26	16
In Aleksandrovsk Department	179	238	123	127
Total	1,118	1,266	744	671
Infants	744	671		
Total	1,862	1,937	grand total 3,799	

Total population in Kodiak Department	7,000
Excluding Russians	84
Total	6,919

Appendix 8

LIST OF FATAL MISHAPS WHICH BEFELL KODIAK ALEUTS
IN THE EARLY YEARS OF BARANOV'S STAY

1792	Killed by Kolosh during an attack on Baranov's home at Chugats Bay	12
1796	Captured by Kolosh during attack at Lituya Bay	20
	Drowned during same attack	2
1798	On return trip, died on shore	8
	Drowned	10
1799	En route from Sitka, poisoned by shellfish	135
1800	Drowned while being transferred to [Kodiak] Island	33
1802	Killed en route to Sitka, by Kolosh	165
1804	Killed by Kolosh during attack on Sitka	16
1805	Drowned en route to Kodiak from Sitka	200
	Drowned in baidarkas during storms in that same year	100
	Total	751

SELECTED BIBLIOGRAPHY

Bibliographies

Fuller, Grace Hadley. ALASKA: A LIST OF SELECTED REFERENCES. Washington, 1943.

_____. ALEUTIAN ISLANDS: A LIST OF REFERENCES. Washington, 1943.

Kerner, Robert J. NORTHEASTERN ASIA: A SELECTED BIBLIOGRAPHY. 2 vols. Berkeley, 1939.

Lada-Mocarski, Valerian. BIBLIOGRAPHY OF BOOKS ON ALASKA PUBLISHED BEFORE 1868. New Haven, 1969.

Phillips, P. Lee. ALASKA AND THE NORTHWEST PART OF NORTH AMERICA, 1588-1898: MAPS IN THE LIBRARY OF CONGRESS. Washington, 1898.

U.S. Coast and Geodetic Survey. PACIFIC COAST PILOT: COAST AND ISLANDS OF ALASKA. Second Series. Washington, 1879. Bibliography, 225-375; compiled by W. H. Dall and Marcus Baker.

Wickersham, James. A BIBLIOGRAPHY OF ALASKAN LITERATURE, 1724-1924. Cordova, Alaska, 1927.

Books

Andreev, A., ed. RUSSKIE OTKRYTIIA V TIKHOM OKEANE I SEVERNOI AMERIKE V XVIII VEKE. Moscow, 1948.
Translated by Carl Ginsburg: RUSSIAN DISCOVERIES IN THE PACIFIC AND IN NORTH AMERICA IN THE 18th AND 19th CENTURIES. Ann Arbor, 1952.

Andrews, Clarence L. THE STORY OF ALASKA. Caldwell, Idaho, 1938.

Bancroft, Hubert H. HISTORY OF ALASKA, 1730-1855. San Francisco, 1886.

_____. HISTORY OF BRITISH COLUMBIA, 1792-1887. San Francisco, 1887.

_____. HISTORY OF CALIFORNIA. 7 vols. San Francisco, 1884-1890.

_____. HISTORY OF THE NORTHWEST COAST. 2 vols. San Francisco, 1890.

Belov, Mikhail I. ISTORIIA OTKRYTIIA I OSVOENIIA SEVERNOGO MORSKOGO PUTI. [History of the discovery and development of the northern sea route.] Moscow, 1956.

Berg, Lev S. OCHERKI PO ISTORII RUSSKIKH GEOGRAFICHESKIKH OTKRYTII. [Essays on the history of Russian geographical discoveries.] Moscow and Leningrad, 1946.

Berkh, Vasilii N. KHRONOLOGICHESKAIA ISTORIIA OTKRYTIIA ALEUTSKIKH OSTROVOV ILI
    PODVIGI ROSSIISKAGO KUPECHESTVA. [Chronological history of the discovery of
    the Aleutian Islands, or the exploits of Russian merchants.] St. Petersburg,
    1823. Translated by Melvin B. Ricks in The Earliest History of Alaska.
    Anchorage, 1963.

Bolkhovitinov, Nikolai N. RUSSKO-AMERIKANSKIE OTNOSHENIIA, 1815-1832. Moscow, 1975.

_____. STANOVLENIE RUSSKO-AMERIKANSKIKH OTHNOSHENII, 1775-1815. Moscow, 1966.
    Translated by Elena Levin, Harvard University Press, 1975.

Brooks, Alfred H. THE GEOGRAPHY AND GEOLOGY OF ALASKA. Washington, 1906.

Campbell, Archibald. VOYAGE ROUND THE WORLD IN WHICH JAPAN, KAMSCHATKA, THE
    ALEUTIAN ISLANDS, Etc. WERE VISITED. Edinburgh, 1816.

Caughey, John W. HISTORY OF THE PACIFIC COAST OF NORTH AMERICA. New York, 1938.

Chamisso, Adelbert von. REISE UM DIE WELT MIT DER TOMANZOFFISCHEN ENTDECKUNGS-
    EXPEDITION IN DEN JAHREN 1815-18 AUF DER BRIG "RURIK". 2 vols. Leipzig, 1836.

Chevigny, Hector. LORD OF ALASKA: BARANOV AND THE RUSSIAN ADVENTURE. New York,
    1942.

_____. LOST EMPIRE: THE LIFE AND ADVENTURES OF NIKOLAI PETROVICH REZANOV.
    New York, 1937.

_____. RUSSIAN AMERICA: THE GREAT ALASKAN VENTURE 1741-1867. New York, 1965.

Choris, Ludovick. VOYAGE PITTORESQUE AUTOUR DU MONDE AVEC DES PORTRAITS DE
    SAUVAGES D'AMERIQUE, D'ASIE, D'AFRIQUE, ET DES ILES DU GRAND OCEAN. Paris,
    1822.

Clark, Henry W. ALASKA: THE LAST FRONTIER. New York, 1939.

Cleveland, Richard J. A NARRATIVE OF VOYAGES AND COMMERCIAL ENTERPRISES. 2 vols.
    London, 1840.

Corney, Peter. VOYAGES IN THE NORTH PACIFIC. THE NARRATIVE OF SEVERAL TRADING
    VOYAGES FROM 1813-18, BETWEEN THE NORTHWEST COAST, THE HAWAIIAN ISLANDS AND
    CHINA, WITH A DESCRIPTION OF THE RUSSIAN SETTLEMENTS AND CALIFORNIA.
    Honolulu, 1896.

Coxe, William. ACCOUNT OF THE RUSSIAN DISCOVERIES BETWEEN ASIA AND AMERICA TO
    WHICH ARE ADDED THE CONQUEST OF SIBERIA AND THE HISTORY OF TRANSACTIONS AND
    COMMERCE BETWEEN RUSSIA AND CHINA. London, 1780.

Dall, William Healey. ALASKA AND ITS RESOURCES. Boston, 1897.

Davydov, Gavrilo I. DVUKRATNOE PUTESHESTVIE V AMERIKU MORSKIKH OFITSEROV
    KHVOSTOVA I DAVYDOVA. [The twice undertaken voyage to America by the naval
    officers Khvostov and Davydov.] Parts I, II. St. Petersburg, 1810, 1812.
    First English translation in preparation by Oregon Historical Society for
    North Pacific series.

DOKLAD KOMITETA OB USTROISTVYE RUSSKIKH AMERIKANSKIKH KOLONII. [Report of the Committee on the organization of the Russian American colonies.] St. Petersburg, 1863.

D'Wolf, John. A VOYAGE TO THE NORTH PACIFIC AND A JOURNEY THROUGH SIBERIA MORE THAN HALF A CENTURY AGO. Cambridge, 1861; Fairfield, Washington, 1968.

Efimov, Aleksei V. IZ ISTORII RUSSKIKH EKSPEDITSII NA TIKHOM OKEANE (PERVAIA POLOVINA XVIII v.). [History of Russian expeditions in the Pacific Ocean (first half of the 18th c.)]. Moscow, 1948.

_____. IZ ISTORII VELIKIKH RUSSKIKH GEOGRAFICHESKIKH OTKRYTII V SEVERNOM LEDOVITOM I TIKHOM OKEANAKH, XVII-PERVAIA POLOVINA XVIII v. [History of the great Russian geographical discoveries in the northern Arctic and Pacific Oceans from the 17th c. to the first half of the 18th c.] Moscow, 1950.

Fainberg, Lev A. OCHERKI ETNICHESKOI ISTORII ZARUBEZHNOGO SEVERA (ALIASKA, KANADA, ARKTIKA, LABRADOR, GRENLANDIIA). [Essays on ethnic history in the north of foreign lands (Alaska, Canada, the Arctic, Labrador, Greenland.)] Moscow, 1971.

_____. OBSHCHESTVENNYI STROI ESKIMOSOV I ALEUTOV. [Social structure of the Eskimos and Aleuts.] Moscow, 1964

Fedorova, Svetlana G. RUSSKOE NASELENIE ALIASKI I KALIFORNII. Moscow, 1971. Translated and edited by Richard A. Pierce and Alton S. Donnelly: The Russian Population in Alaska and California, Late 18th Century - 1867. Kingston, Ontario, 1973.

Gibson, James R. IMPERIAL RUSSIA IN FRONTIER AMERICA. New York, 1976.

Golder, Frank A. RUSSIAN EXPANSION ON THE PACIFIC (1641-1850). Cleveland, 1914.

Golovnin, Vasilii M. PUTESHESTVIE VOKRUG SVETA ... NA VOENNOM SHLIUPE "KAMCHATKE", v 1817, 1818 i 1819 GODAKH. [Voyage around the world by order of His Majesty, the Emperor, on the naval sloop "Kamchatka" in 1817, 1818 and 1819, by Fleet Captain Golovnin.] Parts I, II. St. Petersburg, 1822.

Greenhow, R. MEMOIR, HISTORICAL AND POLITICAL OF THE NORTHWEST COAST OF NORTH AMERICA AND ADJACENT TERRITORIES. Washington, 1840.

K ISTORII ROSSIISKO-AMERIKANSKOI KOMPANII. [Toward a history of the Russian American Company.] Krasnoiarsk, 1957.

Khlebnikov, Kirill T. ZHIZNEOPISANIE ALEKSANDRA ANDREEVICH BARANOVA, GLAVNOGO PRAVITELIA ROSSIISKIKH KOLONII V AMERIKE. St. Petersburg, 1835. Translated by Melvin Ricks in The Earliest History of Alaska, Anchorage, 1963; and by Colin Bearne, edited by Richard A. Pierce: Baranov: Chief Manager of the Russian Colonies in America. Kingston, Ontario, 1973.

[Kostlivtsov, Sergei]. DOKLAD KOMITETA OB USTROISTVE RUSSKIKH AMERIKANSKIKH KOLONII. [Report of the Committee on the organization of the Russian American colonies.] 2 vols. St. Petersburg, 1863.

Kotzebue, Otto von. PUTESHESTVIE V IUZHNYI OKEAN I V BERINGOV PROLIV...[Voyage into the Southern Ocean and through Bering Strait to find the Northeast passage by sea, undertaken in 1815, 1816, 1817 and 1818...] 3 parts. St. Petersburg, 1821, 1823. [Atlas, n.p., n.d.]

Krause, Aurel. DIE TLINKIT-INDIANER. Jena, 1885. Translated by Erna Gunther, The Tlingit Indians. Seattle, 1956.

Kruzenshtern, Ivan F. PUTESHESTVIE VOKRUG SVETA V 1803, 4, 5 i 1806 GODAKH. [Voyage around the world in 1803, 4, 5 and 1806. By order of His Imperial Majesty Aleksandr the First, on the ships "Nadezhda" and "Neva."] 3 vols. plus atlas. 1809-1813.

Kushner, Howard I. CONFLICT ON THE NORTHWEST COAST: AMERICAN-RUSSIAN RIVALRY IN THE PACIFIC NORTHWEST, 1790-1867. Westport, Conn., 1975.

Langsdorff, Georg H. von. BEMERKUNGEN AUF EINER REISE UM DIE WELT IN DEN JAHREN 1803 bis 1807. 2 vols. Frankfurt am Mayn, 1812. English edition, London, 1813-14.

Liapunova, Roza G. MATERIALNAIA KULTURA ALEUTOV: K PROBLEME ETNOGENEZA. [The material culture of the Aleuts: the problem of ethnogenesis.] Dissertation. Leningrad, 1970.

_____. OCHERKI PO ETNOGRAFII ALEUTOV, KONETS XVIII-PERVAIA POLOVINA XIX v. [Essays on the ethnography of the Aleuts from the late 18th century to the first half of the 19th century.] Leningrad, 1975.

Lisianskii, Iurii F. PUTESHESTVIE VOKRUG SVETA v 1803, 4, 5 i 1806...[Voyage around the world in 1803, 4, 5 and 1806 by order of His Imperial Majesty Aleksandr I., in the ship "Neva," under the command of Fleet Captain-Lieutenant, now Captain First Rank and Cavalier Iurii Lisianskii.] St. Petersburg, 1812. English edition, 1814.

Makarova, Raisa V. RUSSKIE OTKRYTIIA V TIKHOM OKEANE VO VTOROI POLOVINE XVIII v. [Russian discoveries in the Pacific Ocean in the second half of the 18th century.] Moscow, 1968.

Markov, Aleksandr. RUSSKIE NA VOSTOCHNOM OKEANE. Moscow, 1849. Translated by Ivan Petroff as The Russians on the Pacific Ocean. Los Angeles, 1955.

Markov, S. N. RUSSKIE NA ALIASKE. [The Russians in Alaska.] Moscow, 1946.

Ogden, Adele. THE CALIFORNIA SEA OTTER TRADE, 1784-1848. Berkeley and Los Angeles, 1941.

Okun, Semen B. ROSSIISKO-AMERIKANSKAIA KOMPANIIA. Moscow-Leningrad, 1939. Translated by Carl Ginsburg: The Russian American Company. Cambridge, Mass. 1951.

Akademiia Nauk, SSSR, Institute Etnografii im. Milukho-Maklay. OT ALIASKI DO OGNENNOI ZEMLI. [From Alaska to Tierra del Fuego.] Moscow, 1967.

Pierce, Richard A., ed. RUSSIA'S HAWAIIAN ADVENTURE, 1815-1817. Berkeley and Los Angeles, 1965.

Pilder, Hans. DIE RUSSISCH-AMERIKANISCHE HANDELS-COMPANIE BIS 1825. Berlin, 1914.

[Politovskii, V. G.] KRATKOE ISTORICHESKOE OBOZRENIE OBRAZOVANII I DEISTVII ROSSIISKO-AMERIKANSKOI KOMPANII S SAMOGO NACHALA UCHREZHDENIIA ONOI DO NASTOIASHCHEGO VREMENI. [A brief historical survey of the founding and activities of the Russian American Company from the very beginning of its establishment to the present time.] St. Petersburg, 1861.

Poniatowski, Michel. HISTOIRE DE LA RUSSIE D'AMERIQUE ET DE L'ALASKA. Paris, 1958.

U.S. National Archives. RECORDS OF THE RUSSIAN AMERICAN COMPANY, 1802, 1817-1867. 92 vols. Accompanying guide edited by Raymond H. Fisher. Washington, 1971.

Ricks, Melvin B. THE EARLIEST HISTORY OF ALASKA. Anchorage, 1963.

Roquefeuil, Camille de. JOURNAL D'UN VOYAGE AUTOUR DU MONDE PENDANT LES ANNEES 1816, 1817, 1818 et 1819. 2 vols. Paris, 1823.

Russia. Morskoe Ministerstvo. MATERIALY DLIA ISTORII RUSSKIKH ZASELENII PO BEREGAM VOSTOCHNAGO OKEANA. [Materials for a history of Russian settlements on the shores of the Pacific Ocean.] Supplement to MORSKOI SBORNIK, nos. 1, 2, 3 and 4. St. Petersburg, 1861.

Sarychev, Gavrila A. PUTESHESTVIE FLOTA KAPITANA SARYCHEVA...[Voyage of Fleet Captain Sarychev over the northeastern part of Siberia, Arctic Ocean and Pacific Ocean, lasting eight years, with the geographical and astronomical expedition under the command of Fleet Captain Billings, from 1785 to 1793.] 2 parts + Atlas. St. Petersburg, 1802.

Sauer, Martin. AN ACCOUNT OF A GEOGRAPHICAL AND ASTRONOMICAL EXPEDITION TO THE NORTHERN PARTS OF RUSSIA ... AND OF THE ISLANDS IN THE EASTERN OCEAN, STRETCHING TO THE AMERICAN COAST... London, 1802.

Shelekhov, Grigorii I. ROSSIISKAGO KUPTSA GRIGORIA SHELEKHOVA STRANSTVOVANIE V 1783 GODU...[The Russian merchant Grigorii Shelekhov's journey in 1783 from Okhotsk over the Eastern Ocean to the American shores.] St. Petersburg, 1791. Translated by Melvin B. Ricks in The Earliest History of Alaska. Anchorage, 1963.

Shemelin, Fedor. ZHURNAL PERVAGO PUTESHESTVIIA ROSSIIAN VOKRUG ZEMNAGO SHARA. [Journal of the first voyage of Russians around the world.] St. Petersburg, 1816.

Tikhmenev, Petr A. ISTORICHESKOE OBOZRENIE OBRAZOVANIE ROSSIISKO-AMERIKANSKOI KOMPANII I DEISTVII EE DO NASTOIASHCHEGO VREMENI. [Historical review of the establishment of the Russian American Company and its activities to the present time.] 2 vols. St. Petersburg, 1863. Translated in part by Ivan Petrov (in Bancroft Library); complete translation by Dmitri Krenov and Michael Dobrynin (in University of Washington Library and Bancroft Library.)

Tompkins, Stuart R. ALASKA, PROMYSHLENNIK AND SOURDOUGH. Norman, Okla., 1945.

U.S. Department of State. GEOGRAPHICAL NOTES UPON RUSSIAN AMERICA, 1868. 40 Cong., 2 sess., House Ex. Doc. 177, Part 2.

Vilar, E. Vila. LOS RUSOS EN AMERICA. Seville, 1966.

Vishnevsky, B. N. PUTESHESTVENNIK KIRILL KHLEBNIKOV. [The traveler Kirill Khlebnikov.] Perm, 1957.

Wrangell, Ferdinand P. STATISTISCHE UND ETNOGRAPHISCHE NACHRICHTEN UBER DIE RUSSISCHEN BESITZUNGEN AN DER NORDWESTKUSTE VON AMERIKA. St. Petersburg, 1839.

Zavalishin, Dmitrii I. ROSSIISKO-AMERIKANSKAIA KOMPANIIA. Moscow, 1865.

Articles

Allen, Robert V. "Alaska before 1867 in Soviet literature." Quarterly Journal of the Library of Congress, Vol. XXIII (July, 1966.)

Andreev, A. I. "Ob arkhive Rossiisko-Amerikanskoi Kompanii." ["Concerning the archive of the Russian American Company.") IZVESTIIA VSESOIUZNOGO GEOGRAFICHESKOGO OBSHCHESTVA, Vol. LXXV, 1943.

Andrews, Clarence L. "Alaska under the Russians - Industry, trade and social life." Washington Historical Quarterly, Vol. VII (Oct., 1916.)

Blomkvist, E. E. "Risunki I. G. Voznesenskogo (ekspeditsiia 1839-1849 godov). Sbornik Muzeia Antropologii i Etnografii, t. XIII (1951). Translated by Basil Dmytryshyn and E. A. P. Crownhart-Vaughan as "A Russian Scientific Expedition to California and Alaska, 1839-1849." Oregon Historical Quarterly, Vol. LXXIII (June, 1972.)

Bolkhovitinov, Nikolai N. "Avantiura Doktora Sheffera na Gavaiiakh v 1815-1819 godakh." NOVAIA I NOVEISHAIA ISTORIIA. Vyp. 1, 1972. Translated, "The adventures of Doctor Schaffer in Hawaii, 1815-1819." The Hawaiian Journal of History, Vol. VII, 1973.

Cordes, Frederick C. "Letters of A. Rotchev, last Commandant at Fort Ross." California Historical Society Quarterly, Vol. XXXIX (June, 1960.)

Crownhart-Vaughan, E.A.P., and Thomas Vaughan. "Dnevnik amerikanskogo puteshestvennika nachala XIX v. Dzhona deVulfa kak istoricheskii istochnik." ["The diary of the American traveler of the early 19th century John d'Wolf as historical source material."] In press in the USSR.

Essig, E. O. "The Russian settlement at Ross." Quarterly of the California Historical Society, Vol. XII (September, 1933.)

Fedorova, Svetlana G. "Ethnic processes in Russian America." Translated by Antoinette Shalkop. Anchorage Historical and Fine Arts Museum Occasional Paper No., 1, 1975.

Gibson, James R. "Bostonians and Muscovites on the Northwest Coast, 1788-1841."
In The Western Shore: Oregon Country Essays Honoring the American
Revolution. Oregon Historical Society, 1975.

_____. "Food for the fur traders: the first farmers in the Pacific Northwest,
1805-1846." Journal of the West, Vol. 7 (Jan., 1968.)

_____. "Problemy istoricheskoi geografii russkoi ameriki." ["Problems of
historical geography of Russian America."] In press in the USSR.

_____. "Russia in California, 1833: Report of Governor Wrangel." Pacific
Northwest Quarterly, Vol. 60 (Oct., 1969.)

Golovin, Pavel N. "Obzor russkikh kolonii v severnoi amerike." ["Survey of the
Russian colonies in North America."] MORSKOI SBORNIK, no. 1, 1862. English
translation in preparation by Oregon Historical Society.

Golovnin, Vasilii M. "Zapiska kapitana 2 ranga Golovnina o nyneshnem sostoianii
Rossiisko-Amerikanskoi kompanii." ["Memorandum of Captain Golovnin on the
present condition of the Russian American Company." MORSKOI SBORNIK,
Supplement to No. 1, 1861. English translation in preparation by Oregon
Historical Society.

Mazour, Anatole G. "Doctor Yegor Scheffer: dreamer of a Russian Empire in the
Pacific." Pacific Historical Review, Vol. VI (March, 1937.)

Pierce, Richard. "Alaskan treasure - the Russian skin money." Alaska--Magazine
of the Last Frontier, November, 1969.

_____. "George Anton Schaffer, Russia's man in Hawaii." Pacific Historical
Review, Vol. XXXII (November, 1963.)

Sherwood, Morgan B. "Science in Russian America, 1741-1865." Pacific Northwest
Quarterly, Vol. LVIII (January, 1967.)

Shirokii, V. F. "Iz istorii khoziastvennoi deiatelnosti Rossiisko-Amerikanskoi
kompanii." ["History of the economic activity of the Russian American
Company."] ISTORICHESKIE ZAPISKI, 1942.

Shur, Leonid A. "Dnevniki i zapiski russkikh puteshestvennikov kak istochnik
po istorii i etnografii stran tikhogo okeana." AVSTRALIIA I OKEANIIA:
ISTORIIA I SOVREMENNOST. Moscow, 1970. Translated and edited by James R.
Gibson, "Russian travel notes and journals as sources for the history of
California, 1800-1850." California Historical Quarterly, Vol. LII (Spring,
1973.)

Zavalishin, Dmitrii. "California in 1824." Translated and annotated by James R.
Gibson. Southern California Quarterly, Vol. LV (Winter, 1973.)

INDEX

catch of furbearing animals, 138-41;
trapping, 23; see also Prices, River
otters, Sea lions, Sea otters, Seals

Garnets, 39
Golovnin (ship Brutus), 56, 60, 61, 66,
78, 79, 86, 87, 122, 130
Grain, 8, 53, 106, 118-19, 131:
storage, 9, 53; see also Wheat
Gray's Harbor, 7, 8, 107
Great Britain:
Eng.-Russ. competition, 2, 3; see
also Trade and commerce
Grudinin, ----, 9, 116
Gyzelaar, Henry, 58

Hagemeister, Leontii Andreianovich,
iii, 14-15, 20-23, 55, 60, 61, 74,
110, 115, 121
Halibut, 3, 29, 36, 54
Hartwell, ----, 59
Hawaiian Islands, see Sandwich Islands
Hay, 78, 105
Herrera, ----, 112
Herring, 3, 29, 36, 53:
oil, 55
Hides, 104, 121, 122:
rawhides, 114
reindeer--
Kolosh exchange, 32
sea lion (lavtaks), 104, 123;
walrus, 16n, 51
Hill, Samuel, 5

Ianovskii, Semen, iii, 23, 74
Icy Strait, 23
Ilmen (brig Lydia), 8, 18, 114
Indians:
n. Calif., 23, 124--
boats, 109; food, 126; friendly
to Russians, 129-30; hostilities;
108-109, 129, housing, 109;
weapons, 108
see also Aleuts, Chugach, Kolosh
Isabella (ship), 7,8
Iturbe, Augustin de, 130

Juno (ship), 5, 9, 113, 114

Kamchatka (sloop), 130
Kamchatka Peninsula, iii, 3, 34, 36
Kamehameha, 65, 66-67
Karpinskii, ----, 9

Katherine (ship), 7
Kenai Bay (Cook Inlet), 1, 5:
census records, 16, 143; settlement,
1
Khlebnikov, Kirill Timofeevich, 94n:
awards, iv, journals, iv; publica-
tions, iv; travels, iii-iv
Khvostov, Nikolai A., iii
Kiakhta (brig), 53, 61, 62, 63, 78, 79,
86, 87, 103, 107, 122
Kitkh-ugin-si (mythical being), 25-27
Kodiak (ship Myrtle), 5, 7-8, 9, 89,
107:
crewmen desert, 8
Kodiak Island, 5:
census records, 16, 40, 144; settlement, 1, 129; supply depot, 2; trade
center, 4
Kolosh (Tlingits), 1:
armor, 30-31; boats and canoes, 32,
33; care of the helpless, 27; ceremonial killings, 32; childbirth, 27;
clothing, 30; dances, 31-32; disci-
pline of children, 27; disease, 29;
firearms, 35; food, 29, 30, 31, 36,
112; funeral customs, 29
handcrafts, 32--
carving, 32, 39; dyeing, 38n;
weaving, 33, 38n
hostilities, 5, 101-102, 106--
harrassment of Aleut hunters, 4-6,
55; kidnappings, 4; Sitka, 3, 4,
39; tribal warfare, 30-31
hunting, 35, 39; lip-piercing, 28,
39; marriage customs, 28; masks, 31,
33; myths, 25-27; no suicides, 32;
physical features, 28; prostitution,
71; shamans, 27, 29, 30, 32; slaves,
31, 32, 71; superstitions, 27;
toions, 32, 38n; totem poles, 31;
weapons, 3, 30, 35, 55, 56
Koniags, 29
Konstantin (sloop), 18, 41, 78, 86,
87, 88, 89
Kootznahoo Inlet, 2
Kostromitinov, Petr S., iii
Kotsebue, Otto von, 115
Krasheninnikov, Stepan P.:
Explorations of Kamchatka, 1735-1741,
cited, i
Krusenstern, Ivan F., iii
Kuglinov, ----, 15
Kuskov, Ivan Aleksandrovich, iii, 5,

Yakutat, 1; see also Ships
Ships, 9, 82:
  guns, 95: lists, 7, 18, 56-62, 78-29,
  86-90, 136-37; purchased, 79; sold,
  116
Shipwrecks, 4, 7, 9, 11, 107
Shur, Leonid A., iii
Sitka (brig), 9
Sitka Bay, navigation, 98
Sitka Island, 36:
  flora, 38-39; geology, 23, 39; lakes
  and rivers, 33-34, settlement, 2-3;
  topography, 23, 33-34; see also
  Climate, New Arkhangel
Slobodchikov, Sysoi, 6, 106
Smallpox, 29
Sola, Pablo V. de, iii, 9, 61, 110, 115
Somoilov, ----, 108-109
Sonoma Bay, see Bodega Bay
Spain:
  claims to Pac. Coast, 130; hostility
  toward trespassers in Calif., 8, 9,
  107, 108, 115, 130; missions, 79, 112,
  115, 116, 130, 131; see also Sea
  otters, Trade and commerce
Springs:
  hot springs, 34, 81; sulphur springs,
  34
Stevens, ----, 59
Strogonov, Paul Aleksandrovich, 92, 93,
  94
Sultan (ship), 59
Surveyors, see A. Baranov, E. Purtov
Suvorov (ship), 15, 18n, 89
Swine, 100, 119

Tallow, 121
Tarakanov, Timofei, 6, 7, 8, 56, 107
Taxes, 16, 19, 21, 22, 43, 81, 85
Tell, ----, 58
Thaddeus (brig), 58
Tides, Sitka Island, 98
Timber, 98
Tlingit Indians, see Kolosh
Toropogritskii, ----, 5
Trade and commerce:
  Amer. competition, 2, 3, 5, 70--
    smuggling, 64
  Amer.-Russ., 4, 6, 8-10, 57-100;
  barter, 5, 7; Canton-Russ., 4, 11-14,
  59; commodities, 4, 8, 10, 11-14, 19,
  23, 57-66, 68-69, 71-73, 84-85, 114-15
  company supplies, 44, 47-48, 51, 53-

55, 113-15--
  dependence on foreign ships, 10,
  101, 131-33; domestic trade,
  71-73; employees' rations, 42-44,
  48, 51, 53-55, 61; Fort Ross
  produce, 106, 131, 132; ship
  stores, 23, 76, 76n; shortages,
  1n, 4, 48, 57, 101, 129;
  storage, 9, 23, 53
Eng.-Russ., 4, 9, 57, 84
Eng. competition, 2, 3--
  smuggling, 64
French-Canton, 34; grain, 8, 53,
  see also Wheat; Kolosh, 5-6, 33,
  57, 68-71, 102; lumber, 98-99;
  Sandwich Islands, 57-60, 64-68;
  ships bought and sold, 9, 60, 67,
  79, 116; see also Fur trade, Prices,
  Russian American Co., Sea otters
Trees:
  n. Calif., 109, 117, 125; Sitka
  Island, 38, Yakutat Bay, 1
Trinidad (Humboldt) Bay, 7, 8, 106,
  107; Indians, 24, 108

Unalaska, 16, 77

Vasiliev, ----, 98
Venereal disease, 104
Volga (brig), 41, 61, 78, 79, 87, 88,
  90, 110, 117
Volunteer (ship), 58
Vosdwit (Wadsworth), ----, 8

Walruses, 16n, 51:
  teeth and tusks, 12, 12n, 139, 141
Washington (schooner), 60
Whales, 29, 35, 55, 125:
  bone, 12, 141; oil, 51, 55; sinews,
  104; whiskers, 104
Wheat, 53, 64:
  efforts to grow, 1; importation
  from California, 8-9; storage in
  ships, 9, 18, 116
Whittemore, Isaac, 7
Winship, Jonathan, 6, 7, 8, 106
Winship, Nathan, 7
Wrangell, Ferdinand von, iii

Yakutat:
  expedition, 1, 1n; settlement, 1,
  1n; survey, 1
Yakutat (Bering) Bay, 1, 34, 35, 56

Zlatoust (ship), 18

BACK ENDPAPERS: 1840 map of "The North-West-
Coast of North America and adjacent territories, Compiled from the best authorities
under the direction of Robert Greenhow to
accompany his Memoir on the Northwest Coast...
drawn by David H. Burr."